A DISTURBING AND ALIEN MEMORY

SOUTHERN LITERARY STUDIES
Fred Hobson, *Series Editor*

A DISTURBING AND ALIEN MEMORY

Southern Novelists Writing History

DOUGLAS L. MITCHELL

LOUISIANA STATE UNIVERSITY PRESS
Baton Rouge

Published by Louisiana State University Press
Copyright © 2008 by Louisiana State University Press
All rights reserved
Manufactured in the United States of America
First printing

Designer: *Amanda McDonald Scallan*
Typeface: *Weiss*
Typesetter: *J. Jarrett Engineering, Inc.*
Printer and binder: *Thomson-Shore, Inc.*

Library of Congress Cataloging-in-Publication Data

Mitchell, Douglas L., 1968–
A disturbing and alien memory : southern novelists writing history / Douglas L. Mitchell.
p.   cm.
Includes bibliographical references and index.
ISBN 978-0-8071-3373-6 (cloth : alk. paper) 1. American fiction—Southern States—History and criticism.
2. Authors, American—Southern States—Knowledge—History. 3. American fiction—19th century—History
and criticism. 4. American fiction—20th century—History and criticism. 5. History in literature. 6. Southern
States—Intellectual life—1865– 7. Southern States—In literature. I. Title.
PS261.M48 2008
813.009′358—dc22

2008019090

The paper in this book meets the guidelines for permanence and durability of the Committee on Production
Guidelines for Book Longevity of the Council on Library Resources. ∞

CONTENTS

ACKNOWLEDGMENTS

Many thanks are due John Easterly and the excellent team at LSU Press. I am particularly grateful for the incisive eye and gracious spirit of my copy editor, Grace Carino.

I would also like to thank my primary mentors over the years, Jim Babin and Bob McMahon at LSU and Fred Hobson at Chapel Hill. I would have little sense of my vocation without their example and encouragement.

This book took its initial form within the companionable confines of the Dead Mule Club in Chapel Hill. The hours spent over drafts with my fellow Mules Farrell O'Gorman and Collin Messer were some of the most enjoyable and profitable I will ever spend. Their friendship and that of others, particularly Todd Stabley, Bob Schaefer, and John Talmage, helped me get through the dry spells.

One's family, of course, is always owed the greatest debt. My parents have given me their faith and support, my children the sacrifice of things left undone, and my wife, Shawn, the gift of constant love and patience.

INTRODUCTION

"The burden of southern history," in C. Vann Woodward's famous formulation, is the single most prevalent topic in the study of southern letters, and with good reason. We look at the history of writers coming to terms with that shifting entity known as "the South" and are continually confronted with people wrestling with the meaning and shape of the past, particularly during the explosion of creativity in the Southern Renascence. Regardless of the accuracy of their perceptions, southerners have had a very different relationship to the past than have Americans generally, and historical concerns continued to pervade southern literature long after they faded (albeit never completely) from the canvas of major writers in other regions; put another way, Jay Gatsby and Nick Adams might serve in the North, but the South must have its Quentin Compson. The burden of the past takes many forms for southern writers—the guilt of slavery, the memory of defeat, the urge to justify—but all these forms have meant at bottom that writers simply could not, until fairly recently, leave the past well enough alone. This concern with history in poetry and fiction has received more than its due scholarly attention, as have various forms of nonfiction prose, but one notable phenomenon has not been treated systematically: the line of southern novelists and poets, all of significant stature in their respective periods, who have turned to the writing of formal history and biography over the course of their careers.

This study focuses on a line of writers stretching from the early nineteenth century to the mid-twentieth. It begins with William Gilmore Simms and the opening of the historical rift between North and South after the emergence of a distinctively southern sectional identity. The failure of Simms's Romantic nationalism—traced through his histories, biographies, essays, and occasional pieces—leads to the cult of memory, epitomized in the work of Thomas Nelson Page in the late nineteenth and early twentieth centuries. Page's treatment of the Old South as a redemptive history illustrates the peculiar hazards of the historical cul-de-sac in the dominant southern consciousness after the war: namely, pastoralism as justification for white supremacy in the South and, more deeply, a failure to shape an adequate artistic response to the civilizational change. Such a response would come with the advent of literary modernism, and two of the South's primary modernist voices, Allen Tate and Robert Penn Warren, would find themselves split between their roles as keepers of memory and as artists. The ambivalence wrought by their encounter with modernism would lead both to abandon the polemical imperatives of Agrarianism and develop new, but very different, visions of history. Only with Shelby Foote's magisterial three-volume narrative of the Civil War, however, would public history and private vision merge and signal the closure of the historical gap.

Focusing on historiography by literary figures allows us to view the question of the southern writer's relationship to history from another angle, through another sort of lens. Since the 1970s, scholars have begun to examine the more strictly literary forms of southern literature—poems, novels, plays—alongside a great many other kinds of texts produced by southern writers.[1] Though this study is limited to writers who are primarily novelists or poets, it builds on this expanded notion of the literary by focusing on the historical works that occupy (with the obvious exception of Foote's narrative) a secondary place in each writer's corpus.

The question of interest here is why southern novelists and poets persisted in writing history long after changes in both historiography and the ideas of artistic vocation had sundered the two realms for most writers. Several of the significant works of southern letters, of course, are histories of one sort or another—Captain John Smith's narratives of exploration, Robert Beverly's *History and Present State of Virginia,* and David Ramsay's histories of the American Revolution among them—but these works were written under a broader dispensation of the man of letters that continued into the Romantic era. In the nineteenth century, Simms and Washington Irving developed reputations as historians equal to their reputations as writers of fiction, James Fenimore Cooper wrote a history of the U.S. Navy, and the literary lions of the age included historians George Bancroft, William Hickling Prescott, and John Lothrop Motley. With the rise of scientific history and specialization, the older literary historians fell out of favor, and the gap between historian and artist widened; Henry Adams is the only major figure of the late nineteenth and early twentieth centuries in American literature who could move with credibility in both realms. In the twentieth century, with the rise of modernism, the artist would occupy a realm apart, and the artist's prerogative—his truth—would be found in subjective vision and the form of art.

After World War II, postmodernism would only heighten the subjectivity while further challenging the coherence of traditional narrative. Carl Sandburg's massive biography of Lincoln stands as a great anomaly among northern writers, but stranger still is that two of the greatest southern writers of the century—Allen Tate and Robert Penn Warren—would make their entrance before the public (in the heyday of modernism, no less) with Civil War biographies, and Shelby Foote would follow them and produce his magnum opus in the form of a three-volume narrative of the Civil War rather than the novel.

One reason for the continued efforts of southern writers along this line is familiar: the southerner's particularly acute awareness of history. "The South," Richard Weaver tells us, "is the region that history has happened to," and the features that have distinguished South from North are its historical experiences: of defeat, occupation and reconstruction, and persistent poverty, as C. Vann Woodward argues in his classic treatment, *The Burden of Southern History*.[2] Since the South lagged behind the other regions in all the indexes of social and economic progress and was set apart by having been on the "wrong side" of history in our nation's great moral crisis, the natural impulse of critic or apologist was to get at what *is* through what *was*. Defeat in the Civil War gave birth to what Lewis P. Simpson calls a "spiritual nation" or, as Robert Penn Warren has it, a "City of the Soul," a hovering entity providing identity and meaning in the present, either for salvation or damnation depending on one's perspective.[3] The conservatives would argue essentially that history is written by the winners, leading to distortion of the nature of the Old South and southern society, though their accounts of the Old South would vary widely, from the chivalric plantation ideal of Thomas Nelson Page to the hardened, frontier ethos of Andrew Nelson Lytle's yeomen in the Upland South. The critics would take aim at the myths of the Old South to show that they masked, and suppressed, the underlying "real" nature of southern culture, whether they posited that nature in W. J. Cash's frontier culture co-opted and dominated by a faux aristocracy or in Lillian Smith's vision of a twisted Freudian family romance splitting the superego of the mansion house and gynolatry from the dark id of the interracial sexual desire in the quarters.[4] Nor was this effort, from whatever perspective, simply a historical exercise; with the continuing legacy of the older South (or Souths) in twentieth-century political dynamics, economic realities, and race relations, this turning to the past was also, as Hobson notes, a turning inward for an image of the self. However much southerners responded to attacks from other regions, there were also promptings from within: "But the siege from without was not all, was not even the principal factor in turning the Southern mind upon itself. Even greater was the pressure from within—the doubt honest Southerners had about themselves and their own past—for the burden of Southern history was a burden primarily self-imposed" (10).

But this general account leaves us with the question of why the southern writers mentioned at the outset turned specifically to historiography when, as has been amply demonstrated in the twentieth century, fiction certainly can be used as a powerful vehicle for historical vision. No one wishes that Faulkner had turned aside from Yoknapatawpha for a historiographic treatment of Mississippi; his corpus stands as the great American testament to the distinct authority of the subjective vision of the artist. In this distinct authority, however, lies the rub for the artist who hopes to exercise a broader cultural authority; the alienated vantage of the high modernist secures a sovereignty in the realm of art—a prerogative of vision—but that sovereignty is purchased at the price of a more direct, if less profound, connection to the public at large. Those writers who maintain a broader currency with the public do so through a connection with science, which has the virtue for pragmatic Americans of having produced tangible results. The social sciences had long since begun to model themselves on the lines of the natural sciences, following the efforts of Ranke and Comte in the nineteenth century, and so shared something of the credibility of those sciences.[5] Even history, once the most humane of the humanities, had crossed into the ranks of the social sciences, and here we have the strongest motivation for the southern conservatives, who were most insistent on art as a separate domain of knowledge, to shift temporarily to formal history when attempting to gain a foothold for their cultural critique with a broader public.

This claim leads to a necessary qualification and extension of an otherwise valid point made by Hobson concerning the difference between apologists and critics in the South: "Liberal or conservative, critic or apologist, each felt compelled to explain the South, and if any generalization might be made at the outset it is that the apologists, the defenders, tended to be of a poetic nature and, since poetry is ahistorical, to protest the injustice that the South should be judged only through its recorded history and not through the integrity of its vision as well; while the critics . . . tended to rest their case on history, on observed fact, and draw their position, their attitude, from the documented Southern past" (7). Though the conservatives did, for the most part, hold to the autonomy of art beyond political concerns and resisted the notions of a politically concerned art prevalent in the interwar period, formal history provided them with a vehicle for dealing in the facts of the past, drawing on the credibility of the historical specialists without compromising their essentially private vision of art. The liberals, in works such as W. J. Cash's *Mind of the South*, Lillian Smith's *Killers of the Dream*, or Clarence Cason's *Stars Fell on Alabama*, were working more in the mode of sociological and psychoanalytic analysis (albeit with a large historical component), while the conservatives went the historiographic route. History is the most conservative of the social science disciplines, refining its methodology but retaining largely the same address to reality it had in the nineteenth or arguably even the eighteenth century; in spite of scientific "advances," it retains traits of the branch of literature it once was and, some practitioners suggest, remains.[6] The conservative champions of poetic vision could don the mantle of historian and draw on its objective credibility without seeming complicit in the scientism that was, for them, one of the major problems with modernity. To adapt Hobson's terms, they could "rest their case on the facts of the past" without compromising their "quality of vision," at least in theory—the matter would be considerably more complicated in practice.

My purpose in this study is not to determine the accuracy of the histories these writers produced but to explore the nature and purpose of their construction. In this approach, I follow works such as Richard Gray's *Writing the South*, which treats southern histories as fictions, created out of certain needs in response to historical pressures.[7] Gray, drawing on contemporary linguistic theory, deals with the creation of the South as a rhetorical act, using certain patterns of rhetoric that shape identity by limiting discourse. Contemporary theoretical perspectives generally have begun to shape our perception of narrative and historiography, in Gray's work and others, and though my methods are more traditional, there are fundamental insights to be gained from theoretical challenges. The most important of these, for my purposes, is the reconception of the connection between narrative and identity in such works as Benedict Anderson's influential *Imagined Communities*.[8] Anderson examines national identity not as growing from a prior reality that is simply manifested in texts but as the product of these texts (broadly conceived to include maps, artwork, official documents, fiction, poetry, and so forth); the texts create the boundaries that allow people to imagine themselves as part of a national community. While this study is not as reliant on Anderson and other theorists as some recent works, it shares with them the assumption that the truth of the works is less important than the "style of imagining," to use Anderson's phrase. The writers dealt with here all had a hand in writing the South, constructing a historical image and a present reality, and I examine the nature of that construction and the imperatives—personal, artistic, and cultural—driving it.

I chose a traditional line of writers because of the difficulties—intellectual, artistic, and psychic—this very tradition involved them in. These writers can all be considered conservative only in a special sense. All of them held (albeit to varying degrees) a conception of the historical South as a traditional order set against an advancing modernity that had overwhelmed it, and all felt the temptation to use this alternate vision of order as the ground of meaning and identity in the present—as a redemptive history. As Simpson writes concerning the relation of the southern writer to southern nationalism: "The Southern writer has tended to be a kind of priest and prophet of a metaphysical nation, compelled in his literary construction of human existence in the South—whether he is historian, philosopher, critic, poet, or novelist—toward representing it as a quest for a revelation of man's moral community in history. The revelation may be ironic, tragic, humorous; it may be all three at once, but it is salvational" (*Man of Letters* 202). The problem for the southern writer taking on this prophetic role is the suppressed reality of chattel slavery as the foundation of the old southern order. The South was not a pastoral alternative to modernity but a unique modern slave society. Only when southern writers in the twentieth century began to realize that the Old South itself was part of "the apocalypse of modern civilization" could they begin to participate in a meaningful critique of modernity and formulate a viable alternative vision of order in literature (*Man of Letters* 226).[9]

My study begins with the career of William Gilmore Simms, the preeminent man of letters in the antebellum South, and the failure of Romantic history after the opening of the sectional divide. Simms worked in his various capacities as editor, novelist, poet, and historian to define and wield the broad cultural authority of the man of letters. As a Romantic nationalist, he saw his role as a nation maker, a keeper of memory who could shape the future course of the nation by a prophetic invocation of its past. In the first portion of his career, this role meant a devotion to the origin and destiny of the United States, with Simms the guardian of a southern component of a national story, but he became involved in the project of southern nationalism by the 1840s. New imperatives led Simms to reenvision the nation and, as a "man of mind," to reshape its history and seek new models of heroism suited to a period of civilizational crisis, particularly in his three biographies of the 1840s. In the heated sectional debates of the 1850s, there was a struggle over the truth of the Republic, and much of the debate centered on the American Revolution, a historiographic struggle to which Simms made the dominant southern contribution with his *South Carolina in the Revolutionary War* (1853). The breakdown of national consensus had revealed an irresolvable tension in the founding of the United States and signaled the end of the viability of Romantic history. In the remainder of his career, his formerly dynamic historical vision gave way to the static gaze of the apologist, and, with the defeat of the Confederacy in the Civil War, Simms found himself trapped in a barren present.

Thomas Nelson Page came of age in the wake of this closure of history on the South and took upon himself the vindication of the Old South. He became the high priest for a nation of the spirit and more than any other figure gave the myth of the Lost Cause expression in the popular mind, in both his collection of stories, *In Ole Virginia* (1887), and the historiographic essays and addresses in *The Old South* (1892). But Page's work for the cult of memory was not simply a matter of nostalgia and the window dressing of chivalric men, saintly women, and graceful manners; in a prophetic role, he both elaborated a pastoral vision of the Old South and attempted to reinscribe the South into the main line of American historical development. His second collection of historical work, *The Old Dominion: Her Making and Her Manners* (1908), casts Virginia as the torchbearer leading the way into an Anglo-Saxon future. Page attempts to synthesize these distinct visions of the South in time and the Old South as timeless Arcadia in his biography of Robert E. Lee. More important, in his work during the decades of American expansionism at the turn of the century, we see the influence of the plantation myth on the form of his nationalism. Page attempts to shift the lines of difference defining the nation by arguing for a racial nationalism as the answer to the threat of "Africanization" and civilizational decline. Such is Page's attempt to belatedly expel the chattel from the garden and so preserve the pastoral and the South as a vision of order.

During the time Simms and Page were shaping their vision of the South, African American writers were attempting to forge a place for blacks in the American narrative, and my third chapter serves as a coda in which we turn for perspective to the most important of the black writers turned historians: William Wells Brown. Brown, one of the earliest African American novelists, worked to raise consciousness of the buried history of blacks both in historical novels such as *Clotel* and in four works on black history. His work represents an entry by an African American man of letters into the historiographic struggle over the shape and content of the nation's past by George Bancroft or, on the southern side, Simms and George Tucker. Like Simms, he would turn frequently to the American Revolution for the meaning of the Republic and the place of neglected patriots, and like Page, he would attempt to shape the meaning of the Civil War and Reconstruction into a vision of a new order emerging from the struggle. In his first histories, his published lecture *St. Domingo: Its Revolutions and Its Patriots* (1854) and *The Black Man* (1863), there is a tension between finding a place for blacks in the American story and raising the specter of slave revolt. Simms's partisan warrior finds his counterpart in Nat Turner and Toussaint L'Ouverture. In the works written after northern victory in the Civil War, *The Negro in the American Rebellion* (1867) and *The Rising Son* (1874), we find Brown, like Page, turning to a renewed nationalism founded on an emerging racial order. For Brown, however, that racial order is based on the defeat of white aristocrats and a newly empowered black leadership; with the failure of Reconstruction, it would be Page's vision, not Brown's, that would win the day. Brown's work is flawed by carelessness and opportunism, but he helped prepare the way for the greater skill and ironic distance of Charles Chesnutt and the writers of the Harlem Renaissance. These writers, too, are southerners, and my treatment of a more traditional line is not intended to exclude them but to lay the groundwork for an appreciation of their alternative histories, their very different construction of the South and the larger nation.

Women writers have also made significant contributions to the literature of memory. Look into any southern family or community, and you will find women as the keepers of the stories and lore. This study, however, focuses on those writers who wrote in formal history and biography and entered the fray over the nation's past. The public form of the writing and its polemical bent set it apart from local, regional history or private memory, and the psychic and artistic costs of such a project are the subjects of this study. Mary Chesnut's *Diary* is the greatest text in the southern literature of memory, far better as literature than most of the texts dealt with here and more valuable as history, but it is a private genre. Grace King's histories of Louisiana focus on a southern subculture rather than defining and placing the South as such; she is the historian of the Creoles. Evelyn Scott's *Backgrounds in Tennessee*, like her novels, is a groundbreaking work in southern modernism, but it is a nuanced exploration of memory different in kind from and superior to the Civil War biographies produced by the Agrarians. Caroline Gordon, during her marriage to Allen Tate, did participate directly by writing portions of Tate's *Jefferson Davis*, but by and large the women avoided the bypath taken by these male figures, and that, in my view, is to their credit. It is the tension between private memory and public history, after all, that would prove most fruitful for southern writing in the twentieth century. The position of public historian is fraught with peril for the poet.

Page never demonstrated any awareness of the problematic nature of redemptive history, but the southern writers who followed him in the wake of modernism were forced to a reckoning, particularly the Fugitive-Agrarians. These writers—John Crowe Ransom, Allen Tate, Robert Penn Warren, and Donald Davidson—had worked to gain a certain measure of detachment from the South and knew the artistic benefits of alienation, but they found themselves drawn back to the South and its history by a sense of crisis that was part personal and part cultural. They assumed the polemical stance so familiar to the southern writer and sought to define a viable southern tradition—agrarianism—in response to what they viewed as an assault by social planners and industrialists; in short, they sought a pastoral alternative to modernity, an alternative that would find expression in *I'll Take My Stand* (1930). Three of the Agrarians—Allen Tate, Robert Penn Warren, and novelist Andrew Nelson Lytle—wrote Civil War biographies during this period, both to put forward models of heroism and to clarify the nature of the cultural difference between North and South. Through a more public form they could assume an authoritative role of mediator between past and present, forgoing for the time their artistic prerogative of alienation and subjective vision, but they could not completely shed their self-consciousness, their awareness of fragmentation and the disjunction between past and present, or their nagging sense of the dangers of a willed identification with the historical image.

Allen Tate was the most committed modernist of the Fugitive-Agrarians and the one most keenly aware of the divide separating past and present. The situation of the modern, as Tate captured it in "Ode to the Confederate Dead," separates him from a past in which a unified sensibility and heroic action were possible. The speaker's question "What shall we say who have knowledge carried to the heart?" haunts Tate's writing, as does the danger that attempting to bridge the gap through force of will is only to "set up the grave in the house."[10]

Tate's effort to lay the groundwork for a society of "*positive* reactionaries"[11] in the South led him to attempt to circumvent the dilemma presented in the poem, both in polemical essays and in the Civil War biographies he wrote in the period culminating in *I'll Take My Stand. Stonewall Jackson: The Good Soldier* (1928) and *Jefferson Davis: His Rise and Fall* (1929) reflect his desire for an adequate model of action and a viable traditional order, but both bear marks of the intellectual violence necessary to gain them. In the case of *Stonewall*, Tate's hero becomes essentially the antithesis of the Agrarian ideal, rather than its embodiment, and in *Jefferson Davis*, his analysis locates the failure of mind in the Old South (and the corresponding failure of the Confederacy) in its blindness to its own nature as a burgeoning aristocratic culture, a conclusion that severely undermines the Old South's strength as a model. Only through his failed effort to write a third biography of the South's greatest figure, Robert E. Lee, and his fictional exploration of the antebellum South in his novel *The Fathers* (1938) would Tate begin to recognize the fatal irony of chattel slavery at the core of the Old South. Though he would never renounce his Agrarian principles, he ultimately moved toward Catholicism and found his transcendent ground in the City of God rather than a City of the Soul.

Tate's younger counterpart Robert Penn Warren arrived at a very different alternative to redemptive history: an existentialist vision of history not as mundane decline and transcendent order but as the self struggling blindly in an "agony of will" in a world of forces beyond understanding and certainly beyond control. The meaning of the past lies only in the experiences of individuals who painfully construct knowledge of themselves through action, but Warren does not see the self acting in isolation; each action impinges on other selves, and consequence rarely matches intention. One must act for self-definition, but there is an inevitable involvement in guilt. The crucial choice is whether to accept responsibility or to reject it in order to maintain the illusion of innocence. Warren's obsession with history dominates his best fiction—especially *All the King's Men* (1946) and *World Enough and Time* (1950)—and much of his poetry, but he also took on the role of historian he so effectively dramatized. In *John Brown: The Making of a Martyr* (1929), his later meditation on history in *Legacy of the Civil War: Meditations on the Centennial* (1961), and addresses and essays such as "The Use of the Past," we can trace the development of Warren's mature vision of history, when he speaks in the broader public realm and prophetically offers redemption. His is not a redemptive history of the South, however, but a tragic vision that offers reconciliation only through the recognition of guilt, beyond the illusions of innocence, national or personal.

While Warren could describe this tragic vision and give it dramatic embodiment in his fiction, Shelby Foote's three-volume *The Civil War: A Narrative* (1958–74) succeeds in restoring the tragic vision of the war by re-creating it in words. Foote was simultaneously closer to the reality of the Old South than the Agrarians and farther removed from it. Coming of age in the heart of the Mississippi Delta and descended from planters, Foote knew the limitations of the planter aristocracy as a traditional order and was highly skeptical of its claims to a benevolent paternalism. Like his lifelong friend Walker Percy, he experienced the best of the older tradition in the person of William Alexander Percy but tended toward irony rather than piety. He began his writing career after World War II and accepted the breakdown of the older cultural tradition, never feeling the impulse of the apologist. Foote remained devoted to modernism as something approaching a religion and was buoyed by a faith in art to create a reality superior to any present; in his great narrative of the war, this devotion allows him to craft not a commentary on the war but a re-creation of it. Form here is meaning, rather than simply an organizing device, and he constructs a highly structured narrative that contains the force of lived experience, bringing the multiple, competing voices and heterogeneous facts of the war into a narrative controlled by a single voice. His narrative is a medium wherein the war itself can play out in the reader's consciousness as a grand completed action with the catharsis of tragedy.

Foote's work represents the culmination of this line of historical texts by southern artists. In Simms and Page we see the identification of the writer with "an aborted national will," as Simpson phrases it, and his entrapment with the imperatives of that nation, translated into new terms. Tate and Warren knew the hazards of that identification and sought to identify a different address to the past, an alternative model of order. Warren in particular succeeded, over the course of his long career, in reconceiving a role for the southern man of letters in the twentieth century that would allow him to speak with authority on a proper relationship to the past, but Foote became something different: the artist as historian. He marries the historically grounded vision of the conservative southern writer with the detachment of the post–World War II generation and re-creates the war and the massiveness of human experience in the event. The two-decade span of the trilogy's composition neatly corresponds to the time of the civil rights movement, and I would argue that there is a deeper correspondence between the two. If the civil rights struggle represented the South's "working through" (in Hobson's phrase) its legacy of slavery and emerging chastened but stronger, Foote's narrative allows us to "work through" the event that produced the specter haunting the South and the southern writer through midcentury. As Foote says at the end of his final volume: "The conflict is behind me now, as it is for you and it was a hundred-odd years ago for them."[12]

1

"MEMORY ENOUGH FOR THE BEST
AND BRAVEST OF US ALL"

William Gilmore Simms and the Failure of Romantic History

William Gilmore Simms (1806–70) dominated southern letters from the time of the development of a distinctly southern sectional identity in the 1820s through the failure of the Confederacy in the Civil War. He was the preeminent man of letters in the region, producing works of fiction, history, drama, poetry, and political and social commentary over a forty-year span. While he is remembered primarily for his historical novels of Revolutionary and pre-Revolutionary America, he also laid claim to the title of "historian of South Carolina" and indeed was the leading recorder of the state's past, especially of its Revolutionary legacy. Though his concern with history is normally treated in the context of his fiction, Simms saw himself as participating in the realms of both formal history and its fictional representation. As a Romantic historian, he viewed the roles of artist and historian as two parts of the vocation of man of letters in service to the nation. Simms, through the early part of his career, was a literary nationalist and saw his contribution in terms of a sectional component of a national story. The growth of sectional tensions pushed him toward southern nationalism later, and it is most clearly in his historical writings that we see the shift in the historical consciousness of the South.

The shift for Simms came in the 1840s, a decade that saw him both championing literary nationalism and beginning to realize that America meant something fundamentally different for New England and for the South. The struggle was over the truth of the Republic, the nature of its destiny as inferred from the shaped, prophetic recording of its past, and Simms's effort as the man of letters was to create the truth of that past. In his historical writings, we can trace the departure of the southern version of history from that of the American mainstream and the national narrative—its movement into that peculiar blind alley it would find its way out of only in the latter part of the twentieth century. In both his histories and his fiction, we have a critique of the South as it was and a model of what it might become. It is the histories, though, that provided him with the credibility he needed as the interpreter of history, the guardian of the past and the prophet shaping the South's future.

Viewing his historical work as a prophetic endeavor in the Romantic mode, we can gain a fuller sense of his idea of the essence of the southern character, the spirit of place and people, which he held to be the key to its destiny. *Views and Reviews in American Literature, History and Fiction* (1846), his *History of South Carolina* (1840), and several addresses provide us with his sense of the role of the man of letters and the importance and proper use of history. His biographies of the 1840s—of Francis Marion, John Smith, and Chevalier Bayard—put forth a composite model of the individual capable of realizing the South's promise and serve the purposes of southern nationalism by moving progressively deeper into the past to define essential differences between North and South.[1] This shift from the chivalric, yet practical, Revolutionary partisan to the abstract ideal coincides with Simms's assumption of the role of southern apologist amid the breakdown in national consensus. This breakdown was reflected primarily in the historiographic struggle fought between North and South over the meaning of the Revolution, to which Simms made the dominant southern contribution with his "South Carolina in the Revolutionary War" (1853). This struggle signaled the end of Romantic history in the United States, which had assumed a coherent national identity made up of diverse components, all engaged in a single progress toward a national destiny. Simms attempted to modify his vision by emphasizing a southern nation that had yet to come into being; in his revised *History of South Carolina* (1860), he emphasized fidelity to the state and region as his highest value and sketched South Carolina's history as preparation for its leadership in a new southern nation. After the Civil War, with the failure of southern nationhood, Simms's found himself the guardian of a history bereft of meaning, and his last major historical work, *Sack and Destruction of the City of Columbia, S.C.* (1865), presents a stark vision of a South trapped in a barren present. The work of the southern historian was no longer to establish the vital connection between past, present, and future in a dynamic unfolding of national destiny but to vindicate the defeated South—to establish the nature and meaning of what had been. But to properly understand the historical dilemma of Simms and the South following the Civil War, we must begin in the early decades of the century, when the southern writer faced a very different set of possibilities.

What was the situation of the writer in 1820s? With the gradual dwindling of the republican period's emphasis on the civic-minded celebrator of the United States as the embodiment of the ideals of liberty and virtue and with the growing distance from the Revolutionary moment, a crisis of sorts set in. Our emancipation from history began to seem an exile from history and civic republicanism a mere gloss over the harsh chaotic reality of democracy: a tendency to demagoguery and leveling; the incredibly rapid growth of industry, markets, and population; and the specter of dehumanization and the subjection of masses of people to forces beyond rational control. Romanticism provided the possibility of a new sort of ordering, from within the self as an expression of human spirit rather than the realization of a rational order. Divorced from the guides of society in church and tradition (having inherited the paradox of a *revolutionary* tradition), society suffered from a vacuum of moral authority at its core, and the man of letters began to function in the priestly role of interpreter and guide for the energies of the new nation. As Lewis P. Simpson argues, this shift had its roots in the broad transference of nature and history into mind and the assumption of the rational, lettered mind as the model of order, which found its classic formulation in Jefferson's Declaration of Independence.[2] "When the Declaration was proclaimed," Simpson tells us, "there no longer stood at the center of the world a king, a bishop, and a hierarchical society, but rather the man of letters and his written declaration of mind's assumption of dominion and power" (*Brazen Face* 25). However much this subjectification might promise unprecedented preeminence for the man of letters (as man of mind), Simpson goes on to note that "though the Declaration symbolizes the right conduct of mind as the pattern of a just society, it intimates uncertainty about the Third Realm, anticipating the development of an ambiguous relation between the man of letters and a political, economic, and social order that he assumes, or wants to assume, is emblematic of the order of rational, lettered minds—between the Republic of Letters and its citizen, the man of letters" (25). The man of letters had been positioned in a prophetic role as keeper of mind, but, faced with the growing complexity of the present and his increasing alienation, his foremost public role shifted more to that of the keeper and shaper of public memory.

The United States saw an explosion in interest in history of all kinds in the first half of the nineteenth century. Instead of complacency on the frontiers of historical possibility, the nation experienced a longing for origins, whether within individual communities and states or in Europe. Developments in German, French, and British historiography, and the rise of Romantic history, with the emphasis on historicism and organicism, deepened concern with the nature of the American regions and with the United States as a whole. As Crèvecoeur asked in 1782, "What then is the American, this new man?" How did these disparate former colonies form themselves into a whole? Far from being uninterested in the past, Americans in all regions were busily constructing the "sepulchres of the fathers," as Emerson unhappily noted, and the histories of their regions, states, and towns. George Callcott claims in his study of history in the United States during the period that "never before or since has history occupied such a vital place in the thinking of the American people as during the first half of the nineteenth century."[3] State and local historical societies were founded in rapid succession, and antiquarians began ranging far and wide in search of documents for posterity.

The search for local, regional, and national identity was partially born out of the historical enigma that America itself presented, its radical newness on the world stage, and partially out of a response to European philosophical trends, particularly German Romanticism. Historical thought in Germany had undergone a radical shift in the eighteenth and early nineteenth centuries with a concern over the question of national identity. Herder, Hegel, Schiller, and others had transformed German historiography in their elucidation of a *Volksgeist* and their concern with history as the progressive revelation of underlying form. The search for ancient Germanic roots, the seeds of the national identity, was no mere antiquarianism: "While Voltaire was simply curious about the essence of a past age, the Germans were desperately searching for themselves. Knowledge of history would create the nation" (Callcott 8). This movement (in Germany and elsewhere) gave rise to historicism, the belief that the truth of the present is to be found in the past, in the line of historical development, not according to the template applied by the Enlightenment of the triumph of reason over superstition but according to the principles of organic growth. What a people had been was the surest indication of what they would become. This view gave a new preeminence to the historian and the philosopher of history as the writing of history became the most powerful avenue to truth.

With the new emphasis on history, and with the need in the United States for a history that would give form and substance to the emerging nation, the work of the man of letters became bound up with the historical project. In the case of George Bancroft, the first great Romantic historian in the United States, this situation would give rise to a formal history of the American people, tracing the genesis of liberty from the earliest plantings to the world stage in the birth of the Republic and its expansion. In the case of writers such as Simms, Washington Irving, and James Fenimore Cooper, it would lead to a fiction deeply concerned with historical themes and to an impulse toward formal history as part of their careers.[4] They worked on the border between history and fiction partially as a result of the vocational crisis American writers faced in the first half of the century. Irving was the first American writer to make a living from his pen, but his younger contemporaries had to deal with the fact that fiction and poetry were still seen as accomplishments appropriate to the gentleman amateur. The writer had to justify himself by working as a public servant and, in addition to working in a number of nonliterary capacities (as Irving, Cooper, Bryant, Simms, and others all did), found that history provided a validation of the public worth of writing. This validation was particularly necessary for the novelist, who worked in a genre regarded in the early part of the century as a subversive, corrupting influence.[5]

In the America of the 1820s, as the Republic had given way to a rapidly expanding democracy and the Revolutionary generation was dying out (marked by the deaths of Adams and Jefferson in 1826), the writer had a clear role as both historian and historical novelist in reminding the people of their past and their promise. Writers of an earlier generation, such as Philip Freneau or the Connecticut Wits, wrote in the afterglow of the Revolution and in the spirit of a republican America; the immediacy of the struggle for independence and the glories of the new constitutional order allowed them to focus on the present as the culmination of history. The next generation, as the Revolution receded into the past, would have to recover the immediacy of the Revolution and the colonial period preceding it. It was no longer enough to marvel that the United States *was*—how did it come *to be?* This need led to a veritable flood of historical fiction after 1820. Cooper led the way in the 1820s with his novel of the American Revolution, *The Spy* (1821), and the beginning of his Leatherstocking series; a host of others followed, including the younger Simms with the first two of his historical romances, *The Yemassee* (a colonial romance of Carolina) and *The Partisan* (the first of his Revolutionary War series) in 1835.

Far from viewing the historical novelist as a lesser sort of historian, Simms, in

Views and Reviews, First Series (1846), makes a claim for the artist as perfect historian. Writing to counter the claims of the new critical school of historiography, which emphasized factual accuracy and rigor above all else, Simms claims that "the chief value of history consists in its proper employment for the purposes of art" and not in laying out "an articulated skeleton" of fact.[6] The artist has the power to elevate readers' souls and make them feel, to put flesh on the "truths of the greatest purpose,—the purest integrity, the noblest ambition, the most god-like magnanimity" (32). Not that the writer can neglect sound research, but his "imagination takes part with his judgment, officers and counsels his thought, wings it to the desired fact, and vividly portrays to the mind's eye the hero and the event. Thence he becomes a limner, a painter, a creator; and the picture glows under his glance, and he becomes a living and authentic witness of the past" (37). "Hence," Simms tells us, "it is only the artist who is the true historian" (36). So long as the writer violates no known facts while supplying the additional ones necessary to bring the past before the reader, "it is enough if his narrative warms our affections, inspirits our hopes, elevates our aims, and builds in our minds a fabric of character, compounded of just principles, generous tendencies and clear, correct standards of taste and duty" (38). Indeed, the historian, insofar as he deserves the name, must be an artist, as were Livy and Gibbon. Simms then goes on to describe the vast field of American history as a potential harvest for the romancer—the very paucity of facts that frustrates the chronicler allows much freer range for the novelist.

Simms's novels certainly provided him with fame and established him as a writer with a national reputation, but one must keep in mind that his stature (especially in South Carolina) was bound up with his authority as a historian. While Simms's historical novels are far better known than his histories and biographies, historians since the 1950s have come increasingly to recognize Simms's fidelity to the facts of the past, especially the Revolutionary era.[7] Simms compiled a vast library of more than twelve thousand primary documents related to South Carolina history, primarily concerning the Revolutionary War. If he would argue, especially in *Views and Reviews,* for the superiority of fiction to a mere recounting of fact, he nevertheless built upon the research of a practicing historian. In addresses, essays, and his *History of South Carolina* (1840), he had firmly established himself as the leading historian of South Carolina, and this authority allowed him to act in the public sphere as more than a mere novelist. During the nullification controversy in the early 1830s, the pro-Union *Courier* praised him with comparison to Britain's great historian and public man Thomas Babington Macaulay, and in the 1840s a writer in a *Southern Literary Messenger* article, "Mr. Simms as a Political Writer," asserted that his historical work (including, but not limited to, his historical novels) equipped Simms for "application of that knowledge to present events and the affairs of nations and society generally."[8] This credibility allowed him to engage in public affairs as more than a commentator—to prepare for his term in the South Carolina legislature in 1844–46 and his prominent role in the sectional controversies of the 1850s.

Simms's task as a historian of South Carolina was twofold: first, to assert South Carolina's prominence in the past of the nation as a whole, especially its role in the Revolution and the formation of the United States; and second, to shape a coherent historical identity for South Carolinians. His work was carried out in the context of a national competition among historians from various states and sections who sought to establish their rival claims to prominence in the nation's founding. George Bancroft's *History of the United States* (1835, first volume), easily the most important of these works, proclaimed the triumph of democracy and freedom with a New England emphasis, while historians from the Mid-Atlantic states and Virginia argued with a distinctly different bias. The response to Bancroft's history written by Nathaniel Beverly Tucker in the first volume of the *Southern Literary Messenger* (which began the year Bancroft's first volume was published) makes clear the stakes in the struggle. Objecting strongly to the way in which Bancroft's notions of liberty run roughshod over regional differences, Tucker condemns "this strange attempt to pervert the truth of history" and goes on to warn his Virginia brethren: "Let them [our northern neighbors] write our books, and they become our masters."[9] In spite of their differences on sources and origins, one must keep in mind that the emphasis was still on a unified national destiny for almost all of these writers; the goal was to put forth the unique contribution of a state or section in such a way that it would be seen as central to the nation's present and future.

Simms's nationalism reached its high point in his participation in the Young America movement in the mid-1840s. "Young America" consisted of a group of writers centered around Evert Duyckinck and the *Democratic Review*; these writers, as C. Hugh Holman captures it, "were liberal and radical democrats in politics, ardent nationalists in literature, and committed foes of conservatism in Whig politics and Anglophile criticism."[10] This group came to include Poe and Melville (with Melville's essay "Hawthorne and His Mosses" being Young America's classic statement). The Young America writers' opponents, the Knickerbocker group, with whom Simms was associated in the 1830s, "were conservative Whigs, Anglophiles and internationalists" (Holman xxiii). This group included William Cullen Bryant and John Lawson, Simms's lifelong friend and correspondent. Simms's primary contribution to these literary wars was *Views and Reviews*, especially the address "Americanism in Literature." In it Simms bemoans the American "enslavement" to Europe and specifically England: "Our writers are numerous. . . . But, with very few exceptions, their writings might as well be European. They are European. The writers think after European models, draw their stimulus and provocation from European books, fashion themselves to European tastes, and look chiefly to the awards of European criticism. This is to enslave the national heart—to place ourselves at the mercy of the foreigner, and to yield all that is individual, in our character and hope, to the paralyzing influence of his will, and frequently hostile purposes" (7–8). The literary nationalists wanted American writers to tap into the nation's vast resources of wilderness, its democratic traditions, and the diversity of its people. The aim was to provide a cultural identity and a distinctive voice for America: "It is but to see these things as we should—to understand the world-wide difference between writing *for*, and writing *from* one's people. . . . To write *from* a people is to *write* a people—to make them live—to endow them with a life and a name—to preserve them with a history forever" (12–13). Not that regional distinctiveness is to be lost in national identity—in the vision of Young America, the very multiplicity of the country's regional identities is part of its distinctiveness: "The very inequalities of things in moral respects, in employments, in climate, soil and circumstance, which we find in these severalities, is at once calculated to provoke the mind in each to exertion, and to endow it with originality. There is none of that even tenor of aspect, in the genius of the country, which somewhat monotonously distinguishes an empire the whole energies of which spring from centralization" (28). One must write from one's region, or, as Simms states, "To be *national* in literature one must needs be *sectional*."[11]

The combination of an ardent nationalism and a pronounced sectionalism in the first half of Simms's career is one of several apparent contradictions in his work and thought. The South for Simms, however, was in a process of becoming, and Simms's role as a Romantic man of letters, a man of mind, was to reconcile opposing tendencies—aristocracy and democracy, tradition and dynamic change, agrarianism and the promise of industry, up-country and low country, seaboard and frontier—and thereby give shape and direction to the unfolding of his civilization. It must be remembered that even while Simms sought to find his place in the highly stratified social structure of Charleston, he remained, as Holman phrases it, "a committed Jacksonian and a consistent Jeffersonian" (xiv). The conflict between the democratic and patrician models of order was by no means peculiar to Simms; the South itself struggled with the potential of Jacksonian democracy and Jeffersonian liberty set against the backdrop of an economy and a social order largely based on chattel slavery. Louis D. Rubin perhaps sums up the challenge for the modern reader best: "Anyone who does not understand that in the antebellum South one could both be a vigorous advocate of chattel slavery and an enthusiastic believer in 'Loco-foco' popular democracy will be unable to understand the antebellum South."[12] The effort Simms would make in history and fiction to balance democratic potential and patrician order was largely informed by his ambivalence toward the frontier and the old Southwest.

For Simms, the frontier represented at once the promise of renewal and the threat of barbarism. Simms struggled with the legacy of his father, a failed Charleston merchant who had gone west, fought with Jackson at New Orleans and in the Indian wars, and made good as a Mississippi planter. Simms remained in Charleston with his maternal grandmother—choosing Charleston and chosen by it—though promised by his father a plantation, a prosperous law practice, and a seat in Congress.[13] His father's indictment of the city in a letter to his young son would haunt his choice: "Return to Charleston! Why should you return to Charleston, where you can never succeed in any profession, where you need what you have not,—friends, family, and fortune; and without these your whole life, unless some happy accident should favor you, will be a mere apprenticeship, a hopeless drudging after bread. Ho! do not think of it. . . . Charleston! *I know it only as a place of tombs.*"[14] Simms often portrays Charleston in this period as stifling, ossified, and sterile, in contrast to the vibrant and expanding West. His three trips to the frontier in 1824–25, 1831, and 1842 allowed him to see the potential of the new country, although he would always return to Charleston.

Even while he was thus drawn to the new region, as were many of his contemporaries, he was troubled by the threat of the breakdown of social order, the loss of civilization. He warned the Alabama undergraduates attending his lecture "The Social Principle" in 1842, after surveying the remarkable progress of the region from his first visit, "Your prosperity is the due result of whatsoever degree of thought has been expended upon your progress, and whatever measure of energy has been concentrated upon the plans and purposes of your intellect. . . . It is only by venerating the mind which has made, that the works of mind may be preserved, unimpaired, for posterity."[15] Mind, for Simms, is intimately bound up with the spirit of a people, and the integrity of that cultural identity was precisely what was threatened by expansion; "the wandering habit of our people" had led to a dissolution of home and hearth, the traditions of the people. Civilization (and thereby mind) was being sacrificed for "the little more to the cotton heap," and Simms's assessment was severe: "We are lamentably sunk in character—not our Government—do not delude yourselves,—but our people,—you, and I, and all of us" (48). Simms, in fiction and nonfiction, found his hope for the South in a dialectic between frontier and tidewater, the one bringing life and promise, the other order and tradition. In his border romances, he constructed plots in which a young man from the East goes to the frontier and meets the agents of chaos on the frontier (usually in the form of outlaws such as the Murrell gang); the young man ultimately chooses to return to the plantation culture (often in the East) but does so both chastened and strengthened by the encounter. Simms was ambivalent about Charleston, but he was no less so concerning the frontier. As Wakelyn notes, "He considered it a land of opportunity, yet he disliked the 'boomer' mentality. He loved the raw beauty of nature but was concerned over what kind of society such freedom would produce" (28). In his effort to reconcile the promise and hazards of expansion, he turned to characters who provided a model of leadership in the midst of it. Further, he turned to the Revolution, a time of dynamic change and potential crisis, to examine the men who had guided the society through it and "preserved the works of mind," bringing forth the new Republic. In his biographies, his history, and much of his fiction, he found the ideal figure in the partisan warrior.

The partisan leader, for Simms, embodied the traits needed in a time of civilizational crisis. The vast majority of Simms's heroic figures, in fiction, history, poetry, and commentary, are really various manifestations of this single type. Looming over them all is the gigantic figure of Old Hickory, Simms's model of frontier leadership projected onto the national and international stage. As Wakelyn points out, Simms continued to look for a new Jackson to assume the reins of southern leadership through the 1850s (163). Jackson had successfully channeled the energy of rough frontiersmen into military victories and guided the forces tending toward anarchy in the Republic into a new democratized political order still capable of united action—in the progressive realization of the nation's destiny. Jackson, whom Simms claimed as a South Carolinian by birth, was heir to the legacy of the great partisan leaders of South Carolina: Sumter, Moultrie, Marion, and the other legendary leaders of the Carolina resistance.

The partisan leader is at once the aristocrat by nature and man among equals in the rough equality of the frontier. He claims his right to rule by natural authority, not by birth or circumstance, and reconciles in his own person the order and grace of the plantation and the vigor of the wilderness settlement. Surveying the leadership of South Carolina, Simms was equally disgusted by individuals who held power by virtue of controlling banks and other institutions, those who claimed authority as a prerogative of social class, and those who sought power through demagoguery. Simms turns to the Revolutionary leaders of South Carolina for models of the leadership suited to the character of the people. In *The Partisan* (1835), he emphasizes time and again the nature of Major Singleton's relationship to his men and his peculiar rapport with all of them, regardless of station: "All were sure, as the Major of Partisans went by, to hear his gentle salutation, in those frank tones which penetrated instantly to the heart, a sufficient guaranty for the sincerity of the speaker. And there was no effort in this familiar frankness, and no air of condescension. He was a man speaking to men; and did not appear to dream of making every word, look, and tone remind them of this authority. His bearing, when not engaged in the absolute duties of the service, was that of an equal, simply. And yet there was really no familiarity between the parties."[16] For Simms, the situation of the partisan warrior holds a particular relevance to the challenges of leadership in the rapidly expanding South. Partisan (or guerrilla) warfare, "the peculiar and most difficult of all kinds of warfare,"[17] forces the leader to act in the face of constantly shifting circumstances, inadequate supplies, and social disorder, but the commander's gift allows him to transcend these circumstances: "Unprovided with the means of warfare, no less than of comfort—wanting equally in food and weapons—we find him supplying the one deficiency with a cheerful courage that never failed; the other with the resources of a genius that seemed to wish for nothing from without" (*Marion* 10). Given the contingencies of time and place, he is "happily dextrous in emergencies to seize upon the momentary casualty, the sudden chance—to convert the most trivial circumstances, the most ordinary agent, into a means of extrication or offence" (*Marion* 23). Most important, he knows the people of his region and works in accordance with their genius to turn citizen-soldiers into an effective, unified force, overcoming difficulties with their wide dispersal over the countryside, the demands of bringing in crops to feed their families, and their native temperament—ill disciplined, impetuous, and independent. Such were the qualities of the leaders who enabled an isolated South to play its role in the struggle for independence and the nation's founding, and such must be the leaders who would ensure it continued to play a significant role in the nation's realization of its destiny, a significant challenge as the agrarian South continued to lose ground in the 1830s and 1840s to the rapidly industrializing North in the struggle for national leadership.

In his three biographies of the 1840s, Simms provides a composite portrait of a partisan leader answering to the character of the region. He worked to put forth a model, especially though not exclusively for the youth, of leaders who represented the finest expression of their people at a moment of radical change. Certainly this would be "philosophy teaching by example," as Simms had it (quoting Thucydides), but rather than turn to a Julius Caesar or an Alexander, Simms dealt specifically with three figures who represent certain facets of the southern character at its finest, set against the tendencies of the South Simms struggled against.

This ideal of leadership, for Simms, did not apply merely to military or political leadership, of course; as several scholars have noted, Simms was deeply concerned about the role of the public intellectual in the South. John McCardell, especially, has emphasized the connection between "poetry and the practical" for Simms—his need to balance the claims of belles lettres with his notion of the intellectual's wider responsibility to his community. As an editor/writer in various periodicals concerned as much with the current political scene as with art, as a writer who produced a geography, histories, and biographies in addition to novels and poetry, and as a lecturer, Simms simultaneously turned intellectual endeavor into a sort of action and created the space for that very action through his crafting and reshaping of notions of leadership and activity. Concerning the biographies, McCardell claims, "Through these four works [counting the biography of Greene] he reexamined the role of the intellectual in society. What most united them, in other words, was the way in which they allowed Simms to speak out in a personal way about himself as a writer in Charleston."[18] While McCardell overplays the mundane autobiographical elements of the biographies, he is certainly right about the connection between the works and Simms's self-image. But this image is equally that of the people Simms cherished as kindred spirits, such as Hammond (most clearly) or another friend, John Izard Middleton, whom he compares to Bayard in the dedication of that work. By cele-brating a certain type of leader in a certain sort of transitional stage in history, Simms attempted to convey both that this was such a time for South Carolina and the South and that such a time demanded such a leader.

Simms's first full-length biography was *The Life of Francis Marion*, and the work provides the clearest expression of the ideal of the partisan warrior in the Revo-lutionary moment. If Andrew Jackson provided Simms with his ideal for national leadership in his own age, Francis Marion looms larger than any other figure in South Carolina history. His symbolic power stems from the purity of his role in the regional imagination. He stands simply and purely as *"par excellence,* the fa-mous partizan of that region . . . the wily fox of the swamps" (9) and rises not from Charleston but from the settlements of the time. Like Cincinnatus, he came from the plow to the field of battle when (as Simms says of Jackson) "the earth had need of him."[19] As a militia commander in regional campaigns, principally those of resistance in the complete absence of the Continental army, he is not a national hero like Washington but exclusively identified with South Carolina and its neglected contribution to the Revolutionary struggle.

In spite of Marion's various personal excellences, Simms stresses his connec-tion to the people of the state, in both the shape of his character in life and the shape of his legend in death. Simms dwells at some length on Marion's Hugue-not ancestry and the honorable role the Huguenots have played in South Caro-lina. Simms, like Carlyle or Emerson, sees the hero as emerging from the people, as the finest expression of their essential character. In praising the Huguenots, Simms praises a distinctive strain in the racial mix of South Carolina. They were a "much better sort of people than those who usually constituted the mass of European immigrants" and, "though a gentle race, were men of soul and strength, capable of great sacrifices, and protracted self-denial" (13–14). Coming of age in a stable culture of virtuous and industrious people, Marion also profited from the frontier circumstances, gaining "hardihood, elasticity, great courage, and ad-mirable dexterity in war" (24). In keeping with his notions of social organicism, Simms stresses the formation of Marion's character by the larger community and sets a harmonious relation between the leader and the people he leads. Heroes are no mere anomalies, Simms explains: "On the contrary, we take for granted, that every distinguished person will, in some considerable degree, betray in his own mind and conduct, the most striking of those characteristics, which mark the community in which he has had his early training; that his actions will, in great measure, declare what sort of moral qualities have been set before his eyes, not so much by his immediate family, as by the society at large in which he lives" (24). Simms goes on to further emphasize the representative character of the leader, and he does so in a way that bears particular relation to Simms's own situation as a public intellectual and advocate of change in Charleston and the South. One even senses the ghost of his wandering father haunting the following passage and hints of his attempt to overcome his problematic relationship to Charleston in his effort to identify himself with South Carolina through his prophetic vocation as man of letters: "He will represent that society rather than his immediate family, as it is the nature of superior minds to rush out of the narrow circles of domestic life; and . . . his whole after-performances, even where he may appear in the garb and guise of the reformer, will indicate in numerous vital respects, the tastes and temper of the very people whose alteration and improvement he seeks" (24–25). Simms's problem was that of the American writer for much of the nineteenth century, closing the widening gap Simpson refers to between the Republic of Letters and the man of letters. Marion, facing no such conflict, provides the perfect example of the visionary man of action who is at one and the same time a leader of the people and their finest expression.

As the culture shaped Marion's character, so the people preserved his fame through legend and tale in the absence of official records, and Simms presents his history as an extension of their work of memory. "'Marion's Brigade' and 'Marion's men,' have passed into household words, which the young utter with an enthusiasm much more confiding than that which they yield to the wondrous performances of Greece and Ilium," he tells us (10). "It is a people's history, written in their hearts rather than in their books" and so "seems to have escaped the ordinary bounds of history. It is no longer within the province of the historian. It has passed into the hands of the poet, and seems to scorn the appeal to authentic chronicles" (11–12). Simms, in his attempt to write a "sober history" of so fabled a character, stretches the bounds of history in a marriage of formal history and popular legend. In his introduction, he situates his own work between the Marion biographies of Parson Weems and Judge James. The Reverend Weems, he says, produced "a delightful book for the young," but he has "rather loose notions of the privileges of the biographer" (vii–viii). The strength of Weems's biographies lies in their vivid embellishment of events and character (with the biographer often supplying them out of whole cloth). Weems is the people's historian, writing out of and for the popular imagination, but Simms at several points faults his lack of respect for the facts and his twisting of Marion's essential character and the concrete historical situation for the sake of a successful formula. Judge James, on the other hand, produced a factually accurate account, but "as a literary performance, it is quite devoid of merit as pretension" (viii). Lacking the imaginative faculty of the artist, James is the "mere chronicler" Simms consistently denigrates, and his account lacks the evocative, shaping character essential to bringing the force of heroes and events to bear.

Simms emphasizes the specific challenges faced by the partisan resistance in South Carolina, far removed from the main theater of war to the north and having the character more of a civil war between loyalist Tories and partisan Whigs. He highlights the isolation of the South following the fall of Charleston and Savannah and the defeat of General Gates at Camden. In the case of Charleston, specifically, he questions the tactical wisdom of sacrificing four thousand sorely needed troops in a doomed effort to save the city in the early stages of the war. To understand the contribution of Marion and the other partisans to the Revolutionary effort, Simms claims, one must understand that, although the South was securely under control by the British regulars, it was imperative that the British be forced to maintain that control and not shift large bodies of troops to the North. The partisans accomplished this aim through disrupting communications and supply lines and harassing outlying, poorly defended posts. Most important, the power of the Tories could not be allowed to grow, as it did during the periods when the South seemed given over to the British and South Carolinians were faced with making the best of their situation. Simms claims here (as he will more emphatically in later years) that South Carolina's motivation for revolt was distinct from that of New England and the rest of the colonies. While the mercantile, manufacturing North was forced into rebellion by tariffs and taxes, the South, with a different economy and largely unaffected by the same measures, acted out of indignation at the infringement on southerners' rights as Englishmen. Although, as Simms has it, their motives were less mercenary and the spirit of liberty on the part of the partisans purer, this difference in motivation made for a much more complicated situation among the people at large. A much larger percentage of South Carolinians remained loyal to England, whether out of an abiding fidelity to country and crown, or to protect their lives and property, or to exploit the situation and ruthlessly rob their Whig neighbors, thus gaining wealth and favor with the ruling powers. Simms, here as elsewhere, characterizes the struggle as a civil war: "Motives of private anger and personal revenge embittered and increased the usual ferocities of civil war; and hundreds of dreadful and desperate tragedies gave that peculiar aspect to the struggle, which led [General Nathanael] Greene to say that the inhabitants pursued each other rather like wild beasts than like men" (162). It was a time of social chaos, when men, if they were governed at all, were governed only by a law within themselves; the partisan leader acted solely out of a sense of firm conviction, being on no payroll and often acting independent of any higher authority.

Simms knew from his experience of the Southwest that rights and law could be used as a mere veil to be hung over private vengeance and the pursuit of power, and he makes clear that these motives were not absent on either the Tory or the patriot side of the Revolutionary conflict. His highlighting of these motives only sets in higher contrast the manner in which the partisan leaders transcended their situation and reflected in their character the finest attributes of their civilization. In spite of their very American aim of securing liberty, they embodied, in refined form, the inheritance of European chivalry, and it is these traits that distinguish them, as conservative revolutionaries, from mere rebels, mercenaries, or outlaws. Their eyes were set on human possibilities, in a new form for a new age but in keeping with the finest examples of human virtue throughout all ages. Marion and the other partisan leaders have these virtues in the highest degree, but they are representative of the essence of their people even at the moment when that essence is determining a new form. In contrast to the brutality among individuals in Revolutionary Carolina, Simms sets forth a strength of soul manifested in the war that bodes well for what might come of these people, as we see after his description of the valiant defense of Fort Sullivan in the opening stages of the war: "The coolness—nay, the cavalier indifference—displayed by the Carolinians throughout the combat, is not its least remarkable feature. There is something chivalric in such deportment, which speaks for larger courage that belongs to ordinary valor. Mere bull-dog resolution and endurance is here lifted, by a generous ardor of soul, into something other than a passive virtue. The elasticity of spirit which it shows might be trained to any performance within the compass of human endowment" (74). Simms is at great pains at times to distinguish fighting for a just cause from delight in warfare, strife to secure a more perfect order from mere rebellion, and partisan tactics from mere banditry. Writing at a time when the very energy that promised the expansion and improvement of civilization threatened to undermine it, Simms focuses on the character of the men and women who ensured continuity in the midst of change and made the Revolutionary frontier a place and time of promise rather than decay.

Simms casts Marion as a force for order by describing him as a knight-errant in the democratic cause. Marion becomes a symbol of the continuity of ancient European traditions in a new historical moment, striking the perfect balance between civilization and frontier. Simms focuses on the character of Marion throughout his biography, not as something evolving but (as we have seen above) formed by his community in his early years and determining his later actions in all circumstances. He is a highly idealized figure, one of those "perfect characters . . . the beautiful symmetry of whose moral structure leaves us nothing to regret in the analysis of his life" (20). This idealized vision leads Simms to rhetorical flights so reminiscent of medieval romance as to be indistinguishable from his later treatment of the good knight Bayard. We are told, for instance, that prior to his encounter with the Cherokee, Marion "had yet to flesh his maiden valor upon the enemy" (33). Simms uses the chivalric rhetoric to set Marion apart from the cruelty and excesses of the times, as exemplified by Tarleton and the Tories on the one hand and backcountry rebels on the other: "No single specification of cruelty was ever alleged against the fair fame of Francis Marion" (144). Simms portrays the partisan as lord of a separate realm, as we see most clearly when Simms describes Marion's encampment on Snow's Island:

> Marion's career as a partisan, in the thickets and swamps of Carolina, is abundantly distinguished by the picturesque; but it was while he held his camp at Snow's Island, that it received its highest colors of romance. In this snug and impenetrable fortress, he reminds us very much of the ancient feudal baron of France and Germany, who, perched on castled eminence, looked down with the complacency of an eagle from his eyrie, and marked all below him for his own. The resemblance is good in all respects but one. The plea and justification of Marion are complete. His warfare was legitimate. He was no mountain robber,—no selfish and reckless ruler, thirsting for spoil and delighting inhumanly in blood. The love of liberty, the defence of country, the protection of the feeble, the maintenance of humanity and all its dearest interests, against its tyrant—

these were the noble incentives which strengthened him in his stronghold, made it terrible in the eyes of his enemy, and sacred in those of his
countrymen. (166)

Serving in the cause of liberty, the chivalrous Marion not only transcended the
base struggle of many of his contemporaries but improved upon a certain variety of the medieval model as well. Simms makes his allusions in such a way as
to leave no doubt that Marion is aligned with the *"mouvement* party" and the progressive emancipation of the human spirit.

Marion is the knight from the hand of nature, escaping the excesses of un-
restrained power while embodying the finest elements of the knightly tradition.
Simms emphasizes that Marion's vigorousness and decisiveness did not exclude
gentleness and forbearance—here again, the hero carries a law within himself in
circumstances in which force seems to be the only law. Simms points to several
actions throughout the book to illustrate "that rare humanity which was one of
the most remarkable and lovely traits of his character" (50–51). Marion and his
men inhabit the green world outside the bounds of civilization, even while their
forays into it will change its course. The bond of Marion's men to their leader is
"characteristic of only the most romantic history": "That he should disband his
men at one moment, and be able by a word to bring them together when they
were wanted, proves a singular alliance between the chieftain and his followers"
(129). The hero of the new world finds his proper analogue in the old in Robin
Hood, struggling against the unjust dictates of a prince. Marion's camp at Snow's
Island, in both its security and pastoral beauty, was "one, complete to his hands,
from those of nature—such an one as must have delighted the generous English
outlaw of Sherwood Forest" (167). Simms shapes his allusions to distance Marion
from the aspects of knighthood that might seem brutal to some of his contemporaries and which found an unfortunate (to his mind) continuation in the present South. Marion was "notoriously the most merciful of enemies" (165) and
scorned certain aspects of the chivalric inheritance: he was not quick to sense
an affront to his pride, and his vengeance was never personal. Simms is writing
for his people, and he attempts to separate the ideal of honor and erroneous notions of it. He tells us of Marion: "His ardor was never of a kind to make him imprudent. . . . We have no proofs that he ever engaged in a single combat" (11–12).
While Marion might accept a challenge from an enemy in the field to a combat
between groups of twenty picked men, "a proposal that savored something of

chivalry," he bluntly refused a challenge to a duel from an officer whom he had disciplined, treating "the summons with deserved contempt" (184).[20] Simms works very deliberately to differentiate chivalry and savagery. In Marion, he creates a balance between aristocratic past and democratic future, enlivening the one and restraining the other.

Of course, there is a latent contradiction in using the chivalrous ideal from a feudal age to portray the democratic hero, and this contradiction comes to the fore when Simms speaks of the order arising out of the Revolution. When the newly formed legislature takes seats, guarded from disturbance by the army of Greene, Marion is among its members, and it is anything but a body of the people at large, as Simms represents it: "Constituting as they did, in a slave community, a sort of feudal aristocracy, and accustomed, as, for so long a time they had been, to the use of weapons of war, its members wore the deportment of so many armed barons, gathered together quite as much for action as resolve" (292–93). It was a body of aristocrats by nature, who had demonstrated their capacity for bringing order out of disorder, and their decisions were marked by power and wisdom, as Simms writes, "Who could so well determine what were the necessities of the country—what the exigencies of the people—what the local resources and remedies—as those who had fought its battles, traversed every acre of its soil, and represented its interests and maintained its rights when there was no civil authority?" (293). Simms here attempts to reconcile a problem that haunts the southern writer from Thomas Jefferson to Allen Tate and beyond when considering the peculiar problem of the antebellum South: how does one reconcile the founding of a democracy with a society built upon chattel slavery? For Simms, the Revolution brought forth leaders who had a connection with the broader community and the land, who had demonstrated their worth in a time that separated character from pretension, and who possessed a selflessness that certainly is not the predominant trait of a hierarchical, "feudal" society. In his mind, though, the promise of the struggle for liberty could be reconciled with slavery, and he suppresses the contradictions and ends with Marion in the traditional figure of plantation patriarch. Of the end of his life, Simms tells us, "He had become fond of rural life, and the temporary estrangement of war seemed only to increase his desire for that repose in action, which the agricultural life in the South so certainly secures" (334). "In the decline of life, in the modest condition of the farmer, Marion seems to have lived among his neighbors very much as an ancient patriarch, surrounded by his flock" (344)—the patriot becomes the patriarch. Because of the conservative character of the American Revolution, as Simms saw it, its energies were directed at the strengthening of the plantation order, not its undermining, thereby maintaining the necessary balance between progress and stability.[21]

From Marion in the Revolutionary period—the shared origin of the United States—Simms turns to Captain John Smith in the period of exploration as he seeks to establish a southern claim on American origins. If Marion embodied, for Simms, the best of Old and New World virtues, Captain Smith quite literally spanned the two continents at the time of first settlement. In his early career he was a knight serving a Christian prince against the Turks and in his later one the savior of Jamestown and the founder of American civilization. Smith is more complicated than Marion, from a ruder age and without the "perfect" character of the Swamp Fox; Simms, in good Romantic fashion, makes clear that the standards and mores of our own age cannot be used to judge conduct in another, but still he tells the reader: "Our object is not to excuse but to represent him justly."[22] Smith embodied the traits that made English colonization so different from Spanish or French; he was no mere explorer or adventurer but a founder. He combined the strength and vigor of a Cortes with the wisdom of a good lawmaker and was therefore the one who could carry civilization into the wilderness not simply for exploitation (as the Spanish) but for the progress of civilization into the new continent. For Simms, he is the great man of the age of exploration, able to bridge the gap between Old World and New, and it is as "one of the master spirits of this period and of modern times, that [Smith] challenges the consideration of our people" (11).

Simms devotes the first portion of his biography to Smith's exploits as a soldier in Europe, a training in action and chivalry as a Christian knight fighting the infidel. Like Marion (or other Romantic heroes, for that matter), Smith is a man of action, one of those people in whom "the blood and the brain work together in the most exquisite uniformity" and who "seem to conceive and to think more justly while in action than in repose" (9–10). Simms emphasizes that Smith was not one to simply find his place in the existing order but one whose spirit demanded new fields of action for an order carried within. He looks upon Smith's failure to gain an appointment to the royal court as a gift of providence, saving Smith "from this sort of degradation" (16). Society, whether in Smith's London or Simms's Charleston, is fraught with the danger of languor and complacency, and Simms characterizes Smith as transcending the normal routes to power and place in his time: "His blood was naturally fretted by inactivity, and the very presence of a crowd, *of a society that was performing nothing*, must soon have disgusted a temper, which, for so long a period, had enjoyed for its daily food the humors and the excitements of a camp, the variety and the animation of a great city, the dangers of the sea, and the thousand stimulating aspects and avocations of a strange land" (19; emphasis mine). Rather than entering the court, Smith retreated to the forests, in the guise and manners of a hermit, and engaged in what Simms presents as an ideal regimen of self-culture, reading Marcus Aurelius and Machiavelli, hunting, and practicing with lance and ring. Simms's observations on Smith's woodland training in the "minor arts of war" echo those he makes both earlier and later regarding the preparation of the southerner for war. Such a preparation befits one who is a "nobleman of nature" rather than of society. Before turning from the forests of England to the wilder forests of America, Smith will complete his training on the older chivalrous fields of the European continent in the struggle against the Turks.

Simms goes to great lengths to establish Smith's credentials as both a chivalric hero and a man of action. Smith's experience on the European continent provided him with training in partisan warfare, activity for both mind and body, and training as a knight of the old school, complete with a patent of nobility. Smith joined the armies of Rudolph of Germany in a campaign against the Third Mahomet, and in the wilds of Transylvania "Smith was employed in a manner which must have afforded him excellent training for his future career among our North American Indians," having to "contend with a people practised in guerilla or partisan warfare" (46). His resources were tested, and in addition to his successes in combat, Simms credits Smith with "certain improvements in the art of war" (ranging from codes to employment of fireworks)—Smith is "that rare combination of thinker and worker" (33). Simms dwells longest on Smith's successes during the siege of Regnall, where he emerges as a full-fledged knight and earns his patent. Simms often balks at the brutality of warfare, but the tournament that follows a Turkish challenge to the Christians before Regnall draws his unabashed enthusiasm. He tells us of the Turkish damsels adorning the walls and the reluctance of the knights to "depart from the city without affording any pastime to the ladies thereof": "The challenge was after the fashion of knightly times, and these had not entirely gone out of the memories of men" (50). It was "in the best spirit of the Middle Ages" (50), and Simms presents the soon-to-be founder of the Jamestown settlement as direct heir to that older tradition.

Smith wins three heads in successive single combats with Turkish champions, gains his patent of nobility (which Simms places as an appendix to the volume), and goes on to further knightly exploits, leading Simms to some of his most notable rhetorical excesses: "He did not repose upon the laurels of Regnall, but in all probability dyed his sanguinary chaplet trebly red in the havoc of that mortal struggle" (66).

Before Smith returns to England and sets out for the new continent, his career is interrupted by a period of slavery in the hands of the Turks, and significantly—considering that he is dealing here with the man responsible for the first settlement of what will become a unique modern slave society—Simms goes into some detail regarding Smith's period of bondage. Smith is captured and sold in the slave markets of Axiopolis to a Turk and given to the man's "faire mistress," Charatza Tragabigzanda. Simms, in history or fiction, cannot pass a good love story by, but here the story is of slave and mistress, and he goes so far as to compare Smith's account to the story of Othello, indirectly introducing the specter of race into the equation. Simms, writing during the 1840s, when the brutality of slavery was directly in question, then proceeds to detail Smith's fate at the hands of a brutal master: "Within an hour after his arrival, our adventurer was stripped naked, his head and beard shaven 'so bare as his hand,' his body clad in undrest skins and haircloth, and a heavy ring of iron, 'with a long stalke bowed like a sickle riveted about his neck'" (76). He is pushed "beyond the endurance of a dog" by a master: a "petty tyrant; who, for all [his slaves'] pains and labours, no more regarded them than a beast" (76). Smith *kills* his master, with the full approval of Simms, and escapes back to Christendom. Even granted that part of the polemical effort of the slavery apologists during this period was to cast southern slavery as a benevolent institution in contrast to other (and earlier) forms of it, Simms comes dangerously close here to something that might have provided fodder for the abolitionists (and, with slight modification, might have spiced up an issue of *The Liberator*). In any case, Simms does not downplay the fact that the founder of Jamestown had been bought and sold, though he does make it into something of a romantic adventure.

Simms dwells upon all these experiences as preparation for Smith's voyage to the new continent, and he portrays Smith as well suited to resist the temptations offered by the new frontier. Simms tells us that Smith, never idle, returned to England: "He was now better prepared than ever to convert these admirable qualities of courage into useful and efficient agencies for the prosecution of great designs" (92). Of course, it was an age of great designs, and Simms is careful to distinguish the noble motives of Smith from those of most of his contemporaries. However much he might praise Smith, Simms certainly does not gloss over the more troubling aspects of Virginia's founding. The frontier, in Simms's age as well as Smith's, could bring out the worst as well as the best aspects of human character. Of the New World generally, Simms writes, "To the boy-dreamer about Arcadia and the golden age, it offered all that imagination could conjecture and Astraea could supply. To the veteran, grown grey in stratagems and spoils, without having grown strong in their retention, it opened the most easy paths for the attainment of his selfish objects. Freedom from all restraints of law, and conflict only with a people entirely without its pale and protection, were considerations beyond price to the habitual ruffian, who, in the world itself, found nothing more precious than an oyster which he was permitted to open with his sword" (94). In contrast to these adventurers, men such as Sir Walter Raleigh and Smith constituted "another class . . . who loved adventure for its own sake, who never looked to the mere personal rewards, and not often or too closely at the consequences, and who were better pleased to be doing and achieving, even if suffering also, than in the acquisition of spoils, or even the honors of the achievement" (96). Simms continues in a critical vein when he turns to the Jamestown settlers specifically, noting that the "exceeding disproportion between the gentlemen and the mechanics and laborers reminds us irresistibly of the limited allowance of bread to sack in the domestic economy of Falstaff" (103). Smith is the heroic figure who can make Jamestown something more than a shipping station for plunder; he is the settler, the lawmaker, and the good soldier in one, but his efforts meet with resistance from lesser men of more limited aims. Even his rivals for leadership, according to Simms, have to recognize that he is "the true man," "the king-man . . . a sovereign by the appointment of nature," but they realize that his character stands in the way of their personal designs for power and wealth: "The world-man cordially hates the God-man, and will destroy him if he can" (105).

Smith's main occupation in Virginia was "to protect the greater number of his followers from themselves," and Simms's indictment of them reads much like his comments on contemporary Charleston and the South. The early Virginians were lazy malcontents who were unwilling to change even when stasis meant destruction, and Smith acted repeatedly (in his own account as in Simms) to force them to provide for their own survival and eventual prosperity. He is the actor/thinker who wakes his contemporaries to their own situation and its potential. Simms tells us that the "moral of his progress" for his own age is found in Smith's own statement of his "general principles": to "'discover the contrey, subdue the people, bring them to be tractable, civill and industrious;' in order that the resources of their own nature, and the virtues of the soil and climate, might at once be brought into just fruition" (286). The wildness to be overcome was in the settlers as much as, if not more than, in the land to be settled, as the infertility and barrenness of the southern soil of Simms's own time he saw as stemming from the people rather than the soil. In his treatment of this earliest phase of the southern plantings, Simms provides his readers with a model of action and leadership in Smith and prepares them to accept such leadership in their own age. The biography is a cautionary tale as well, since Smith was finally forced from the colony and back to England; it ends, after other voyages, with Smith as a man who had served two countries and had no holding or reward in either (much as Simms might have seen his situation serving an inappreciative South in exile from the northern publishing centers). Smith ultimately is the great prototype of the man of mind as actor and writer, since he became "something of a literary man," who "held the pen quite as vigorously as he did the sword," and his own chronicler (327). In fact, given his contributions to New England through his writings (in advising on settlement), Smith's literary acts are quite as significant as his physical and political ones.

Smith's founding of Jamestown and Virginia also provides Simms with a counter to the myth of the Puritan origins of America and the American genesis at Plymouth and Massachusetts Bay, which had gained increased currency through the writings of Bancroft and others. Simms treats Smith's voyages to New England (and his naming of it) as a mere afterthought; his focus is on the genesis of America in the ruins of the Jamestown settlement, and it inspires the most extended rhetorical flight in the book:

> But the foundation of the city was a small and trivial event to that of the great nation which has yet grown from this small beginning: and he whose eye beholds now upon this memorable but neglected spot no trophy more significant that the rents of ruin in the arches of a single tower overgrown with ivy, and the rank forest growth which denotes the mound where sleep the bones of the early settlers, will scarcely be persuaded that he beholds the obscure nest and birth-place, as lowly as that

of the sea-fowl which leaves her eggs along the shore, of the great nation whose wing now spreads, or is fast spreading, over the whole vast continent of North America. . . . From this memorable movement the tree takes root, in the future shade of which a mighty people are to find shelter, and in the fruits of which a thousand generations are to gather strength and sustenance. Verily, we may not look upon that ruin of a town, that low and lonely remnant of our royal hamlet, on the north side of the river Powhatan, with unconcern and indifference! (111)

This is a southern version of the national story, a version still consonant with the aims of literary nationalism but already tending toward the southern nationalism Simms will champion by the 1850s.

After Smith, Simms moved to a figure more central to the South's self-conception and the embodiment of the South's chivalric ideal: Chevalier Bayard, a legendary French knight who served Charles VIII and Francis I during the late fifteenth and early sixteenth centuries. His *Life of the Chevalier Bayard* (1847) completes a movement from Marion, the hero of liberty with a chivalric character, to Smith, the Christian knight who had begun New World settlement by the English, to Bayard, a figure so ideal as to be an anachronism even in his own time and certainly far removed from the reality of the antebellum South. The Chevalier, *sans peur et sans reproche*, "furnishes the most admirable model to the generous ambition of the young that we find in all the pages of history," but it is a model with only the most tenuous connection to American life.[23] *Bayard* marks a shift that would grow increasingly noticeable after 1848, away from the South's part in a larger democratic project toward a defensive posture and abstract argument. Scott's influence here is pronounced, but it is more of the idealizing, enervating sort assailed by Mark Twain in later years, rather than the dynamic vision of the past that had inspired much of the best historical writing. Bayard, as noted by Wakelyn, is "the classic embodiment of romantic nationalism" (122) of a sort peculiarly well suited to contrast with the crass materialism and base motives of the Yankee. Bayard is the "model of a perfect character" who kept the "whiteness of his soul free from spot, in spite of the contagion in which he lived" (3–5), and his one great distinguishing characteristic (apart from his general excellence) was his fidelity to his country and king.

Again, Simms chooses a figure at a transition point in history, as Europe passed into the modern world. Bayard lived in a time of deceit and treachery, when the spirit of chivalry had ebbed and he was the last bloom, "the fairest flower of knighthood," on a withering vine. As Simms writes in the opening passage: "It was a time when chivalry was at its lowest condition in Christian Europe; when the fine affectations of the order, erring always on the side of generosity and virtue—its strained courtesies, its overwrought delicacies, its extravagant and reckless valor—every thing, in short, of that grace and magnanimity which had constituted its essential spirit and made of it a peculiar institution—had given way to less imposing and less worthy characteristics" (1–2). Unlike the examples furnished by Marion and Smith, Bayard functions only as a rebuke to the crass present (of his own age and Simms's); he is certainly a man of action, but, in contrast to the others, he does not act to bring something new into being. His is a rear-guard action of a passing age, and the nobility of his life lies partly in its futility. Simms characterizes his life simply and well: "If it is greatly honorable to found an illustrious family, it is no less meritorious to maintain its character, and finish nobly its career" (6).

As much as Simms celebrates the chivalric virtues of Bayard, he is by no means uncritical in his approach to chivalry; Simms carefully qualifies his admiration to suit the standards of a more enlightened age, and he is blind to the incongruity between celebration of the knightly ethos and his strictures on its excesses and contradictions. Apart from the obvious barbarity of siege and sack, Simms is most severe in his condemnation of single combats to defend one's honor, a practice that had continued in the United States, particularly in the South, and reached its height in the Jacksonian period. He praises Francis Marion in the earlier biography for the fact that "no duel took place among his officers during the whole of his command" (331) and notes that "we have no proofs that he ever engaged in a single combat" himself (12). Even though he sketches the single combats themselves rather romantically, he provides a gloss to convey his disapproval, as he does when Bayard kneels to pray before his combat with Don Alonzo of the Spanish army: "We shall comment hereafter upon what seems to us a strange inconsistency in this act of pious devotion, at the very moment one is about to violate the laws of that Being before whom he kneels in hope and supplication" (102). The tension between romantic appeal and moral judgment is encapsulated in one sentence: "Certainly, seen through the medium of our more prosaic era, this institution of chivalry was a thing of marvelous caprice and inconsistency" (102). Simms still strikes the progressivist note—"Civil regulations, accordingly, interposed at an early day, under the dawning light of civilization, in checking the frequency of single combat" (104)—even while he laments the passing of the chivalrous age. He seeks to set before the reader an ideal of chivalry shorn of its latent barbarism, an ideal he had already embodied in Marion.

The question to be asked is, what sort of model is Simms attempting to provide for his audience? Oddly enough, Simms continues to treat his hero in terms of the partisan warrior throughout, but with Bayard it is merely a matter of the limited scope of his command and his ability to turn long odds to his advantage. With Marion and Smith, he had emphasized their practical virtues as much as their knightly ones and presented them as unlocking the peculiar potential of a given set of people to the benefit of the nation and humanity at large. Bayard's status as partisan warrior is used here merely to set him apart from the petty strife and mean objectives (albeit on a grand scale) of the warring princes. "Indeed, it is in contrast with the deeds of the army, at this period, that his own acquire reputation," Simms tells us (121). Bayard's single most distinctive virtue is one that would become increasingly important and overriding for Simms at the time of the Civil War: absolute fidelity to his country. Simms had used Marion and Smith to critique certain aspects of southern culture, whereas Bayard can serve only to embody traits the South already complacently prided itself upon: gentleness with women, courtly bearing, benevolence, and so forth. While Bayard is devoted to his country above all else and acts according to the fairly arbitrary dictates of a king, Smith and Marion had acted to shape a nation coming into being, and that difference speaks volumes about the shift in Simms's perspective on the South and his role as keeper of memory. After describing the French defeat at Ravenna, Simms writes of the French in a way that presages generations of southern chroniclers of the lost ideal to come: "All that remained to them . . . was the glory of Gaston de Foix and the famous deeds of Bayard. These make their monuments, and fill their chronicles, and furnish them with models and with morals, which have endured, perhaps equally for good and for evil, for successive centuries" (304).

In the same year Simms published *Bayard* (1847), South Carolinians were stung by an assault upon the state's honor that would destroy any remaining consensus on the question of the nation's origin and destiny, Lorenzo Sabine's *Biographical Sketches of Loyalists of the American Revolution*. Sabine, a Maine politician and historian, enhanced the laurels of New England by arguing that "the adherents of the crown were more numerous at the South and in Pennsylvania and New York, than in New England," directing his scorn particularly at South Carolina.

"It is hardly an exaggeration to add," Sabine writes, "that more Whigs of New England were sent to . . . [South Carolina's] aid, and now lie buried in her soil, than she sent from it to every scene of strife from Lexington to Yorktown."[24] This was the opening salvo in a war of words that would lead to Preston Brooks' employment of his cane in the Senate chambers, and in the midst of the controversy was William Gilmore Simms, writing in his capacity as South Carolina's leading historian.

Historiographers point to Sabine's book and the responses to it as marking the end of the dominance of Romantic history in American writing.[25] Romantic history demanded a rough consensus on national values and character and a sense of common origin. While there certainly had been disagreement from the earliest days of the Continental Congress over the question of slavery, a sense of common purpose had united first the colonies and then the states, a sense of a common destiny as a nation and a shared love of liberty: blood from Vermont to Georgia had mingled in the Revolutionary struggle. Sabine was not arguing a point of divergence on a national question, such as the annexation of Texas; rather, he was calling into question the very nature of the Revolution by questioning the South's (and its leading voice in the contemporary debates, South Carolina's) role in it. Historians like George Bancroft in his first volumes and, earlier, David Ramsay of South Carolina may have differed on questions of emphasis, but they were largely aligned on questions of values and underlying principles; for there to be an *American* people, there had to be a common movement toward a common goal from a shared origin (at least in the Revolutionary moment). Callcott treats the demise of Romantic history toward the end of his volume, noting the damage done to this conception of history by "new contradictions appearing in historical works." He points out that "often they were related to the growing sectional hostility and they cast doubt on the basic assumption that history illustrated truth" (217). Simms was certainly suspicious of northern versions of history before, but 1847 proved a watershed year for his, and the South's, sense of the struggle over the nation's history.

The following year, Simms made his reply to Sabine in a *Southern Quarterly Review* article, "South Carolina in the Revolution," later published in pamphlet form.[26] Simms had assumed a defensive posture concerning the South at times earlier in his career, as, for instance, in his response to the accounts of slavery published as part of Mrs. Trollope's *Domestic Manners of the Americans* (1832) or in his attack on Harriet Martineau's book a few years later.[27] Earlier, however, he was a sectionalist only on very specific issues, and his writings on these must be placed in the context of his broader nationalism; during the 1840s, ironically the high point of his literary nationalism, his perspective had begun to shift toward a more purely sectional view under the pressure of the continuing tariff issue, the question of Texas annexation, and growing abolitionist power (and anti-abolitionist ferment). He had already begun to emerge as a leading advocate of the cooperationist position in the 1840s, working with Hammond and others of the Young Carolina movement to outflank Calhoun's group by assuming the more radical position (Wakelyn 104). His disillusionment with the prospects for the nation and democracy generally would be complete with the sweeping failure of the European revolutions of 1848 and the promise of Zachary Taylor's presidency (he had abandoned Loco-foco democracy to support Taylor as the more pro-southern candidate). As much as any other single event, however, Sabine's work was the firebell in the night for Simms, and Simms was well aware of the shift his response reflected; following the publication of his article, he wrote Nathaniel Beverly Tucker, asking him to read it and proclaiming, "You will see how much of a Southron I am and how little of a Yankee."[28]

Simms recognized that Sabine's work represented a historiographic challenge being turned to the purposes of contemporary politics. The new critical history threatened to undermine the consensus that was crucial to maintaining the mythic aura of the Revolutionary period and the nation's birth. In *Views and Reviews, First Series,* Simms had argued for the superiority of Romantic history to the new critical mode in European historiography associated most strongly with Leopold von Ranke, and Sabine's work was among the first American fruits of the new historiography. Sabine had denigrated South Carolina's role in the Revolution on the basis of the preponderance of hard evidence—the numbers of loyalists versus patriots, numbers of troops in the Continental army, and so forth. According to Simms, this "wretched skeleton of facts" completely missed the underlying truth of the Revolutionary struggle in his state, the manner in which certain individuals of exceptional courage, wisdom, and virtue had advanced the cause of liberty in spite of statistical odds. The representative man, for Simms as for Emerson, is not the average one but the one most attuned to the spirit of his age and his people. Simms's Romantic presuppositions had allowed him to emphasize those individuals possessed of a "vision so prophetic"—the partisan leaders who could see the "shapes and claims of the future" and play their part in shaping the destiny of the nation. Sabine's account, "worthless as the contents of last year's almanac," dealt only with the facts of a static present. In answer to Sabine's charge that the partisans were but "whig leaven" (in a Tory loaf), Simms answers that "the character of a country does not depend upon the opinions of the mass, and is not determinable by the direction which its mere numbers may please to take" (13). But Simms understood that the battle was to be fought on a new sort of historical ground, and he warms to the challenge of answering the facts presented by Sabine.

Rather than just defending the role of the patriots in South Carolina, Simms takes the battle to the North and questions the pretensions of Sabine's New Englanders. He argues that the vast numerical superiority of New England over the South on paper is simply the result of New Englanders' tendency to exploit the potential for profit in any situation. Where, Simms asks, was this "horde" of New Englanders in any given conflict? While Sumter, Marion, Moultrie, and their followers were serving for years as militia without pay in territory usually controlled by the enemy, the New Englanders, having charge of the payroll, were simply profiting by swelling the ranks of the Continental army on paper. He notes John Adams's claim that the British never had more than 25,000 troops on the continent at any one time and points out: "Certainly these ought to have been but a mere mouthful for these fierce fighting New-Englanders, 118,000 strong, who should have swallowed them with as much ease and eagerness, as a French *gourmand* swallows a fricasee of frogs" (54). He marshals evidence from contemporary sources on the difficulty of recruiting in New England, even in conflicts on its soil. While the South remained largely an occupied region during the war, New England availed itself of the opportunity to swell the payroll and gain a disproportionate share of the general officers. "The fact is," Simms tells us, "that this pretension of Eastern states to numbers in the army, would be the most ridiculous thing in the world, in view of the actual fact, if it were not for the enormous robbery of the national funds, of which it has been made the pretext" (43).

Simms argues that the continued occupation of the region by the British for the duration of the war indicates not a lack of patriotism on the part of the South but a preoccupation of the New Englanders with their own interests at the expense of other regions. He disputes Sabine's claim that the South had to rely on northern troops for its eventual liberation. In answer to Sabine's charge that the number of northerners who died in South Carolina was greater than that of the men that state sent to the remainder of the Union, Simms claims that

Sabine and others err in reading "Northern troops" in the contemporary records; "Northern" refers to north of South Carolina, and Simms claims that *no troops from New England ever crossed the State of Virginia*" (34): "The tide of battle rolling southwardly, left them in a condition of comparative security, and their patriotism was then of a sort to enable them to snap their fingers at the distresses of the southern people;—it is certain that they snapt nothing more potent in the ears of either friends or enemies" (28). One of Sabine's primary pieces of evidence was the inadequate defense of Charleston before its fall, and Simms answers, after demonstrating the valiant defense of the city against overwhelming odds, that the defense of the city was in the hands of a New England general and that promised reinforcements from the rest of the country had failed to materialize: "These phantom troops . . . were pretty much the same order of soldiers as were enrolled on the New England establishment—never to be seen except at the serving out of rations" (35).

Simms had noted the fact of New England's absence from the campaigns south of Virginia in earlier works, but his purpose then had been simply to heighten the contribution of the southerners, especially the South Carolina partisans; in this piece, however, his purpose is to demonstrate that the revolutions of New England and the South were qualitatively different. Disillusioned with what had become of the nation, Simms retreated from the very idea of the Revolution as a unified (and unifying) event and carefully qualified South Carolina's "revolution" to distance it from that of New England. William Taylor points out the shift in Simms's idea of revolution by 1850: "No longer did he speak hopefully of revolution in the sense of overturning an established order. . . . The two sections thus represented two different kinds of insurrection in Simms's typology of revolution. New England had engaged in a 'modern' revolution, in the sense that it had fought to acquire property; South Carolina had fought the kind of struggle characteristic of the 'Anglo-Norman race,' a war fought in the name of liberty to vindicate the rights of property."[29]

Mounting an apology for South Carolina leads Simms to present a highly idealized picture of the South Carolina patriots, idealized to a degree formerly reserved for a few exceptional figures such as Marion. He emphasizes South Carolina's lack of the "base and selfish interests" that had guided New England in the war and argues that South Carolinians fought not because of "those pecuniary considerations" but to resist the "denial to the native mind, of its proper position" (14–16). He goes on to make claims for the sons of his state that would be more appropriately applied to the mythic Bayard than even the Swamp Fox: "We contend that purer patriots were never found; that hands cleaner of offense, freer from the stain of base and selfish motives, never grasped the sword of war; never more truly and faithfully carried life, property, and sacred honor, as their pledges, for the prosecution of a glorious national purpose" (18). Most important, he defends the plantation slave culture that had come under attack as a source of southern weakness in Sabine's history (and, of course, was assailed by northern critics of the South generally). Far from being a weakness, South Carolina's slave system had allowed the slaves to continue to produce needed agricultural products for the war effort while leaving the whites free to conduct the business of warfare: "It secured protection for the one who toiled, and sustenance and food for him who fought" (33). This feudal vision is a marked shift from his earlier treatments of the yeoman farmers slipping in and out of the militia ranks as the demands of the farm dictated. Further, the conditions of southern life produced the ideal warrior, according to Simms, and his arguments anticipate those to be made at the onset of the Civil War:

> He was born, we may almost phrase it, on horseback, and with the rifle in his grasp. His ordinary exercise made these his familiar companions. His ordinary amusement was the chase; and, as a hunter, horseman, and rifleman, he was almost naturally trained to war. It is in these possessions, indeed, that we may boast of a militia in the South, such as the world has never elsewhere seen. These possessions combine the most powerful elements and agents of the military—habitual stratagem and adroitness in snaring and baffling game—a perfect mastery of the horse, and an unequalled excellence in firearms. Exercise in these is naturally the source of spirit and vigilance, of confidence and courage in the field, which ordinary militia never possess; and of a peculiar capacity for guerilla or partisan warfare, in which the South has especially been distinguished whenever her troops have been led by native officers, who knew how to appreciate and manage them, and who understood the business themselves. (33–34)

Simms had always been the champion of the southern soldier, but his argument here is of a piece with a broader defense of the southern way of life, one that admits no faults outside the family and uses the aspects of the South most often attacked by critics as its greatest strengths.

The lines had been drawn, and Simms called upon the South to take charge of its history. "It is the misfortune of the South that the lion does not often write the history of his own career. In this history, he has left it almost wholly to the jackal," he writes (32). *South Carolina in the Revolutionary War* also contains a reprint of his review of John Pendleton Kennedy's *Horse-Shoe Robinson* in 1853. The review restates many of Simms's claims about the truth of South Carolina's role in the Revolution and its misrepresentation by northern historians. Simms makes his call for the South to write its own history more explicitly here and again ties his defense of the Revolutionary history of the state to a broader defense of southern culture. Even when northern historians admit the merit of the South Carolina patriots, they honor them as exceptions "where all besides is vacancy and waste—a dull, monotonous region, either stagnating or senseless, or in feverish disturbance from gales and storms of eccentric passions" (61). The seeming sluggishness of the southerners in responding to the war was due to a difference in temperament, and Simms quickly warms to a pastoral theme: "It must be admitted that our forest population are dilatory in their movements. All agricultural people are of this character. They differ from the citizens, from those who dwell in active business communities, in respects that derive heir [*sic*] controlling influence from the inevitable laws of nature. While the merchant has to watch all the fluctuations and caprices of trade, and the manufacturer all the variations of fashion in the community, the agriculturist obeys only the natural, gradual and successive progresses of the seasons" (173). Seeming faults become evidence of cultural superiority, a transformation seen repeatedly in the debates of the 1850s. Slavery, of course, provides the subtext for all these debates on the South's culture, and a brief perusal of the back cover of this volume reveals that the Revolutionary debate was intimately bound up with a defense of the peculiar institution. At the top is an advertisement for Fletcher's *Studies of Slavery*: "This valuable work has been prepared with the most careful attention to well-attested facts by the author, and is not only a faithful *exposé* of the institution of Slavery, but also the *basis* of that institution. The work is well worth the study of not alone the *pro-slavery man*, but also of the most *fanatical abolitionist*" (italics in original). This advertisement is followed by: "ALSO READY, 'The Pro-Slavery Argument, containing papers on the subject from Chancellor Harper, Governor

Hammond, Dr. Simms, and Professor Drew.'" It is no wonder that, placed in this company, the *South-Carolina in the Revolutionary War* volume smacks more of defiance than dialogue, of polemic than persuasion.

Simms's work in answer to Sabine placed him squarely in the midst of the sectional controversy of the 1850s. As McCardell notes, during this period Simms was playing to perfection the role of the practical poet he had striven to play all of his career (208). As a man of letters, he wrote novels and poems, edited the important *Southern Quarterly Review* (1849–54), lectured, continued to advise Hammond and others on political matters, and generally agitated for secession and a united southern front against the North. His stock was running high as a spokesman for South Carolina. Simms's work in answer to Sabine was cited in Congress by Laurence Keitt and others in the wake of the Sumner-Brooks affair (Van Tassel 136–37). He embarked on his ill-fated northern lecture tour in 1856 to repeat many of his earlier claims about South Carolina's role in the Revolution. After the original publication of "South Carolina in the Revolutionary War" in the *Southern Quarterly Review* in 1848, he had written Hammond that he had carried the war into "Yankeedom," and his lecture tour was a continuation of this effort (and it might be noted that, although he was repulsed prematurely, he made it farther north than Lee would in 1863).

Simms published the final four volumes of his Revolutionary romances from 1851 to 1856, and he turned these volumes to the purpose of the southern cause. In the two lesser works, *The Forayers* and *Eutaw* (1855 and 1856), he deals again with partisan warfare but emphasizes the roots of the sectional split in Revolutionary times. More important, in two of his better works, *The Sword and the Distaff* (1852, later renamed *Woodcraft*) and *Katherine Walton* (1851), he writes of a South that had "won its battles but lost the war" (287). His overriding concern in both his fiction and his writings in reviews and lectures is southern unity—showing a South that emerged from the Revolutionary conflict unified and ready to enter upon its own distinct destiny. In the last novel published during his lifetime, *The Cassique of Kiawah* (1859), he turns to a South Carolina settlement of 1684, to "the source of the South's separate life," as Wakelyn puts it (229). His concern is no longer with the nation born of the Revolutionary War and the South's place in a vibrant union but with the sources of that nation yet to be born in his own time, to the birth of which he contributed his best efforts.

His focus on a separate South did not, however, mean that he blindly celebrated his city, state, and region; if anything, the push to secession meant that he had to work harder to make the South recognize its faults and remedy them in preparation for nationhood. *Katharine Walton, The Cassique of Kiawah, Father Abbot; or, the Home Tourist,* and other writings all contain satire—sometimes veiled and sometimes explicit—of Charleston society. In the *Father Abbot* essays, he decried the division of society into one branch that was energetic and ambitious and one that was complacent and committed only to the maintenance of a social hierarchy. The second branch had lost sight of the dynamism of history and the need of a people to progress: "Its people could boast of a *past.* They could look back with pride to their ancestry" (qtd. in Guilds, *Simms: A Literary Life,* 410). Most important, Simms was bitterly disappointed by the quality of the emerging leadership in South Carolina. As Wakelyn notes, "He felt that a new breed of mediocrity was replacing intelligent politicians and statesmen in a period of extreme crisis. Instead of leaders, men who played up to mass sentiment were everywhere in evidence. Simms continued with renewed impatience his search for a young Hickory, a prophet to carry the South out of the wilderness" (163). There were a great many things to be done, and rapidly, in his state: expanding manufactures and the industrial base, improving agricultural techniques and encouraging their application, reforming education, and, above all, setting a clear political course for the South in a time of shifting power relationships nationally. The extremity of the times called for a revision of his model of leadership: instead of his chivalrous, romantic model of the military hero, "Simms praised the fanatic who could inspire men to action through his powers of concentration" (Wakelyn 165).

Now even more than in the past, the man of letters had a key role to play as the reconciler of stability and change, of the effeminate virtues of civilization and the masculine virtues of industry and ambition. Simms as editor and writer could at once celebrate the South and the glories of its past and castigate a society that seemed unwilling to change even at the cost of its survival. As Simms had done throughout his career, the writer must provide appropriate models for action and behavior, and Simms worked to encourage others to provide southern models of both the practical politician and the political theorist: "He encouraged Beverly Tucker to write a life of John Randolph of Roanoke, Hammond to study the career of George McDuffie, and John Pendleton Kennedy to write a life of his kinsman, William Wirt" (Wakelyn 165). Not that Simms turned solely to practical concerns. He and a group of younger writers formed the Russell's Bookstore group in Charleston in the mid-1850s, a coterie that was able to find a balance between polemic and high aestheticism. Simms was the grand old lion of this group, but at the same time he struggled with his feeling that the writer was peripheral in the South and growing more so.

As novelist, poet, editor, and historian, Simms had worked to position the man of letters, the man of mind, in a central position in the life of his people, guiding their self-understanding, and he had acquitted himself well in the task, but he suffered reminders toward the end of the decade that the role was largely illusory and maintained by force of will. It was through his role as historian, as keeper of the state memory, that he had gained the credibility as a defender of the South—the credibility that had largely propelled his successful bid for a seat in the state legislature in the 1840s and placed him in the middle of the national debates surrounding the Sumner-Brooks affair in the 1850s. His place was challenged in the most public of ways when James Louis Petigru, a staunch Unionist whose credentials paled in comparison with Simms's, was chosen as the first president of the newly formed South Carolina Historical Society in 1859. Insult was added to injury when his newly revised *History of South Carolina* (1860) met with silence and apathy in the state he intended to serve. "In S. C. I am repudiated," Simms lamented; his history, intended to instruct future generations of a new southern nation, had "fallen dead from the press" (qtd. in Guilds, *Simms: A Literary Life*, 278).

Simms revised his history to emphasize the origins of the sectional split and to inspire the youth of South Carolina with the necessity of defense against aggression, of loyalty to the state above all else. In his preface, Simms laments the ignorance of young South Carolinians of their state's past and notes, "Circumstances, of late days, also seemed to demand that a frequent survey should be made of the general condition of the country, in order that the reader should be able, of himself, to decide upon the resources, and so properly to appreciate the responsibilities of the state and people."[30] He heightens the role of South Carolina in the Revolution and points to northern (especially New England) failures in the same manner as in his response to Sabine, albeit in a somewhat softer tone. Most significant, in the crucial revisions and additions to the final portion of the book (covering 1782 to 1860), he emphasizes that a proper understanding of this period is necessary to understand the position of the South in the Union and the necessity of preparing for an irrepressible regional conflict. The Revolutionary history of the state was a preparation of the people for just such an event: "Such crises, in the affairs of a people, are, perhaps, ordeals of training and preparation; ordeals of fire; by which they are to be at once purified for a great service, and a goodly development of moral strength and stature" (393). What we are to learn from the war is that, in spite of God's goodness, "it is yet very certain that, in the avarice, insolence, and restless ambition of men, there will be found always some portions of the human family prepared to make war a human necessity! Nations are required to accept it as one of the evil conditions inseparate from the assertion of their rights, their liberties, and independence" (392). He goes on to sketch the rise of its necessity in the present moment in no uncertain terms, underscoring the flaws present in the Union from the start and devoting a fair portion of his narrative to the nullification controversy. Greatness becomes measured by fidelity to the state and its defense, and he includes a paean to the greatness of Calhoun, whose hold on power he had so often opposed. He gives the overriding lesson of his revised history at the close of the Revolutionary section: "It is that which teaches the citizen to cling to the soil of his birth in the day of its difficulty, with the resolution of the son who stands above the grave of a mother and protects it from violation. This will be a safe rule for the citizen, whatever may be the cause of war or the character of the invader" (391).

Throughout his career, Simms had acted on the premise that the man of mind could act as a shaping force on the destiny of his people, but by the 1850s we see Simms responding more to historical contingency and a mind shaped by a pressing current of events. By the late 1850s, Rubin argues, "he was witnessing the utter collapse of the equilibrium that he had managed, however unevenly, to maintain between his literary interests and ambitions and his involvement in the political and social life of his community. It was no longer possible to be a professional man of letters in the South; henceforth he must put aside his artistic vocation and sink his entire hopes into his identification with the secular, political southern community" (*Edge of the Swamp* 101). In the 1830s and early 1840s, Simms had been committed to reconciling his dual identity as a "born Southron" and an "ultra-American" (*Letters* 1:319) in a validation of the meaning of the Revolution and the Republic born from it. The Revolution had been for him the primary evidence undergirding his Romantic faith in the destiny of the American people and South Carolina's role in that destiny. As Simpson argues in *Mind and the American Civil War*, it became increasingly clear that there were two competing truths of the Republic, that of New England and that of the South (35). The Revolution, for Simms in the late 1840s and 1850s, had only led to the necessity of further rebellion for the South, and the outcome of the struggle was far from clear. The Romantic view of history depends upon what *has been* to determine the nature and truth of what *is*, but Simms was forced from this position to a dependence upon what *might be*—whether, that is, the South would prevail (its rightness thereby vindicated) and Henry Timrod's vision of a southern empire in "Ethnogenesis" be fulfilled. Should the course of events prove otherwise, the South would find itself in a barren present, with a past bereft of meaning. As William Taylor says of Simms's state of mind in this period: "He seemed to welcome the idea of a war which he saw not as a revolution but as an explosion which would clear the air. Only some cataclysmic event, some great purgation, seemed capable of restoring the South to political health" (284).

The war, of course, proved devastating for Simms. His plantation house, "Woodlands," burned twice during the war, accidentally in 1862 and at the hands of Sherman's troops in 1865. Simms's collection of more than ten thousand primary documents concerning the Revolutionary war and South Carolina history was lost with the house. His second wife died in 1863, and his eldest son, Gilmore, was wounded late in the war. The war years were a time of intense financial hardship, beginning even before the conflict itself, as reflected in a letter from 1860: "This year, dreadfully unfortunate in my crop & overseer, I have been driven to the necessity of selling Milton for a bushel of corn, Shakspeare [*sic*] for a bunch of onions, Chaucer for a string of fish, and Bacon for a barrel of beans" (*Letters* 4:215–16). Cut off from northern publishers, he lost the principal supplement to his plantation income. Warned of Sherman's approach, he removed to Columbia with his children in 1865 to protect his family and witnessed the destruction of the city. If Rubin is right in his claim that, earlier, "for all his fascination with the past of South Carolina and the nation, he could not view history as something that was happening to *him*," he had now suffered it with a vengeance.

History *happened* to William Gilmore Simms in February 1865, and Simms's final volume of formal history was his record of the event: *The Sack and Destruction of the City of Columbia, S.C.* (1865). After the reduction of the city by Sherman's troops, he worked with others to begin publication of the *Columbia Phoenix* and published his account in that newspaper before issuing it as a separate volume. The work stands out in the Simms canon because of the extreme contrast with his earlier vision of history and the purpose of historical writing. *Sack and Destruction* was written to establish the facts of the case, not to elevate the reader or to provide a narrative framework that would imbue the facts with meaning. It portrays a scene of chaos and brutality in an incoherent narrative, one that includes instances of humanity and virtue but is unredeemed by them. Sherman and members of the northern press had attempted to portray the fire as the result of retreating Confederates firing stockpiles of cotton and "drunken negroes," and Simms writes to place the blame squarely on Sherman and the troops acting on his orders.

The accuracy of the facts here is of primary importance, whereas it had been subordinate to the "higher" aims of the imaginative writer in most of Simms's work. Simms amasses facts and points to a uniformity that testifies to the "general authenticity of the whole."[31] To demonstrate that the destruction of the city was carried out according to plan, Simms cites the discipline of the soldiers on entering and leaving the city, the numerous instances in which citizens had been warned beforehand by northern soldiers that the city was "doomed," and the indications that the lawlessness of the soldiers was allowed within certain set boundaries. In his conclusion he writes that the northern version of events might be credible were it not for certain facts to the contrary: "If it could be shown that the one-half of the army were not actually engaged in firing the houses in twenty places at once, while the other half were not quiet spectators, indifferently looking on, there might be some shrewdness in this suggestion [that the drunkenness of the soldiers and local blacks was to blame]. If it could be shown that the whiskey found its way out of stores and cellars, grappled with the soldiers and poured itself down their throats, then they are relieved of the responsibility" (84–85). Simms relies on anecdotes, letters, and other documents and provides an extensive list of property destroyed as an appendix to the volume. History has favored the North in the war and will lend authority to accounts of northern writers, but Simms gathers his facts for the vindication of memory.

Simms's account is no mere catalog of facts, but the passages of sublime horror, instances of nobility, and even occasional humor attest to no larger meaning than the experience of suffering and vain struggle. The fire itself calls forth Simms's most effusive prose: "It was a scene for the painter of the terrible. . . . The winds were tributary to these convulsive efforts [of the flames], and tosses the volcanic torrents of sulphurous cloud—wreaths of sable, edged with sheeted lightnings, wrapped the skies, and, at short intervals, the falling tower and the tottering wall, avalanche-like, went down with thunderous sound, sending up at every crash great billowy showers of glowing fiery embers" (42). However much such a passage might recall earlier ones in his work, such as the description of the hurricane in *The Partisan*, here there is no suggestion terror will lead to hope, that it has meaning beyond the present moment. In the same way, when we find instances of nobility on the part of southern women, as when a young lady relinquishes her claim to a stolen riding whip rather than comply with the demands of the Yankee who has stolen it, it seems pointless defiance rather than the meaningful sacrifice of the patriotic lady in Simms's Revolutionary writings. Everything, however vivid in itself, takes its place in a largely random narrative of destruction and dispossession.

Any meaning to be found in the suffering of the city and its inhabitants is simply in the measure of what has been lost. Simms emphasizes the futile efforts of the Columbians to preserve art, books and archives, and historical buildings and monuments, and he records the blindness of the northern troops to the worth of what they are destroying. The most telling instance comes when Simms describes the vain effort to save the library collections of South Carolina College. The fervent pleas of the college officials are answered only with Sherman's contempt and remarks on the blighted state of the South. The same treatment was accorded private scientific collections, the new capitol building, and even a statue of Washington. The war may have been decided on the field, but a more subtle (though no less intense) struggle then ensued over the worth, the very nature, of what had been lost. Simms's last significant historical work is written in memoriam.

Sack and Destruction represents the final closure of the historical field that had been open to Simms earlier but which had gradually closed as the destiny of the South diverged from the larger American one that had guided Simms's historical thinking in his early years. Not that he lost all hope, but the story of the new American Republic, the Second one emerging from the Civil War, was to be distinct from that of the First, born of the Revolution. The war created a historical rupture in the southern mind, which would remain for many generations beyond Simms's time. Simms had devoted his life to the study and celebration of the American Revolution as no one else, but he had witnessed its final issue in the flames of Columbia. Calling on the citizens of Columbia to begin anew in the *Phoenix*, he found his hope in a new South "superior even to this past," and, in an 1867 letter to Paul Hamilton Hayne, he would go so far as to say, "Let us bury the Past lest it buries us!" (*Letters* 5:214) Clinging to the old ways of understanding the nature and place of the South in the new, postbellum era would only leave it as Simms described it in a letter to his New York friend Duyckinck: "The people are hopeless—in despair—surrounded by Ruin & threatened, in addition to the loss of their liberties, by the immediate pressure of famine. The whole South is in this condition and is doomed to be the Ireland of the Union—a perpetual incubus" (*Letters* 5:36). The degree of his disillusionment with the promise of the Revolution in these circumstances is most evident in a review of Cornelia Spencer's *The Last Ninety Days of the War in North Carolina*, in which he "accused the author of making worthless allusions to colonial times. . . . There was no use to look back eighty years while 'the memory of five or six years is almost enough for the best and bravest of us all'" (Wakelyn 259).

In the last years of his life, Simms would continue his historical work, but he would do so in a defeated South coping with a new historical situation. He began biographies of Washington and Hammond and wrote an introduction to the war correspondence of "the Southern Bayard" of the Revolution, John Henry Laurens. He wrote amid the emergence of a new pantheon of southern heroes, and the older figures would take their place beside Lee, Jackson, and the others. The separate destiny of the South had been driven underground, into the region of myth and memory.

2

"IT WILL BE AS I NOW REMEMBER IT"

Thomas Nelson Page and the Old South

One of the unnoticed little ironies of literary history is that two of the foremost literary salons in Washington, D.C., at the close of the nineteenth century and the opening of the twentieth were conducted in the homes of Henry Adams and Thomas Nelson Page. Harriet Holman, in the biographical portion of her work on Page, mentions among the "lacunae" in Page's career his "withdrawal from the society of Henry Adams" in Washington.[1] One finds more similarities between the two than might at first be suspected, judging by the intellectual chasm separating them. They had a number of friends in common, including Theodore Roosevelt and the New York editor Richard Watson Gilder, and Page appeared in the society of northern men as comfortably as did Adams with the quintessential southern politician L. Q. C. Lamar. More important, both were of families whose prominence reached its peak in the Revolution and the days of the early Republic. These storied figures from Massachusetts and Virginia—governors, generals, and presidents among them—bequeathed an enormous burden to their descendants. Page might have asked Adams's famous question from the opening of his autobiography: "What could become of such a child of the seventeenth and eighteenth centuries, when he should wake up to find himself required to play the game of the twentieth?"[2] The difference in their answers to this question defines the difference between the two men and provides us with a good starting point for considering Page's work in the context of his time.

This difference can be briefly stated: Adams woke to history while Page remained asleep, lulled by his own sweet dream of antebellum peace. Where Adams came to reckon with every major intellectual and cultural current of his time—Darwinism, biological determinism, positivism, Marxism, the implications of technological change and capitalism—Page fell victim to his own myth of the Old South and reckoned with almost none of them. Adams experienced history as a matter of live forces impinging on his consciousness, to such an extent that he became a cipher in his own autobiography; the past for Page was a matter of the Arcadian land that was a myth with power to shape identity in the present. He lived and moved in the mundane world after Appomattox but had his being in the world before it.

My concern in this chapter is with the implications of this divided consciousness on Page's historical work. Page came of age in the wake of the closure of history on the South that we saw with Simms in the previous chapter, but what had been experienced by Simms as entrapment in a barren present soon gave way to the development of a curious backloop of memory for his successors—Arcadia had found a local habitation and a name, the Lost Cause. Page, more than any other writer, gave definition and life to the myth, most notably in *In Ole Virginia* (1887) but also in the historical addresses and essays contained in *The Old South* (1892). In this early work he treats the beautiful but doomed plantation society like one who had briefly known it in early youth. His concern here is to set forth in loving detail the civilization that parted ways from the mainstream of American development and at last fell victim to it. But Page's concerns changed after the heyday of local color, and in the new century he emphasized the place of Virginia in the main line of American civilization. His second collection of historical work, *The Old Dominion: Her Making and Her Manners* (1908), treats Virginia not as a distinct civilization set apart from the other regions but as the inheritor of the legacy of progress in the West, on the vanguard of Anglo-Saxon civilization. He sketches the colonial and Revolutionary life of Virginia and presents it as the nation maker before turning to its unjust humiliation during Reconstruction. By leaving aside the earlier years of sectional strife, he presents a progressive model of the South but a peculiar one—progressive yet highly stratified along the lines of race and class. There is a great deal of overlap between his visions of the Old Dominion given in these two volumes, but the final synthesis resides in his biography of Robert E. Lee, also published in 1908. Lee, as Page presents him, willingly puts aside the temptation of command of the Union armies to sacrifice himself on behalf of the South and, in the strength of his nobility, rises from defeat and humiliation to transcend history. Lee's victory in defeat brings about the "apotheosis of the South," as Page elsewhere puts it, allowing the rebirth of the South as a spiritual nation. The two nations can then coexist, and Page's role as man of letters is a prophetic one, offering the redemptive power of memory in the mundane present; the redemption, however, proves hollow.

Some critics have treated Page as though he had no personal knowledge of the war or the Old South of which he wrote, discounting his experience because of his age. Granted, Page did not experience battle firsthand, but Page indeed experienced the war in a very immediate sense, and far from making such recollections dim, his age (eight to twelve) enhanced and selectively enlarged the war—its figures, its events, and his own exploits around the fringes—as only childhood memory can do. Mark Twain's clearest, and most powerful, memories of Hannibal and the Mississippi certainly were not furnished by his mature perceptions. These memories surface in much of Page's historical writing and in such fiction as *Two Little Confederates* (1888) and several stories. Harriet Holman provides a nice digest of Page's childhood experiences in her biographical sketch:

> During the war years Page participated in activities that would make a modern child-psychologist shudder; he went to see the fire-gutted warehouse at Beaver Dam; he haunted the site of skirmishes because he wanted unexploded cartridges to supply him with powder and ball for squirrel-hunting; once in his search he went so close to actual fighting that a Northern officer sent him hurrying out of danger. . . . Hanover County lay in the path of McClellan's campaign of 1862 and Grant's campaign of 1864. Seven Pines, Chickahominy, Old Church, Mechanicsville, Gaines Mill, Cold Harbor, and the Seven Days Battles were fought there, and Kilpatrick, Stoneman, and Sheridan went through Hanover on raids. (10–11)

Page's stories and sketches are evocative precisely because they are drawn from personal recollection and have both distant grandeur and fond immediacy—the combination often present when preadolescent memories are recalled to the adult mind. It is this highly personal quality that provides his history with a certain charm, even while it robs it of much of its potential power as historical inquiry.

At the same time that Page was breathing life into the romantic history of the Old South in his fiction, a very different movement was afoot in American historiography. A new generation of American historians was beginning to transform the practice and teaching of history in America. Fresh from seminars in the great German universities, younger scholars were returning with missionary zeal to reform historical practice along new, scientific lines, and the first major sign of the change was their meeting at Saratoga Springs, New York, in 1884 to form the American Historical Association. Herbert Baxter Adams, Andrew D. White, Alexander Johnston, and John Fiske—the most prominent of the group—came of age in a milieu beginning to feel the force of Comtean positivism and social Darwinism, and they sought to move the domain of the historian from the realm of letters to the university. On this change, David Van Tassel writes, "As literary artists the great mid-century historians received the respect of the newcomers, but history was no longer to be considered a branch of literature; it was a science whose practitioners marshaled and classified data and published monographs modeled after the laboratory report of the natural scientist" (173). Objectivity was their byword, and the older "literary" historians' celebration of feeling, evocative power, and conscious artistry was put aside in its name. In the face of this change and the professionalization of history, writers such as Page were hard pressed to gain the mantle of historian, once their right as men of letters.

Page insists repeatedly on the authority of private memory in the face of critics and public records. He spends the first two pages of his unpublished "Recollections and Reminiscences" on just such justification and in fact opens with a section dealing with the remarkable power (of human beings generally) to remember far back into childhood. He pairs one example of his distinct memory from a very early visit to "Shirley," the old place on the James belonging to his relatives the Carters, with the historian Edward Gibbon's memory of a gold watch being dangled before him as an infant. The credibility of his early memory is crucial to him because all his subsequent experience is located in relation to his remembered world of the plantation at Oakland in antebellum and Civil War days: "When I learned that there were other places they took location and position in my mind relative to Oakland, as newly discovered worlds are designated as being so far from such and such a star or sun."[3] Page does recognize the distance from these memories and his childhood perspective as he speaks of the "change" that has come over Oakland since his childhood years: "Its dimensions have now shrunk until it is only an ordinary old plantation of the type common in the poorer part of Eastern Virginia, with an old wooden, weatherboarded house of two and a half stories, on a hill, with a yard around it, commonplace enough except for [three] fine hickories and two magnificent oaks which would dignify any spot on earth . . . but at the time of which I speak, before the paltry experience of the relative size of things which we are pleased to term knowledge,—a poor exchange for the absolute acceptance of childhood,—had diminished its bounds and abbreviated its distances, it was the world" (4). Page's phrasing—"the paltry experience of the relative size of things which we are pleased to term knowledge"—is revealing here. Even at the moment when he is qualifying his recollections, he gives them standing as somehow a higher, purer form. The break represented by the South's defeat, remembered as a series of discrete, personal events in a child's experience, prevents the normal process of assessment, the normal recognition of nostalgia in recalling one's early past. His memories of the lost age were those of a child, and these memories are invested with the authority of a privileged witness of a lost past. Had he been a mere ten years older, like Adams, his memories of the old regime would have had to pass through the normal adult process of reassessment, even before the time of the war. Lucinda MacKethan points to the significance of his childhood memories: "The war and its aftermath emphasized for Page the values of the old world just at the moment that they were disappearing, leaving him with a sense that the re-gime that had been destroyed had a tragic grandeur and his childhood memo-ries a special importance that might serve as instruction for posterity."[4] If Page made the preeminent contribution to the creation of the Old South, with its idyllic combination of innocence, high civilization, peace, and nobility, his ac-counts draw their power from the fact that his memories of the old culture and the doomed struggle are identical with his memories of childhood.

Of course, Page had to live in a new South, though his heart might have re-mained with the old; he more than adapted to the new conditions but certainly suffered from what C. Vann Woodward refers to as the "divided mind" of the New South: "The deeper the involvements in commitments to the New Order, the louder the protests of loyalty to the Old."[5] The height of Page's fictional ca-reer spanned that of the greatest of New South proponents, Henry Grady, who spoke from his pulpit at the *Atlanta Constitution* from 1880 until his death in 1889. Grady and compatriots such as Baltimore's Richard H. Edmonds and Louis-ville's Henry Watterson pushed for the radical social and economic reform of the South in accordance with the northern model. They urged the South to take advantage of its enormous natural resources and supply of cheap labor (of a particularly strike-resistant variety) to draw northern and foreign capital into the region. They championed railroads and ports to improve infrastructure and mills and mines to develop an indigenous industrial base.[6] Page's famous stories of the 1880s (collected in *In Ole Virginia* (1887)—"Marse Chan," "Meh Lady," and "Unc' Edinburg's Drowndin'" most prominently—satisfied the need for a unifying sentiment in the face of a rather chaotic social, political, and economic situation. His vision of noble gentlemen, pure ladies, and contented darkies, all enveloped in the golden haze of fond recall, provides a refuge from the complexity of the present and constitutes a sort of pastoral rebuke to an impoverished time.

Far from being hostile to the chroniclers of the Old South, such as Page or his frequent companion on the lecture circuit, F. Hopkinson Smith, the proponents of the New South used nostalgia for the Old South to great effectiveness in advancing their aims. As Wayne Mixon writes, "The New South professed to have no quarrel with the Old, for the magic of the Lost Cause, the source of its appeal to the North and to New South spokesmen, was that it was so irrevocably and satisfyingly lost."[7] Nostalgia for the Old South suited the purposes of the New South proponents because the political climate (in the wake of defeat and Reconstruction) demanded conservative leaders and the appearance of restorers of the old order—whether the "Redeemers" in politics or the industrialists and their advocates, they were nothing of the kind. In fact, as Mixon points out, the plantation tradition "lent itself to sentimental romance that, by its bathetic treatment of the Old Order, offered no real alternative to the industrial, urban ethos. Often, in fact, the plantation romancers were quite effective propagandists for the New South movement" (8–9). The New South, as Grady claimed, was "simply the Old South under new conditions," a proposition given almost identical formulation by Page, and the new leaders of the South went to great lengths to maintain this appearance by studiously applying a coat of Confederate gray to whatever project they had in hand. In the most striking instance of this trend, the directors of the notoriously corrupt and immensely powerful Louisiana Lottery brought in Generals P. G. T. Beauregard and Jubal Early to supervise and confer credibility on their drawings. Woodward captures the situation perfectly: "It was a poor subsidiary of an Eastern railroad that could not find some impoverished brigadier general to lend his name to a letterhead. General Robert E. Lee's austere example in this regard was much admired but rarely followed" (*Origins* 14).

If the Old South, as presented in Page's fiction, could not provide a tenable alternative for the young southerner, neither did the family plantation at Oakland provide an adequate object for Page's ambitions as a young Virginia law-yer. Once Page finished his law work at the University of Virginia in 1873, he began his practice of law on the Hanover Circuit in 1874–76. He had the chance to remove from Hanover to Richmond "to take a desk in the office of his cousin, Henry T. Wickham, attorney for the Chesapeake and Ohio Railway" ("Recollections and Reminiscences" 61). Page recognized that the most direct route to power and preferment went through the cities, not the country seats of his ancestors, and he remained in practice in Richmond until his retirement from the law in 1893. Page quickly learned to transform stock holdings in the rail-roads into profit and influence, in the best New South style, and went on to in-vest in land speculation both at home and abroad (none of which worked out as he planned) (Harriet Holman 21, 29). Page was not the only young scion of an Old South family to find new routes to success—as Woodward notes, one came across names such as John C. Calhoun and Beverly Tucker on railroad legal staffs (*Origins* 149). As Harriet Holman insists repeatedly, "Page's real interest then as later was the common ambition of his generation—power" (20), and she points to a letter in which Page deals directly with his response to the plantation life he so potently celebrated in fiction: "If I thought I shd be contented I wd go to the country and never let anyone mention money or schemes or honors to me again. But I fear I shd not be."[8] The plantation was an image for Page—nothing more— and he came to identify its very nobility with its inevitable failure. Henceforth, he would celebrate the old and act in the new.

When Page published *The Old South: Essays Social and Political* in 1892, he was about to marry Marshall Field's widowed sister-in-law and move from Richmond to Washington for the remainder of his life. *The Old South* collected several of Page's articles and essays of the 1880s, the earliest a piece on colonial Yorktown published in 1881, the same year he sold "Marse Chan" to *Scribner's* (the Yorktown article was incorporated into "Two Old Colonial Places"). It presents Page's apo-logia for the Old South and its civilization and provides an implicit rebuke to the new age of skepticism, materialism, hurry and push. The title piece was origi-nally delivered as an address at Page's alma mater, Washington and Lee, in 1877 and—as Hobson and others have noted—was consciously titled in response to Henry Grady's famous address "The New South." Grady and Page agreed that the "New South is simply the Old South with its energy channeled in new di-rections," but there was a decided difference in their notions of the function of memory and the man of letter's role as guardian of that memory.

Page strives here to create a space for the man of letters in his prophetic role as keeper of memory, but where Simms and earlier writers had made the same effort in regard to first the United States and then the Confederacy, emerging in history, Page seeks the role of prophet of a land of the spirit. Lewis P. Simpson, in *The Man of Letters in New England and the South*, uses Page to mark a transition point at which the southern myth gained coherence as a "spiritual nation." The South's experiment with a uniquely modern form of pastoral grounded in chattel slavery had failed, and its role as a "redemptive community" now functions in the realm of spirit rather than pragmatic history. The South, Simpson writes, "as a spiritual nation became subject both to the nostalgic and apocalyptic modes of perception in the literary mind" (221), and these would be the modes that would dominate the Page's work: "I dwell on Thomas Nelson Page because it seems to me that he is the continuator of the literary plantation who is the direct prophet of the literary apocalypse that is modern Southern storytelling. In setting up an image of the South as a redemptive nation, he was motivated both by the conviction of an apostasy from the Southern moral order and by nostalgia for the Old South. In Page apostasy and nostalgia fuse to provide a mythic perspective for the Southern storyteller" (225). This position as prophet (and indeed high priest) of the cult of memory grants the man of letters power because he is the custodian of memory in a more absolute sense than before the war—the South as it was is no more, and we hear the incantatory power of the new prophet of the land of the spirit in Page's words, "It will be as I now remember it."[9]

Page makes a direct appeal to young southerners to seize the mantle of historian in "The Want of a History of the Southern People." He claims that the true history of the South is yet unknown and that it is the duty of the young southerner to write it and thereby body forth the South as a redemptive community. The address opens with a striking challenge: "Do we know the true history of the South? I confess that I do not, nor do I know where it may be learned" (*The Old South* 345). He continues, "There is no true history of the South. In a few years there will be no South to demand a history" (346). The keeping of the South is now given to memory, and the young writer must assume the burden of not merely preserving it but of creating it on the page: "A people has lived, and after having crowded into two centuries and a half a mightiness of force, a vastness of results, which would have enriched a thousand years, has passed away, and has left no written record of its life. A civilization has existed more unique than any other since the dawn of history, as potent in its influence, and yet no chronicle of it has been made by any but the hand of hostility. . . . Is there any history of this country which you can place in your boy's hands and say, 'This is the true history of your native land?'" (348–50). The true history lies beneath the existing accounts, the scattered documents and fragmentary recollections, accessible only to the native eye of piety: "The history that has been written is as an ancient palimpsest, in which the writing that is read is but a monkish legend, whilst underneath, unnoticed and effaced, lies the record of eternal truth" (362). Page here skillfully reverses the normal charge of bias and claims objectivity for the redeemer.

Like Simms and the other earlier advocates of a "true" history of the South, Page couches his appeal by reference to the alternative: the history of the South as written by northerners. Having sketched the historical differences between North and South, Page states, "It is to this section [the North], heretofore inherently incapable of comprehending her, that the South has left the writing of the history of her civilization. It may appear to be not a matter of importance who writes the story of this country. Manifestly the South has so regarded it. It is, however, a sad fallacy" (360). The result is baldly stated: "By the world at large we are held to have been an ignorant, illiterate, cruel, semi-barbarous section of the American people, sunk in brutality and vice, who have contributed nothing to the advancement of mankind: a race of slave-drivers, who, to perpetuate human slavery, conspired to destroy the Union, and plunged the country into war. Of this war, precipitated by ourselves, two salient facts are known—that in it we were whipped, and that we treated our prisoners with barbarity" (346). The Civil War pronounced the verdict of history with the defeat of the South, and if the situation is left unchanged, "we shall go down to posterity as a blot on our time, and a reproach to American civilization" (360). Page, however, answers with what becomes a recurring theme: that the verdict of history and the verdict of the historian need not be the same. The surface narrative of mere facts will inevitably indicate that the South suffered a deserved fate, but there is yet another history, the deeper, spiritual one. The South, for Page, did in fact suffer defeat in the realm of mundane history and was shunted aside in the progress of the nation, but this defeat provided "the apotheosis of a race" (366). With the translation of the South beyond history in defeat, a unified myth may be established for the race, centered on that very conflict and bridging the gap between upland and lowland, plantation owner and yeoman, man and woman.

Not that Page is arguing for a return to southern nationalism—far from it.

He seeks to establish a fund of memory from which southerners may draw to act in very different historical conditions. The power of the Lost Cause depends on its being beyond the realm of pragmatic action. Page makes the point very clearly: "I belong to the new order of Southern life. I am one of those who can feel the thrill of new energies fill my heart; I think I can see and admit the incalculable waste, the narrow limitations of the old. I give my loyal and enthusiastic adherence to the present, with all its fresh and glorious possibilities; but I shall never forget that it is to the Old South that the New South owes all that is best and noblest in its being" (363). The renewed allegiance of the southerner to a unified national destiny, to the "fresh and glorious possibilities" of a South remade in the image of the North, gives promise of power and prosperity, even while fidelity to the past, in mythologized form, redeems the Old South from history. The unified myth gives substance to a southern "race" to be incorporated in the nation as an almost autonomous force, as Page implies in this passage:

> The deliberate and persistent endeavor to hold in contempt the people that could produce so sublime a spectacle [as the Civil War] and to forbid them participation in the Union, is a greater wrong to the Nation than was secession. It is an attempt to keep alienated from the Union a race that has ever hated with fervor but loved with passion; of a race that withdrew from the Union under a belief in a principle so sincere, so deep, that it was almost idolatrous; of a race that has now under new conditions turned to the Union all the devotion which under different teaching and conditions was once given to the several States; devotion which when directed against the Union shook it to its foundation, and now is destined to guard it and preserve it throughout its existence. (368–69)

By renewing the allegiance to the nation while simultaneously maintaining a sharp distinction for the southern "race," Page makes clear that this allegiance is contingent on the South being allowed to set its own terms for participation, particularly as regards its social and political order. In short, Page's fingers are crossed during his pledge, and they are crossed in the interest of white supremacy.

In the title essay, "The Old South," Page sets out a sweeping vision of the "truth" of the old civilization, from its founding to its remnants. He opens with a nod to the two great namesakes of the university, the two who mark the high points of the South's prominence in the United States and its brief but noble career as an independent nation on the historical stage. He addresses the college students as though in attendance on a shrine: "Broad enough to realize the magnificent ideal of its first benefactor as a university where the youth of this whole country may meet and acquire the grand idea of this American Union, it is yet so distinctly free from the materialistic tendencies which of late are assailing kindred institutions and insidiously threatening even the existence of the Union itself, that it may be justly regarded as the citadel of that conservatism which, mated with the immortal devotion to duty, may be termed the cardinal doctrine of the Southern civilization" (3–4). In its martyrdom, the South assumes its role as a redemptive community, and Simpson calls our attention to the overtly Christian imagery that infuses Page's original treatment of the South's defeat, burial, and resurrection:

> Two-and-twenty years ago there fell upon the South a blow for which there is no metaphor among the casualties which may befall a man. It was not simply paralysis; it was death. It was destruction under the euphemism of reconstruction. She was crucified; bound hand and foot; wrapped in the cerements of the grave; laid away in the sepulchre of the departed; the mouth of the sepulchre was stopped, was sealed with the seal of government, and a watch was set. The South was dead, and buried, and yet she rose again. The voice of God called her forth; she came clad in her grave-clothes, but living, and with her face uplifted to the heavens from which had sounded the call of her resurrection. (*The Old South* [1892 ed.] 4)

Simpson claims that here "the redemptive South is obviously transformed from the Arcadian image into one primarily derived from the Christian eschatology" (224), and his claim is certainly borne out by the passage. Page's later revision of this passage toned down the specific parallel with Christ (though leaving the outlines of death and resurrection), but this version best represents the import of the Page's message and his sense of mission—what Harriet Holman assesses as his "semi-messianic compulsion to justify the South to the nation, and, incidentally, to techy Southerners" (56).

The man of letters has a particular role in the propagation of the gospel of the

Old South and its message to the southerner and the wider nation of the present. Page makes the intriguing claim that the failure of the Old South was at bottom a literary failure. Toward the end of the essay he writes,

> It was to this that the South owed her final defeat. It was for lack of a literature that she was left behind in the great race for outside support, and that in the supreme moment of her existence she found herself arraigned at the bar of the world without an advocate and without a defence.
>
> Only study the course of the contest against the South and you cannot fail to see how she was conquered by the pen rather than by the sword; and how unavailingly against the resources of the world, which the North commanded through the sympathy it had enlisted, was the valiance of that heroic army, which, if courage could have availed, had withstood the universe. (59–60)

Page reveals here a conception of literature as cultural self-justification. Ironically, as he makes clear in another essay in the volume, "Authorship in the South before the Civil War," it was the very pastoral attributes he elsewhere praises that led to the South's literary failure—that it was primarily agrarian, that it had a dispersed population marked by a spirit of independence, that it was non-materialistic and so failed to support its authors or develop a publishing industry, and that the slavery controversy limited southern thought to a narrow orthodoxy. With the historical nation lost and the spiritual nation risen, however, the man of letters can begin to fulfill his proper function, as defender of the lost civilization: "Now at last the writer is himself to become a redemptive figure in the fulfillment of the South as a redemptive community. Page discovers that the Southern literary imagination is the medium through which the revelation of the meaning of the interior and spiritual history of the South is to be completed" (Simpson 225).

Two essays in *The Old South*, the title essay and "Glimpses of Life in Colonial Virginia," both cover basically the same ground: the essential character and development of Old South civilization (as found in its most perfect embodiment, the Old Dominion). Page sketches the planting and rise of the South as largely a movement and transplantation of British aristocracy to a plantation society that allowed the heightening of class distinctions while fostering a love of liberty, thereby providing the future United States with the conservative leader-

ship necessary to carry it through the time of the Revolution into its existence
as a nation. He emphasizes the role of the English aristocracy in the founding,
dwelling on the efforts of the planners, especially Sir Walter Raleigh, in establishing a stronghold on the new continent for "the rule of the Anglo-Saxon race"
(120). The emphasis on the racial character in his account is marked:

> Thus Virginia was settled with a strong English feeling ingrained in her,
> with English customs and habits of life, with English ideas modified only
> to suit the conditions of existence here.
>
> Among the chief factors which influenced the Virginia life and molded
> it in its peculiar form were this English feeling (which was almost strong
> enough to be termed a race feeling); the aristocratic tendency; the happy
> combination of soil, climate, and agricultural product (tobacco), which
> made them an agricultural people, and enabled them to support a gener-
> ous style of living as landed gentry; the Church with its strong organiza-
> tion; and the institution of slavery. (121–22)

Page stretches his argument at many points to maintain the aristocratic and
Anglo-Saxon character of the South (and therefore of the early nation). He argues from a principle of influence and assimilation. For example, at one point he
dodges the controversy over whether the inhabitants of the southern colonies
were descendants of the Cavaliers by asserting,

> It may, however, be averred that the gentle blood and high connection
> which undoubtedly existed in a considerable degree exerted widely a
> strengthening and refining power, and were potent in their influence to
> elevate and sustain not only the families which claimed to be their im-
> mediate possessors, but through them the entire colonial body, social
> and politic.
>
> I make a prouder claim than this: the inhabitants of these colonies
> were the strongest strains of many stocks—Saxon, Celt, and Teuton; Ca-
> valier and Puritan. (10)

Slavery and the plantation system established the "environing conditions" that
led men of personal force to follow an aristocratic model of ambition: "Each man,
whether gentle or simple, was compelled to assert himself in the land where per-

sonal force was of more worth than family position, however exalted; but having proved his personal title to individual respect, he was eager to approve likewise his claim to honorable lineage" (10). As he says elsewhere, "Undoubtedly many, both at first and later on, came to Virginia who were not of gentle birth; but the lines were too clearly drawn to admit of confusion; those who possessed the personal force requisite, rose and were absorbed into the upper class; but the great body of them remained a class distinct from this" (126). The growth of slavery gave them "the means to support their pretensions as landed gentry"; it "emphasized class distinctions and created a system of castes, making the social system of Virginia as strongly aristocratic as that of England" (123–24). Even in the Shenandoah Valley, where new immigrants came to settle, the patriarchal model was adopted. Page, following earlier accounts, distinguishes three classes of whites: poor whites (the cockfighters and uncouth rowdies), the middle class, and the gentry; and he clearly reserves the lion's share of virtue and leadership for the aristocracy.

Even as Page seeks to highlight the patriarchal character of Virginia, he sees the main legacy of its influence in that it "preserved the spirit of civil and religious liberty pure and undefiled, and established it as the guiding star of the American people forever." "I believe," he continues, "that the subordination of everything else to this principle is the key to the Southern character" (16). The Virginians, for Page, are clearly the key to the American Revolution, and it was precisely the aristocratic sentiment that made them so jealous of their rights from the time of the Jamestown settlement forward. It was aristocracy with a difference: "Yet there was that in the Virginians which distinguished them, for all their aristocratic pretensions, from their British cousins. Grafted on the aristocratic instinct was a jealous watchfulness of their liberties, a guardfulness of their rights, which developed into a sterling republicanism, notwithstanding the aristocratic instinct. The standard was not birth nor family connection; it was one based on individual attainment" (126–27). He cites the zealously guarded charters of Jamestown and Bacon's Rebellion as examples of this trait—the same people who offered a crown to an exiled king were those who knew themselves in possession of a kingdom and its rights.

These were the ardent patriots who guided the burgeoning nation through its conservative revolution and founding. As an aristocracy with large responsibility for land and slaves, the southerners, Page tells us (echoing Edmund Burke), were formed to the task: "Government was the passion of the Southerner.

Trained from his early youth by the care and mastery of slaves, and the charge of affairs which demanded the qualities of mastership, the control of men became habitual with him, and domination became an instinct" (55). This environment led to what Page holds to be the "guiding principle" of the South: "public spirit; devotion to the rights and liberties of the citizen, the embodiment of which in a form of government was aptly termed the Commonwealth" (28). The South, particularly Virginia, was the highest expression of the English spirit on the continent for Page, and he never lets pass a chance to recite the litany of its contributions to the nation: Washington, Jefferson, Marshall, Monroe, and other great men; the Declaration of Independence; the Louisiana Purchase; and so forth. As Page asserts at one point: "The Old South made this people. One hundred years ago this nation, like Athene, sprang full panoplied from her brain" (48). (It takes a Page to cast the South as both Lord Zeus and Lord Jesus in the same speech.)

The virtues of the Old South entailed corresponding faults. As Fred Hobson demonstrates, *The Old South* can be read as Page's indictment of the antebellum South on several scores: "In this volume he emerged as the most eloquent champion of the antebellum South—and one of its most perceptive critics" (138). The Old South's conservatism and independent-mindedness had led to the struggle for liberty, but this same provincialism—"self-esteem and self-content as unquestioning and sublime as that which pervaded Rome"—placed it outside the main line of progress in the very nation it had created. It was "one side and apart from the general movement of contemporary life," and Page views the history of the nineteenth century as the result of the South's new position in the nation, brought about by changes elsewhere, not within the region itself: "But the world was moving with quicker strides than the Southern planter knew, and slavery was banishing from his land all the elements of that life which was keeping stride with progress without. Thus, before the Southerner knew it, the temper of the time had changed, slavery was become a horror, and he himself was left behind and was in the opposition" (30). The nation advanced, and Page here recognizes a common standard of advancement, while the South remained unchanged: "It held by its old tenets when they were no longer tenable, by its ancient customs when, perhaps, they were no longer defensible. All interference from the outside was repelled as officious and inimical, and all intervention was instantly met with hostility and indignation. It believed itself the home of liberality when it was, in fact, necessarily intolerant;—of enlightenment, of progress, when it had been so far distanced that it knew not that the world had passed it by" (30–31). The cause of this situation, Page asserts, was African slavery—the very institution that had given the South its "distinctive character." He emphasizes that slavery was brought on the South from without (largely in the ships of New Englanders) and that the South was left to deal with it as best as it could: "Through the force of circumstances and under 'an inexorable political necessity,' the South found itself compelled finally to assume the defence of the system; but it was not responsible for either its origin or its continuance, and the very men who fought to prevent external interference with it had spent their lives endeavoring to solve the problems of its proper abolition" (31). His treatment of the institution of slavery will be dealt with below; suffice it to say here that he recognizes the evil of slavery (though not for the slaves themselves) but spreads the responsibility for it beyond the borders of his region. The important fact for Page is that it largely cut the South off from progress and formed a Gordian knot that could be cut only by war. The South had to pay the price for the only available solution: "It was reserved, in the providence of an all-wise God, for the bitter scalpel of war to remove that which had served its purposes and was slowly sapping the life-blood of the South" (43).

In this way Page recasts the cataclysm of the Civil War as an unwilling sacrifice on the part of the South. Zeus brought down from his Olympian isolation and made to face Golgotha and the tomb (to return to the mix of Page's metaphors). Slavery had served its purpose in providing the basis for a landed aristocracy and "the sweetest, purest, and most beautiful life ever lived" (115), and the South had brought forth the nation and shaped its course, but it was a doomed civilization. Its faults were those of excess: "The tendency of the civilization was the reduction of everything to principles, and not to disturb them by experiment. In this way there was enormous waste. The physical resources of the country and the intellectual resources of its people were equally subject to this fault" (58). Or, in the case of dueling, "it was an obedience to a sentiment which although grossly abused, had this much justification—that it placed honor above even life" (58). The "apotheosis" of the South in the war destroyed the civilization but left future generations with "the heritage of an untarnished sword" and the memory of an unspotted civilization: "Whatever assaults may be made on that civilization, its final defense is this: The men were honorable and the women pure" (57). The verdict of history fell on its viability, not its virtue. As Hobson points out: "Such was Page's indictment of the Old South, but it was an indictment of a very special kind—criticism of the South as a cultural and political unit whose leaders had been *strategically* in error, but not of the Southerners who had lived under such a regime. For in his 'Old South' address Page envisions a heroic race trapped within a faulty system, a noble people captured by their institutions. Antebellum Southerners were no less worthy than Page had maintained all along; they were victims of circumstance" (142). Having risen from the grave of the war, southerners have been purged of what for Page was merely the semblance of guilt, and they are free to live as citizens of the spiritual nation without confronting past evils or their continuation into the present.

In spite of his pretense to historical analysis, Page again relies on the authority of private memory—the dim recall of a society he scarcely participated in, of a world he barely knew. He devotes the central essay in the volume to describing that world in detail, largely from his family's experience at Oakland and his boyhood memories. "Social Life in Old Virginia before the War" was the most famous of Page's addresses, and it was published separately in 1892. It has a tone of familiar reminiscence and the authority of personal recollection. The previous essays deal with the South as a whole and tend toward the long historical sweep, but this essay focuses on the microcosm at Oakland and allows it to stand for the whole of the Old South. It presents an image of harmony, beauty, and order but leaves no doubt that such a civilization was too good for this world and inevitably fell victim to history and the intrusion of the outside. Here Page is not concerned with establishing facts and dates and setting forth their interpretation but rather with the evocation of an ideal order. The opening sentence leaves no doubt of the mode in which Page is operating: "Let me see if I can describe an old Virginia home recalled from a memory stamped with it when it was a virgin page. It may, perhaps, be idealized by the haze of time, but it will be as I now remember it" (173).

Page opens with an extensive description of the house and lands at Oakland, presenting an image of peace and modest prosperity. The description begins with the house itself, an unpretentious structure made of plain "weather-board" of Revolutionary-era vintage; the trees, bushes, and flowers; the "office" in the yard, a strictly masculine domain, where tales were swapped and the guns were kept; the orchard; the simple furnishings in the interior of the house; the outbuildings—"servants'" houses, smokehouse, and others; the vegetable garden and the flower garden; and lastly (and most extensively), the fields. The plantation is viewed as a harmonious whole, with the plantation house as its center— the plantation order emanating from it through the servants' quarters, outbuildings, gardens, and fields. Most notable about the description is that it moves from a brief recounting through concrete detail to an idealized pastoral portrait. The early concrete paragraphs are those like the following, where we glimpse the age of the establishment and the fact that it is already verging on decline: "The fields that stretched around were poor, and in places red 'galls' showed through, but the tillage was careful and systematic. At the best, it was a boast that a dish of blackberries could not be gotten on the place. The brown worm fences ran in lateral lines across, and the ditches were clean except for useful willows" (173). He quickly moves on to moonlit landscapes, the mythic and chivalric associations of rose bushes, and other pastoral trappings. This movement from the concrete to the abstract and idealized sets the stage for Page's turn to a consideration of the interior life of the plantation house and its social structure. In contrast to the deeper aims of a greater artist, as he moves inward, style replaces analysis, evocation supplants probing.

Page's description of life inside the plantation house centers on the master and mistress—saying that it is idealized would be putting it mildly indeed. He opens with their competence in the management of affairs, within the house and outside it. The mistress has been brought up to skillfully manage all the affairs of the household, but, as Page has it, her power is more to be found in her presence than her skill. We see the effect portrayed here: "It would no more have occurred to him to make a suggestion about the management of the house than about that of one of his neighbors, indeed not so readily; simply because he knew her and acknowledged her infallibility. She was, indeed, a surprising creature— often delicate and feeble in frame, and of a nervous organization so sensitive as to be a great sufferer; but her force and her character pervaded and directed everything, as unseen yet as unmistakably as the power of gravity controls the particles that constitute the earth" (183–84). The master stands before his wife "as he might before the inscrutable vision of a superior being" (185), but his awe is the requisite awe demanded of chivalric duty. Page, in good New South fashion, emphasizes that that master is both a gentleman and a man of affairs and capabilities. He is not an idle aristocrat: Page tells us that "any master who had a successfully conducted plantation was sure to have given it his personal supervision with an unremitting attention which would not have failed to secure success in any other calling" (184). Further, "The ease of a master of a big plantation was about that of the head of any great establishment where numbers of operatives are employed; and to the management of which are added the responsibilities of the care and complete mastership of the liberty of his operatives and their families" (184). Page presents the master as a profoundly conservative type: "He believed in God, he believed in his wife, he believed in his blood" (189); he is formed by his environment for success in certain special conditions but generally doomed in contact with changing times and the wider world. The master and his wife are at the head of the great patriarchal family of the plantation, encompassing all from the immediate family in the great house, to the house servants and driver, to the field hands: "They all formed one great family in the social structure now passed away, a structure incredible by those who knew it not, and now, under new conditions, almost incredible by those who knew it best" (200).

Page's primary emphasis in describing this "family" falls on the importance and position of the house servants and the social hierarchy among the slaves. Drawing heavily on his personal experience, he insists that (contrary to images drawn from such books as *Uncle Tom's Cabin*) the three primary servants—the driver, the butler, and the ever present mammy—occupied honored places in the immediate family household. Page's description of their roles in the family might be found in any number of similar accounts. His detailing of the social roles of the slaves within the larger plantation hierarchy serves to portray social complexity without social tension—the sort of tension that might arise if one were to consider matters such as the humanity of the slaves or the individuality of any of the figures (including master and mistress). This effort resolves the tragic potential of the scene into a comic portrait (in the larger sense) in which all tensions are happily resolved and safely beyond the reach of history.

In his harmonious portrait of social life on the old plantation, Page builds to a climax (as he does in several of his stories) with an account of the wonders of the plantation Christmas. Christmas is a revel, a festival of social harmony, and it is perhaps fitting that the essay begins with images drawn from the Passion and Resurrection and moves steadily back toward Christmas. All the other festivities "paled and dimmed before the festive joys of Christmas" (209), and Page pays it its due in a full ten pages of loving detail. "It had been handed down for generations," he tells us; "it belonged to the race. It had come over with their forefathers. It had a peculiar significance" (209). It was a time when plantation life brimmed full and ran over, with homecomings, gift giving (including "Chrismas gifs" to the slaves, of course), feasts and parties, and weddings among the slaves—most important, it was particularly timeless. Page's essay moves steadily away from one of defense to one of celebration in the dim reaches of memory. Christmas had a ritualized significance set apart from the changes of the years, and it is with a sense of that that Page wishes to leave us.

For Page, the glory of the Old South is doubly lost—even in its mature blossom it was already beginning to wither. He viewed the entire course of the South's history after the Revolutionary War as one of decline, with only the final glorious burst in the time of the Civil War to redeem the century. He pays the requisite tribute to the "languid, philandering young gentlemen of Virginia" who became "the most dashing and indomitable soldier of modern times" (193) and the courage of the women who endured conditions he describes as worse than war. But one has in all of Page a sense that the war is simply the South's swan song and that it had been in the process of a graceful dying for the better part of a century. Indeed, Page presents the plantation master's resolve to maintain his way of life in spite of history as a matter of stoic resolve in the face of certain defeat: "The greatness of the past, the time when Virginia had been the mighty power of the New World, loomed ever above him. It increased his natural conservatism. He saw the change that was steadily creeping on. The conditions that had given his class their power and prestige had altered. The fields were worked down, and agriculture that had made his class rich no longer paid. The cloud was already gathering on the horizon; the shadow was already stretching towards him. He could foresee the danger that threatened Virginia" (190). Page presents a culture overwhelmed by history, but one that has been translated into another form to exert a force on the present through memory. In the final essay of the original edition, "The Negro Question," he turns to the legacy of chattel slavery and what for him is the most pressing concern in the present, white supremacy.

In "The Negro Question," Page argues for a realignment of national identity around the black-white racial dichotomy rather than the North-South divide. As the postmodern theorist Homi K. Bhabha argues, the nation "is *internally* marked by cultural difference and the heterogeneous histories of contending peoples," and it is on the manipulation of the lines of difference that national identity depends.[10] "The history of nationalism," in Lloyd Kramer's gloss on Bhabha's work, "is a history of contestation between those who seek a fully coherent narrative of the community's existence and those whose presence, ideas, color, or culture undermine the possibility of that coherence."[11] Identity, in this view, depends on difference, and Page seeks to replace the dominant narrative of cultural (regional) difference with one of racial difference in a white nation. At the outset, he considers the question of the traditional sectional divide between North and South in a nation in which the more natural divide might have seemed to be between East and West, leading him into his discussion of its cause, the legacy of chattel slavery. He then makes his argument that North and South are equally responsible for the legacy and that it is American civilization as a whole that is threatened by the "great race issue" he repeatedly invokes. National unity and, as he presents it, survival can be guaranteed only by suppression of the "alien" population and measures guaranteeing white supremacy.

The issue, as Page introduces it, is whether to see the "Negro question" in terms of rights due to citizens or in terms of the proper relation of superior and inferior races. Because of the "exigencies" faced, Page acknowledges, southern whites have subverted the law in the interests of political control, and northerners seem intent on seeing only a simple issue of justice; as he observes in a memorable understatement, "It is charged that the written law is not always fully and freely observed at the South in matters relating to the exercise of the elective franchise" (281). But Page argues that the problems following the demise of the chattel system are not so easily solved and spends a large portion of the essay reminding the North that its detachment is merely an accident of history. He recalls slave laws in Massachusetts and widespread hostility to the abolitionist movement in the North before Providence intervened to rid the region of an institution for which it had not much practical use in any case. This detachment has led, he argues, to a warped perception on the part of the North. The South has to deal with the very immediate threats posed by noble ideals, but the North will not much longer have the luxury of distance: "The only thing that stands to-day between the people of the North and the negro is the people of the South" (284). While acknowledging slavery to have been an evil, he recasts the struggle over it (apart from the role of Providence) as a political and economic contest in order to turn the North's attention to the power issue at stake in the present. He casts it in stark enough terms: "The North sees in the negro's attitude only the proper and laudable aspiration of a citizen and a man; the South detects therein a determination to dominate, a menace to all that the Anglo-American race has effected on this continent, and to the hopes in which that race established this nation" (312). To buttress his point, he claims the fallacy of the very idea of responsible citizenship on the part of blacks.

Page's Anglo-Saxon nationalism demands that blacks be rendered as a race different in kind from whites. If blacks are an alien presence and an inferior race, rather than simply an oppressed portion of the citizenry, then all claims about the rights due a citizen are mute: "If it is a question of mere perverse imposition by the white on the black, by the stronger on the weaker, a refusal to recognize his just rights, then the advocates of that side are right. If, however, it be the other ["a great race issue"], then the stronger race should be sustained, or else the people of the North are guilty of that fatuity which destroys nations" (306).[12] Page then embarks on a sweeping historical tour, beginning with conditions in Liberia, the Congo, and Haiti and moving to black rule during Reconstruction and blacks' development in the North, in order to establish that as a race blacks are incapable of self-government and, with rare exceptions, full human development. "Whatever a modern and misguided humanitarianism may declare," he writes, "there underlies the whole matter the indubitable, potent, and mysterious principle of race quality. Scientifically, historically, congenitally, the white race and the negro race differ" (313). Only with the aid and management of the "stronger race" can blacks achieve a modicum of individual development and stability as a people. Given full autonomy, they become a dangerous element in Page's view, and the specter of San Domingo and the slave uprising led by Toussaint L'Ouverture haunts much of the essay. This specter is the dark side of the pastoral vision set out in the rest of the book, a reminder of the presence that disturbs the boundaries of the coherent identity Page narrates, even while defining them. In the essay, Page concludes that the Negro will simply disappear over time (quite literally), but in later editions of the book, he substitutes a figure adapted to the southern version of pastoral, "The Old Time Negro." Page drew one principal lesson from the various currents of thought in his age, the necessity of Anglo-Saxon supremacy and some semblance of aristocracy, but altogether missing is any indication that he felt the pressure on the individual consciousness of the new forces shaping his world. Page, in his history and his fiction, sketches a world of peace in the antebellum years—the function of memory for him is to provide refuge, not to identify patterns that connect past with present. Henry Adams again provides the clearest contrast here, with his obsessive desire to map out the forces that move men and nation across history and into his own confused present. He wrestled with Darwinism (and its progeny, social Darwinism), the lessons of physics, and the dynamics of energy and matter in a way that renders all of history grist for the scientific historian's mill—data with which to identify lines of force. His sensitivity to the changes taking place in the nineteenth century places him squarely in the com-

pany of the naturalists, of Émile Zola and his American successors, Frank Norris
and Theodore Dreiser. Like them, he identified forces other than individual vo-
lition that work far beyond the capacity of consciousness to channel them or
even adequately grapple with them. The extent of the disorientation of the individual in the midst of these finds its classic expression in his *The Education of
Henry Adams*, in which education is a haphazard process indeed and consciousness badly fragmented. When he does find unity, as he does in *Mont Saint Michel
and Chartres*, the unity of the thirteenth century is presented simply as a moment
of equilibrium giving way to ever increasing multiplicity, not as an Arcadia transcending history.

Page found his image of unity in the antebellum South, and the Virgin he
knelt before found its highest expression in the southern belle and the dream-
land of the old days before the war. Although he does identify such vague forces
as "progress" as what ultimately undermined the Old South, he fails to reckon
with the internal divisions and contradictions in that society. For Page, at bottom, the character of the Old South was something like this: it was a highly
stratified society made up of conservative lovers of liberty who inherited a slave
system foisted upon them by the traders and the Crown, which succeeded in ex-
tending the best of the aristocratic European traditions beyond its their age—a
civilization doomed by its very success in transcending the dominant currents of
its time. Not for him was it to delve into the channels of power and the new lines
of force developing as the old mercantile order gave way to the new capitalist
one; not for him to question the harsh economic realities of chattel slavery; nor
for him to raise doubts about the democratic ideals of those people who perpetu-
ated rigid distinctions of class and race. His "historical" South was a shimmering
dream of pastoral peace, a late flowering of an older order. The result was a historiographic sleight of hand by which the New South was made to conform to a
romanticized myth of the Old, thus evading the question of the underlying realities in both. It allowed Page, and a great many others, to walk the earth and participate in the newest of new schemes as citizens of a kingdom not of this world.
As Woodward puts it, "The bitter mixture of recantation and heresy could never
have been swallowed so readily had it not been dissolved in the syrup of romanticism" (*Origins* 158).

Page never intended to sacrifice his pursuit of power in the new order to his
fidelity to the Lost Cause. His path could not have been farther from that of the
poet Paul Hamilton Hayne, that literary lingerer of old Charleston, who lived

until his death in exile in middle Georgia.[13] Page, following his marriage to the widowed sister-in-law of Marshall Field (the Chicago magnate), set his course to Washington and the supply lines of Virginia patronage. There he could set up a premiere literary salon and position himself as a Virginian ambassador to the halls of national power. He removed from Richmond in 1893 and maintained his permanent residence in Washington for the remainder of his life, returning to Virginia only to check on affairs at Oakland and visit his mother and family. Not that he became any less of a Virginian; on the contrary, as with many other expatriates, his situation only increased his awareness of his origins. Though dealing with a great many contemporary political and economic questions on a daily basis, he became more than ever the defender of the Old South and the memory of Virginia.

In *The Old Dominion: Her Making and Her Manners*, published in 1908, Page turned his attention to the relation of Virginia to the nation. Most of the essays deal with the Old Dominion from the time of its founding through the years of the early Republic, the heyday of its national prominence. None deal with the antebellum period sketched in *The Old South*, but he includes an essay dealing with Reconstruction, the period of the defeated state's reincorporation into the nation. In doing so, he sets the contrast between Virginia as the cradle of the nation and its prime mover and Virginia the defeated, having to struggle to regain its self-determination and rightful place among the states. By eliding the years of sectional tension, he establishes a continuity between the Virginia of the First Republic and the Virginia of the Second and sets the state squarely once more on the path of progress and national destiny. Where, in the earlier volume, he had striven for an affective evocation of a lost cultural life, drawn from memory and the personal accounts of his acquaintances, here he strives for the mantle of the objective historian, assessing events and currents and the just claims of Virginia on the nation's past and future. Where civilization in the Old South had been treated as a charming special case in the nation's annals—a dreamy otherworld only wishing to be left alone—Virginia here is a realm of action, the nation maker that builds the United States into a power capable of surviving and acting on the national and world stage. These are the essays of a Washingtonian writing in an age that demands vigor and action, and he crafts an image of Virginia suitable to the time of his friend Roosevelt and a profoundly active United States.

The preface might lead one to expect in the volume another recounting of the grace and beauty of a doomed civilization, but Page evokes the Old South only indirectly in the opening of the volume and the final essay, turning his attention instead to its vigor and activity before the paralysis brought on by the slavery controversy. The volume is dedicated to his brother Rosewell Page, "a Virginia country gentleman, who by his character, unselfishness, his devotion to duty and his lifelong habit of spending himself for others, has preserved in the present the best traditions of the old dominion's past." And one also finds in the preface a stock tribute to the glories of the old order: "[Virginia] brought forth in time a new Civilization where Character and Courtesy went hand in hand; where the goal ever set before the eye was Honor, and where the distinguishing marks of the life were Simplicity and Sincerity."[14] But Page has a purpose other than another romantic paean such as befitted the 1880s with its love of atmosphere and gentle strokes of color.

He begins his first essay with an attempt to do no less than connect the founding of Virginia with the progress and emancipation of the Western mind from medieval darkness. He writes,

> To comprehend truly the achievement of the settlement of Jamestown and what it has signified to the world, and still signifies today, if we but knew it, it is necessary to go back among the forces that were at work in Western Europe during the time when the Dark Ages were giving way to the light of the New Learning. Many forces combined to produce the results, working with that patience which characterizes the laws of Nature. The energies of men had been engrossed by the exactions of war, and of a civilization based on war. The mind of man had been for ages monopolized by war militant and spiritual. Person and intellect alike lay under rule. Then gradually, after long lethargy, men began to think. (3)

This address is pointedly titled "The Beginnings of America," and Page, like Simms before him, argues that it is indeed to Jamestown, far more than to Plymouth and Massachusetts Bay, that we trace our origins as a nation. Indeed, the need for such a claim was more pressing following the divine verdict of the Civil War, which left a stain on the Virginian contribution while embellishing all the more the "purer" motives of the New England colonists. As Page presents it, the main course of the Anglo-Saxon ascendancy lay south of the Potomac, and he sets up the address with a long account of the struggle between Latin and Saxon culture for world dominance and the importance of the foothold at Jamestown in ensuring the coming dominance of the Saxon. Turning the tables on the South's critics, he uses the bogeyman of dark Spain to set the Virginia project in the vanguard of light and progress:

> Spain, cohesive within her own borders at home, abroad dominant on Land, Mistress of the Seas, possessing a vast empire at home and an even vaster one abroad, yet contained a radical and fatal vice which was to destroy her. She was the embodiment of the old as opposed to the new; of the past as against the future; of the out-worn as against the fresh and vigorous; of the narrow as opposed to the broad. She held to the established with unspeakable pride and blindness, and permitted no growth, no advance. She excluded the light which was breaking on all sides and remained in darkness, and whilst others advanced and grew, she stood still and dwindled. Nor was it unnatural. Progress moves on natural lines; nations rise and fall by natural laws. (29–30)

Page, the champion of plantation life and antebellum Virginia, writes with no intended irony of Spain's "radical and fatal vice," its "unspeakable pride and blindness," of a climate in which "no new ideas were allowed to grow, no differences of opinion were tolerated" (31). As we have seen above, Page himself did note these very tendencies in antebellum Virginia on other occasions, but here his purpose is to set the Old Dominion on the opposing side—the side of progress and dawning enlightenment. Jamestown, with its charters of 1606, 1609, and 1612, laid "the foundation of the liberties of the American people on which our fathers based their rights when they stood out for them in 1776" (49).

With the climate at the turn of the twentieth century and America's own imperial aspirations coming to the fore, Page exploits the imperial project of Great Britain—with Virginia as its crown jewel—to cast the Jamestown settlement as the truly representative American settlement. This legacy, like the settlement itself in Page's day, was lost to the present, and Page begins with a meditation amid the vines and ruins (and the requisite lone chimney) such as one might have found in Simms and the earlier historians. The obscurity of the place is contrasted with his proclamation of its role: "Yet here on this very spot, at the head of this little island was Jamestown, the Birthplace of the American People: the first rude cradle in which was swaddled the tiny infant that in time has sprung up to be among the leaders of the nations; the torch-bearer of civilization, and the standard-bearer of popular government throughout the world" (59). Instead of portraying Jamestown as a flawed settlement with peculiarly southern vices leading to its peculiar, and doomed, civilization, Page presents the character of the settlement with no apology as the fountainhead of American liberty: "It was this new band of settlers who on this May day, 1607, finally seized and permanently held the outpost, which was the key to the continent, and led to the supremacy of the Saxon Race with its laws, its religion, and its civilization in North America" (61). He emphasizes the energy of the settlers, the "cupidity, ambition, the chance of sudden wealth and power, and fame" (79), and makes a comparison with the spirit that later sent Americans to California, Alaska, and even as far afield as South Africa in search of gold. Far from portraying the South as lazy and indolent, Page gives us an image of activity and vigor, which, in spite of its excesses, is more in keeping with the age that held the capitalist, the adventurer, and Teddy Roosevelt dear.

Page marries the energy of the explorer to the class consciousness of the aristocrat in his composite portrait of the early Virginian. In emphasizing vigor and the main chance, he is careful to insist that Jamestown had an aristocratic character from the outset and, in spite of setbacks and infighting, established a sound footing. He uses John Smith's account to establish that, although there were problems early on because of the gentlemanly resistance to hard labor, the aristocrats proved more than the equal of the commoner once they had adjusted to the situation. Further, he deemphasizes Smith's role, lest he be seen as an anomaly, and places him on equal terms with Wingfield and the other governors and council members in the enterprise. "Who," he asks, "except for the small class of seekers for historic truth, knows anything of their fortitude, sacrifices and historic deeds? The histories which have circulated for nearly a century have dealt mainly with what they have deemed blemishes on the colony" (97). He asserts that both Wingfield and Smith were good and able governors, and he resists the tendency to praise one at the expense of the other, claiming, "My own study of the case has led me to the conclusion that, as in most discussions of the kind, feeling has been allowed to usurp the place of calm, judicial investigation" (102). The effort was a cooperative one, and its success more than vindicated the aristocratic character of the rulers: it produced the charter of 1612, "the Magna Carta of American liberties"; allowed the founding of the New England settlements; founded the first college and hospital on American soil, at Henrico; and established the proud claim to rights that would lead to Bacon's Rebellion. They strove for liberty, "the same cause as that which a hundred years later was led by George Washington. The immediate occasion was different, but the basic cause was the same in both: the inalienable right of British subjects to have self-government" (132).

The establishment of the society begun at Jamestown continued, marked, for Page, by the same combination of aristocracy and virility, and he treats this period in "Colonial Life." His purpose is to establish several things: first, that the ruling class of Virginia was a landed gentry and continued so; second, that Virginia's aristocratic tendencies did not in any way tend to luxury or dissipation; and third, that Virginia was the primary shaper of American civilization. As Page says on this last point: "The life of the Old Dominion was in a manner distinctive, and that it was not more so was due to the impress that it extended to the life beyond its borders" (134). As he had in the earlier volume, he points to the feudal character of the society in its early days and claims that other classes of immigrants only served to strengthen class distinctions. Not that society was static—the conditions of the frontier tested and strengthened men and women, and there were opportunities for men "of push and enterprise" to rise into the landed class. As Simms did, Page presents a picture of aristocrats without the vices of aristocracy rising in the frontier conditions; even with the emphasis on class, these were to become ardent republicans: "Aristocratic in its form, [this society] contained the essential principle of Republicanism. Every freeholder had a vote. There was much wealth; but little luxury in the modern acceptation of the term. The great landlord must be as hardy as his hunter; the mistress of the plantation must be as brave as her ancestress who defended her castle or her grange" (139). Much of this thought, of course, had been in his earlier addresses, as had his claim that Virginia contributed the lion's share of emigrants to the opening territories of the interior of the country: "Thus, the population of the Old Dominion was composed of sundry strains, all virile, and as the race pushed westward they carried with them the distinctive civilization which still shows to-day along the lines they travelled" (146–47). If historians have overlooked Virginia's contribution, Page's argument goes, it is because Virginia so profoundly impressed itself on the American character as to be recognizable only by distinctive traits, rather than the bulk of shared ones.

Virginia's great contribution, of course, is to be found in the Revolutionary years and the time of the early Republic. "Events have followed each other so rapidly in the last century," Page tells us at the outset of "The Revolutionary Movement," "the current has swept us so swiftly from the old moorings that the time appears longer than it is" (153). Page, without saying so, refers to the "old moorings" of a time when men could proclaim both the love of liberty and the right of slavery, the distinctions of class and the equality of all men, the primacy of the Old Dominion in all things political, and, last but certainly not least, the greatness of the names Page and Nelson. It was also a time of relative racial homogeneity in all the colonies, according to Page, and he emphasizes at the outset the dominance of English blood (while noting the exceptions of the Huguenots and the Negroes). Racialism is important for Page because it allows him to connect the Revolutionary movement with the Anglo-Saxon love of liberty, in accordance with the Anglo-Saxon thesis that had been in vogue for several decades at the time. The connection of blood allowed common action when the colonies "were not united by the ordinary bonds of a common religion and a common interest" (155).

Strangely enough, the long second section of the address deals not with the Revolution as a national movement but with the Virginia Convention at Williamsburg and the role of Page's ancestor Thomas Nelson. Though he does include the necessary high-flown tribute to Washington (culminating in a thirteen-line sentence), he views Washington and Jefferson as simply expressions of Virginia's people at large. The greatest accomplishment, as he paints it, was the preparatory work done in Williamsburg—laying the groundwork for the national convention and the Declaration of Independence. Thomas Nelson played a major role in the Virginia Resolution, and Page does not lose the opportunity to increase his ancestor's prominence in the drama. Nelson offered the resolution to the delegates, and Page insists that "the real author of a resolution is not the man who writes it, but the man who offers it and carries it through" (182). Though acknowledging the obvious contributions of Jefferson, Page pays him scant attention in order to highlight the work of his forebear, both at Williamsburg and in Philadelphia. He presents the work of the Virginians as the product of their civilization, not simply as the work of specially gifted men: "This was the ripest fruit of the Virginia civilization, and the Virginians know that though these might have been equalled by few in genius, in character they were not exceptions, but only types of the Virginian" (197). Character, whether in Page's fiction or history, proves a rather vague characteristic that is all-determining, and the products of a certain character always overshadow any other possible explorations of conflict, the confusion of motives, and so forth.

Of the one glaring inconsistency in the Revolutionary generation, the possession of slaves, Page has little to say. He notes only that Virginia had taken the lead in protesting against the slave trade and made plans for its practical abolition. The character and the work of this generation of Virginians are, for him, beyond reproach or argument. This was a time when Americans of all regions could agree on the cause of liberty and transcend regional differences. Page provides a not-so-subtle reminder of the slavery controversy with his characterization of the struggle against King George in terms that apply as well to the relation of North and South (as Simms had in his long-ago Fourth of July address), claiming that the "conduct of that Government was the oft-repeated story of self-centered phariseeism, thinking that it knows the problems of another region better than those know them of whom they are as vital as the breath they breathe. And as in such cases always, the result was a fiasco" (161). More important, a link is made between the British attitude and that of the North during Reconstruction, the period Page turns to in the last piece in the volume: "the essential and inherent vice of governing by absentee rulers, and the inherent weakness of it" (161).

Page places Virginia's early role in the vanguard of American civilization in contrast to its prostrate, humiliated condition during the Reconstruction era. His focus in this volume as a whole is on Virginia's contribution to American progress, not its separate life during the antebellum years. He leaves aside the decades in which Virginia and the South turned aside from the path of progress and advancement and took on much the conditions he describes of old Spain. The defeat of the South in the war provided the shock needed to wake the South from the idyll Page had earlier painted, but he focuses on Reconstruction as the true death of the Old South. The Old Dominion, as Page presents matters, had launched the nation on the path of progress and human advancement, then lagged behind, only to find itself crushed beneath the might of the very government and civilization it had helped to establish.

Page ardently wishes Virginia to reassume the mantle of national leadership, and in this final essay he sets forth (by means of a negative example) the conditions necessary for the South, and hence the nation, to flourish. Dixie had willingly embraced the necessary economic changes (and many of the political) to conform to new American model, but the race question remained the one on which the South could not yield—the Negroes must know their place in the new order. Reconstruction marks, for Page, the destruction of the plantation model of race relations and provides a cautionary tale against interference with the white southerner's handling of the matter. This piece comes from the same period as his infamous book *The Negro: The Southerner's Problem* (1904), in which he set forth the doctrine of racial inferiority, the blacks' incapacity for self-government, and the justification for paternalism, force, and Jim Crow. Much of what he says in this essay is a repetition of his remarks in "The Old Time Negro," in which he laments the loss of the old ways of mutual affection (and black subservience) and the "new" spirit of rancor in southern race relations. Negroes had their place for Page in the stories of the Old Dominion and the sketches of social life in old Virginia, but once they become an autonomous force, white hegemony must be established by fair means or foul in the absence of the old paternalism.

Once again, he strikes the note of white racial solidarity at the outset of the essay, setting out its racial and ethnic homogeneity as the key to the civilization. In contrast to the North, the South had remained almost exclusively English, Scotch, and Irish (with a healthy Huguenot infusion), receiving little of the foreign-born stock pouring into the other regions. These groups were the true inheritors of the legacy of the Saxon: "These people inherited the traits and tendencies of those from whom they had sprung; were bred on the traditions of the past, and loved the land on which they had been reared with a devotion little short of idolatry," much as the ancient Saxons had established themselves on "a hill or a grove beside a spring" and defended it to the death (235–36). The plantation system fostered individualism (through the distance between neighbors) while tending to "create an aristocracy of the governing people, and to give the dominant race a feeling of superiority and the habit of control" (237). "Against this benefit," Page tells us, "the institution of Slavery must be charged with having secluded the southern people from the movement of the outer world as with a wall. They knew little more of the modern outside foreign world than they knew of Assyria and Babylon; that is, they knew it almost exclusively from books" (237–38).

How such a people had managed to be on the vanguard of progress earlier and completely isolated only decades later (under the same system) Page does not pause to consider, though he does note that southerners had attempted to solve the dilemma of slavery by their own means, and even at the time of the war most of the southern leadership had been Whigs and opposed secession. Antebellum southerners, as he presents it, had been victims of historical forces beyond their control—the rise of abolitionism, the invention of the cotton gin, and so forth. Slavery was an evil that had to be rooted out, he acknowledges; the real question was whether southerners would be granted the right of self-determination in the aftermath of the war.

Page argues that for a time after emancipation and the end of the war, the slaves returned of their own will, and "their return was marked by a revival of the old plantation life, and in a short time, the old regime appeared to have begun again, with every prospect of continuing" (253). For a time, it appeared that "the old time Negro" might yet survive in the land: "The slaves had been emancipated, and labor had been disorganized; but the laborers yet survived, full of health, skilled in many kinds of manual work, trained to habits of industry, and disciplined to good order. . . . Moreover, outside the question of emancipation, the blacks were generally in full sympathy with the whites, and the ties of personal association and affection were recognized on both sides" (243). This relationship, for Page, is a natural, organic one, but "the outside world . . . saw only a relation of brute power and of enforced subservience" (251). Far from recognizing the peculiar traits of chattel slavery and the necessary economic components of it, Page sees only the disturbance of this "natural" order as the product of political action backed up by military force.

Reconstruction marks the true end of the Old South for Page because it substitutes an artificial order enforced by military power and political maneuvering for an order subsisting in the culture itself. Following the assassination of Lincoln, the South, with the imprisonment of Jefferson Davis, the imposition of Republican regimes, and countless other measures, suffered a humiliation Page regards as unprecedented in the annals of war: "with the South prostrate, the Constitution a thing to be tinkered with or overridden as partisan expediency suggested, and 'the party of the Union' burdened in the South with the most ignorant, venal, and debauched representatives that ever cursed a land" (236). He sees the blacks as victims of northern manipulation and measures taken by southern whites as the only course available to reestablish order.

As Page would have us believe, the ordeal of Reconstruction served to leave the South, which formerly had several distinct classes, with only two: the white and the black. The war had heightened the "race pride" on which the strength of

the South was founded, and it presented the whites with a dangerous development: "The laboring population of the South [by which Page means only blacks
here] had been diverted from its former field, and changed from a blessing to a
curse; the former relation of dependency and sympathy had been changed to
one of distrust and hostility; their habits of industry had fallen to those of idle-
ness and worthlessness" (243). The heroes of Page's drama are the Redeemers
and the whites who took back political power by any means necessary and reestablished white hegemony, as he chronicled in his early novel *Red Rock* (1898)
and his late, unfinished work *The Red Riders* (1924).

Page's view of Reconstruction and its significance is much that of the Redeemers and the later New South advocates: southerners could reorganize the
region along radically new lines while acting under the guise of restorers of the
true legacy of the South. Under the guise of controlling the Negro, the whites
of the new ruling class could consolidate political control and thereby prevent a
serious challenge along party lines and control the lower-class whites. As Woodward notes, by invoking the menaces of Negro power and foreign control, they
turned to the only reliable basis of white solidarity: "Almost any other issue
was hushed whenever possible. The Redeemers tried by invoking the past to
avert the future. The politics of Redemption belonged therefore to the romantic school, emphasizing race and tradition and deprecating issues of economics
and self-interest" (*Origins* 51). The new paternalism allowed the erection of the
powerful Democratic edifice largely on the basis of a manipulation of the black
vote and control of black labor. In the more immediate foreground to *The Old
Dominion*, Page had seen the full threat of a loss of white solidarity in the Popu-
list challenge to Democratic control. The New South, from which Page profited and of which he was a part, demanded a certain political and economic buf-
fer against serious reform efforts, and the key to stability (of a sort) proved to be
the doctrine of white supremacy.

In *The Old Dominion*, Page writes for a popular audience, for the pious sons and
daughters of "the South" at large, but he keeps an eye toward his most dangerous
critic, the scientific historian. Assuming the guise of historian, Page uses his authority in the role to correct erroneous views of old Virginia and its relationship with the nation. He seeks to project a Virginian ethos suitable to the vigor
and energy of the new century, and this effort is ultimately more important to
him than any set of facts or the sound methodology of the historian. At several
points, such as when he is dealing with chivalric episodes in the life of Raleigh

or the John Smith and Pocahontas story, he pauses to rebuke the "scientific historians" for their tendency to doubt anything and everything, with or without good cause. Page, acting in the obsolete role of man of letters as historian, essentially acts on the higher prerogatives of the artist (much in the manner of Simms); unfortunately, Page's conception of literary art is severely limited, and his history, like his fiction, is heavy on atmosphere, fixed traits of character, and romantic pronouncements. The contemporary assessment by historian William E. Dodd, writing in the *American Historical Review*, has stood the test of time better than the work he had under review. "The by-products of a litterateur" he calls the pieces collected in *The Old Dominion*, noting their conventionality, before going on to strike at the foundational premise of Page's fictional and historical world: "A note which runs through all that Mr. Page has ever written is evident here also: the judgement of one who supposes character to be absolutely determined by status. All heroic characters are gentlemen; the villains are outside the charmed circle. This is not life; it is not even ante-bellum Virginia life."[15]

Not life, indeed, for what Page sought was not the life but an image of the life useful in the present for consolidating southern identity around the patriarchal ideal, an ideal that would find its highest expression in his biography of Robert E. Lee. Page published a fairly short character study, *Robert E. Lee: The Southerner*, in 1908 and then, shortly before leaving for his ambassadorship in Italy, worked the materials into a larger, more extensive study in *Robert E. Lee: Man and Soldier* (1911).[16] If the war represented the "apotheosis" of the South, the new divinity was figured in Lee—the ideal gentleman soldier who embodied the Old South in its purest form and who was allowed to linger in the Virginia mountains as a living reminder of what had been. As Hobson notes, "It is fitting that when he came to write about a Civil War general he chose not Stonewall Jackson, the stern Calvinist to whom Dabney was drawn, but rather Robert E. Lee—the gentleman" (134). Richard Gray points out that the other generals were taken to represent "some particular aspect of the patriarchal ideal, some facet of the aristocratic model," but Lee was the "sum of all virtues" for southern historians whose aim was "the perpetuation and development of the patriarchal image in the South" (*Writing the South* 78). Everything that the Old South meant for Page is encapsulated in his portrait of the valiant, defeated general.

Page's portrayal of Lee is deeply colored by his personal experience of him at Washington College during Lee's presidency. Page had known the Old South only as it slipped away in his childhood, and he knew Lee only as the great defeated hero attempting to guide young men into a new order. As Page tells us of Lee in that period: "He passed life's close among his own people, a hallowed memory forever to those who knew him, an example to all who lived in that dark time, or shall live hereafter; the pattern of a Christian gentleman, who did justice, loved mercy, and walked humbly with his God."[17] There is enough ambiguity in the syntax here to allow us to read this statement as saying that Lee "passed life's close" *as* a "hallowed memory," a revered ghost encountered with trembling and demanding much. Late in the volume he recounts a day when, running late to class, he met Lee on the campus and received a gentle, albeit powerful, rebuke from him. His memory of Lee, and his earlier experience of Lee the Memory, force upon him the pious debt of remembrance. His writes the biography, as he tells us in its opening page, not to add anything to the fame of the hero "but rather in obedience to a feeling that as the son of a Confederate soldier, as a Southerner, as an American, he owes something to himself, and to his countrymen, which he should endeavor to pay" (ix).

Paying this debt of piety leads Page to even greater extremes in his use of Christian imagery to convey his sense of the meaning of the war. The South, for Page, was redeemed by the nobility of its suffering during the years of the war and its aftermath. The South as a spiritual nation found its birth only in defeat, and Lee underwent his transfiguration only after Appomattox. He tells us early and late that it is not "Lee the Victorious" to whom he will call the reader's attention but "the greater Lee: the Defeated" (xiii). The war years are treated as the time of Lee's Passion, from weeping tears of blood (in his wife's account) over his decision to go with Virginia rather than accepting command of the Union armies to his final review of his troops at Appomattox, of which Page writes, "If that was the very Gethsemane of his trials, yet he must have had then one moment of supreme, if chastened, joy" (257). Page emphasizes that these sufferings were willingly undergone for the sake of duty, and that Lee had no illusions about the significance of his decisions. He would be defeated and given into the hands of his enemies, forced to submit to their tribunals and indictment for treason. Only then would the perfection of his character become evident: "From this inquisition he came forth as unsoiled as the mystic knight of the Round Table. In that vivid glare he stood revealed like the angel bathed in light; the closest scrutiny brought forth new virtues and disclosed a more rounded character" (286).

For these sufferings to have the significance Page intends, Lee has to be made representative of his people, of Virginia and (by a mystical extension) the South.

In the preface Page tells us, "His character I deem absolutely the fruit of the Virginian civilization which existed in times past. No drop of blood alien to Virginia coursed in his veins; his rearing was wholly within her borders and according to the principles of her life. Whatever of praise or censure, therefore, shall be his must fairly fall on his mother, Virginia, and the civilization which existed within her borders. The history of Lee is the history of the South during the greatest crisis of her existence" (xiii). He goes to great lengths in the first chapter to establish that "Lee was essentially the type of the Cavalier of the Old Dominion to whom she owed so much of her glory" (6). He traces the history of the Lees from the first emigrant, Richard Lee, to the builder of Stratford, Thomas, to the two signers of the Declaration and heroes of the Revolution, Francis Lightfoot Lee and his brother, and Robert E. Lee's father, Richard Henry Lee ("Lighthorse Harry"). With the final element of Lighthorse Harry's marriage to a Carter, Lee has the pedigree of the scion of the noblest blood in Virginia. Lee becomes the standard by which Virginia civilization is to be judged, for the best of Virginia went into his making. Page further states toward his close, "I question whether in all the army under his command was one man who had his genius; but I believe that in character, he was but the type of his order, and as noble as was his, ten thousand gentlemen marched behind him, who, in all the elements of private character, were his peers" (289).

This identification, of course, involves a sleight of hand, since Page heightens the excellence of Lee's character to an incredible degree. Page's treatment of Lee's dominant public virtue, obedience to duty, is credible enough, but his intent is to defend not merely Lee but his civilization, and so he includes several extended, highly sentimental asides on his private, domestic virtues as the ideal patriarch. Of his marriage to Mary Parke Custis he claims, "Their domestic life was one of ideal devotion and happiness" (17). He returns time and again to his love for his sons, various incidents illustrating his love of children generally, and (reaching the nadir of banality) his kindness to animals, culminating in a sketch of his concern over a bird in harm's way at a battlefield. In keeping with the Old South's version of the plantation patriarch, Page repeatedly follows his tributes to Lee's fondness for children with those for his love of his slaves with no transition whatsoever. Lee's actions in regard to his slaves provide vindication of the South's long-held position on the matter: Lee opposed slavery and freed his slaves as soon as he declared for Virginia (in contrast to U. S. Grant, Page notes), and he continued to express concern for their welfare. Lee, as Page presents him, was both the ideal slaveholder and freed from the onus of slavery by his own act. The issue for Lee, and by extension Virginia and the South, is thus clarified as a defense of state's rights and the great Anglo-Saxon tradition. Apart from illustrating the perfection of Lee's character, his domestic virtues as patriarch perhaps are intended by Page to demonstrate the primacy of the domestic and thereby the purity of the South's motives. The South responds to threats according to the law of the clan: "The basic principle of Anglo-Saxon civilization was the defence of the inner-circle against whatever assailed it from the outside, and nowhere was this principle more absolutely established than in Virginia" (40).

On Lee as a military commander, Page sets out to demonstrate that he was indeed a great commander, and not simply for defensive operations. He accomplishes this largely by insisting that the "measure of a captain's abilities must rest, at last, on his achievement as gauged by his resources" (61) and by setting out to illustrate that these resources were relatively scant at best. He details several campaigns to show Lee's initiative and audacity when engaged with the enemy—what he did in the face of greater numbers and superior equipment. Whereas "it was to the science of arithmetic that the South yielded at last" (62), Page argues that Lee's victories were produced, apart from tactical genius, by superiority of character and knowledge of the character of his opponent. Not that the South, as Page presents matters, had any corner on valor, but the character of its commanders and soldiers was distinctive. Ultimately, however, this same distinctive character, as embodied by Lee, contributed to the South's defeat. Page points out Lee's humanity, his clemency, and his magnanimity as private virtues that proved professional liabilities. Again, as argued above with Page's treatment of antebellum culture, the South's vices are excesses of virtue, and, finally, Lee's reach exceeded his grasp. Page sums up his assessment of the failure of Lee's plan at Gettysburg by claiming, "It failed because his lieutenants failed, and his orders were not carried out—possibly because he called on his intrepid army for more than human strength was able to achieve" (152).

Although the biography contains some good passages on the movements of men and armies, Page's purpose is clearly not a realistic treatment of Lee or the battles in which he fought; his purpose is to create a sanctified object of memory out of Lee the Defeated. As I argued above, one of his consistent concerns is to establish that the verdict of history is not to be judged by mere outcomes.

Washington, whom Page sees as "the only absolute parallel" to Lee, founded a nation by his victory, but Lee founded a spiritual nation, a people of memory, in his defeat. Page presents the magnanimity of Grant at Appomattox as an illustration of the potency of Lee in defeat: "The greatness of the occasion appears to have lifted Grant to a higher plane than that of the mere soldier from which he had looked apparently unmoved on the sacrifice of thousands of the gallant men and officers who, from the Wilderness to Cold Harbor, had died at his bidding" (250). Grant here plays Saul to Lee's Christ, and Page ends the chapter on Lee's surrender on an prophetic note: "Yea, ride away, thou defeated general! Ride through the broken fragments of thy shattered army, ride through thy war-wasted land, amid thy desolate and stricken people. But know that thou art riding on Fame's highest way: 'This day shall see / Thy head wear sunlight and thy feet touch stars'" (260).

Page presents the Lee as the redeemer of southern history, the founder of the South as a spiritual nation; in his apostolic role, he offers redemption through memory to his readers. Once we properly understand the failure of Lee and the Old South, we can experience the reality of the South in memory, the transcendent truth now beyond the reach of history. Judging the Old South simply as a failed project in the realm of pragmatic history misses the truth Page wishes to present: "Unhappily, the world judges mainly by the measure of success, and though Time hath his revenges, and finally rights many wrongs, the man who fails of an immediate end appears to the body of his contemporaries, and often to the generations following, to be a failure" (x). But, Page promises, "through the history of sublime endeavor . . . He who loses his life for the sake of the Truth shall find it" (x).

The problem with such a plan of redemption is that is leaves the young southerner trapped in an abstracted realm of memory. To bring in Mixon's assessment once more, Page's vision offered no viable alternative to new order, and "by necessity then, if not choice, postbellum romance implicitly and explicitly promoted the industrial ethic, though disguising its message in the trappings of tradition" (31). If Page offers a form of redemption, it comes at no cost to the individual soul in the present—he offers "cheap grace," to adopt theologian Dietrich Bonhoeffer's phrase.[18] The paean to tradition and the icons of the Old Order serve only to mask the individual's involvement with the new order and to artificially partition the consciousness. Memory cannot be contained behind the barrier of Appomattox, since even the experience of our present is mediated through memory, as the modernists to come (and the great Romantics before) well understood. The great historian-artist to chronicle the impingement of history on the self would not be Page but Henry Adams. What was needed for the southern writer, as Ellen Glasgow noted so forcefully, was "blood and irony," and a treatment of memory adequate to the conditions of the new century would have to wait for the great modernists to come.

3

"THE EXASPERATED GENIUS OF AFRICA"

William Wells Brown and African American History

If the white writers of the South had to shoulder the burden of history in the nineteenth century, the black writers took on an even more massive task: providing a history for a people denied a history. Simms and Page entered the lists on behalf of the South in a war of competing national narratives; African American writers had to tell the story of the "nation within a nation" that had been neglected within all the accounts. After the Revolution, American nationalisms of all stripes developed a racial undercurrent, and if competing visions of the Republic emerged north and south, both involved white triumphalism. Black writers and orators strove to insert themselves into the national debates and, by their very presence in the realm of letters, to indict the nation for its failure to recognize African Americans and point the way toward a fulfillment of the Revolutionary promise. At the same time, their recovery of an African American and African past would provide the historical basis for the formation of African American identity.

In William Wells Brown, one of the most prominent black men of letters in his time, we find the African American counterpart of Simms and Page. Brown, like his contemporary Simms, focused on challenging the dominant narrative of America's founding and development by recasting events to highlight a neglected contribution. His historical writings (apart from his slave narrative) begin in 1855 with his published lecture *St. Domingo: Its Revolutions and Its Patriots*. His real stature as a leading African American historian stems from the wartime publication of *The Black Man* (1863), a volume of collective biography highlighting the lives of prominent blacks in the United States, Europe, and the West Indies; this volume emphasizes the contributions of black patriots in the Revolutionary War, in slave uprisings, and in Santo Domingo. Following the war, Brown was the first black writer to chronicle the contributions of black soldiers in a book-length volume, *The Negro in the American Rebellion* (1867). What Brown had begun in this work, establishing the place of blacks in the new American Republic emerging from the war, he would bring to culmination in his best historical work, *The Rising Son* (1874).

After the Revolution, the most prominent black writers and intellectuals worked toward assimilation within the new Republic. In the age of such figures as Phillis Wheatley, Benjamin Banneker, and the prominent minister Lemuel Haynes, the effort was not to create a distinctive African consciousness; protests against the status of blacks and slavery there were indeed, but these protests, such as the string of appeals to state legislatures, were grounded in republican rhetoric and the guarantees of individual liberties already secured by the Revolution. Much as in the narrative of Olaudah Equiano, African identity is subsumed under the larger rubric of republican citizenship and Christian identity, as we see frequently (albeit with some irony) in Wheatley's poems. No career better illustrates the hope of the period that African Americans might take their place in the public sphere than that of Lemuel Haynes, who (like several other black ministers) served largely white congregations in New England and remained a conservative. As Dickson Bruce writes, "Creating what was as nearly as possible a color-blind career in early-nineteenth-century America, Haynes made his mark more for his theological rigidity—and staunch Federalism—than for anything having to do with his African background."[1] These hopes for a color-blind society and access to the prerogatives of the white intellectual would prove illusory even during this period, but the place of blacks within a distinctively Christian discourse would have lasting importance for the beginnings of public intellectual authority. The early nineteenth century also saw the formation of more independent black churches, including the African Methodist Episcopal Church; schools; and civic organizations such as mutual benefit societies in all of America's major cities (including, to some extent, Charleston) that allowed for "the emergence of a self-conscious urban elite" (Bruce 92).

But blacks were still a people set apart, and they grew more so by the second decade of the nineteenth century. They were treated as invisible to history and incapable of world-historical action, and the task facing black writers and intellectuals was writing African Americans back into history. The older inheritance, from eighteenth-century evangelical traditions, was to see African Americans as a dispossessed people, broken and driven over the Middle Passage, in terms of the ancient Hebrews. This redemptive history made them a chosen people of

God in a corrupt society, set apart by their very chains, poverty, and weakness, and made their treatment the criterion by which the nation would be judged, the chosen ones who could provide the key to the nation's redemption or the remnant that could survive its fall. By the nineteenth century, this vision gave way (though not fully, as attested by innumerable sermons and spirituals) to a claim on the monumental history of Egypt as the fountainhead of civilization. In the words of Wilson Jeremiah Moses, "In the years immediately following the American revolution, African Americans typically sought solace in the idea that they were people of a new covenant, a newly chosen people whose messianic destiny must in some way be analogous to the biblical Hebrews. By the [mid-nineteenth] century, at least among the literate population, this idea came to be less attractive than the idea that blacks were ethnologically linked to the pharaohs, who had oppressed the biblical Hebrews."[2] Moses succinctly describes the impulse, saying that "black Americans wanted to be children of Pharaoh as well as children of Israel" (47). The writings of Volney and Henri Grégoire provided much of the impetus for the rediscovery of the glories of ancient African civilization, along with, ironically enough, the formation of the African Colonization Society and the beginning of its journal, *African Repository*, in 1825. The proponents of colonization, who were mostly white but included such prominent black figures as Paul Cuffe, celebrated the once and future greatness of the African continent; as one writer opined in the first volume, "And why may not America, the best and brightest of this wonderful series of revolution, carry back *by colonies* to Africa, now in barbarism, the blessings which, through ages that are passed, and nations that are perished, were received from her?" (qtd. in Bruce 155).

Lingering in the background of the post-Revolutionary years was the specter of Santo Domingo and the Haitian Revolution. Jefferson and Tom Paine notwithstanding, the American Revolution was distinct in being at its core a conservative revolution, intent on preserving the rights of Englishmen and the dignity of self-rule for the colonists. The Constitution resulted from these conservative instincts, carefully balancing competing powers and, while protecting the individual from the government, protecting the Republic from the excesses of democracy. Their carefully limited aims were far removed from the wild-eyed dreams of the fiery Jacobin, but if the degeneration of the French Revolution into bloodshed and tyranny provided the major cautionary tale, it was nowhere near as frightening as the tales emerging from the successful slave revolt in Santo

Domingo. Fears of the excesses of democracy in the early years of the United States were clearly tied to the contradiction between the claims of liberty and the fact of chattel slavery in the heart of the Republic. As Eric Sundquist writes: "The Revolution itself became in many instances a conservative constraint on reform impulses; in the case of slavery, defenders of the institution identified potential slave rebellion not with the achievement of liberty in the American Revolution but with the forces of license, madness, and primitive energy often attributed to the French Revolution."[3] Aborted slave revolts such as the plot in Richmond in 1800 and the Denmark Vesey plot in Charleston in 1822 were clear reminders of the revolutionary potential hidden beneath the surface of the slave-holding order. This potential would come to the fore around 1830 with the publication of David Walker's militant *Appeal* (1829) and the slave uprising of Nat Turner in 1831.

The primary mode of resistance, however, would be the pacifism and uncompromising opposition to slavery of William Lloyd Garrison, and the most important historical documents produced in that mode were not formal histories but the stories of individual freedom contained in slave narratives. These autobiographies documented the realities of slavery, but their primary function was to attest to the abilities of the author and demonstrate black potential for responsible freedom. Although Frederick Douglass's autobiography stands as the greatest of slave narratives, one of the other authentic accounts to garner a large amount of attention was the *Narrative of William W. Brown, a Fugitive Slave* (1847), produced two years later. In it, Brown attests to the contradictions of slavery through the experience of life on Dr. Young's farm as a mixed-race child. Apart from the standard cruelties of slavery, Brown evokes (though not as forcibly or memorably as does Douglass) the growth of his consciousness and his desire for freedom. It was on the river, first working on steamboats and then accompanying the slave trader James Walker to New Orleans, that he gained a sense of the nearness and possibility of freedom, and he made his first (failed) escape attempt with his mother in 1833. Brown succeeded in escaping the next year, made his way north, and spent the next nine years working on a Lake Erie steamer. In the meantime, he became involved in abolitionist and temperance activities, particularly after his move to Buffalo in 1836. There he began to move in the wider circles of the antislavery movement, meeting such figures as Frederick Douglass and Henry Highland Garnett, addressing a national convention, and appearing in print for the first time. He made his first lecture trip to New England in 1843, but his real national stature resulted from the publication of his slave narrative. He was selected as a delegate to the Peace Congress in Paris and left in 1849. With the passage of the Fugitive Slave Law, Brown could not safely return to the United States, but the time abroad proved valuable as a time of education and the formation of a public identity.

During his three years in Europe, Brown gained a new confidence in his abilities as a man of letters. He published his landmark novel, *Clotel*, of course, but equally important he received recognition from highest circles of the literary and intellectual elite in England. He moved in circles at the Peace Conference in Paris that included such luminaries at Alexis de Tocqueville and Victor Hugo; in London, after a lecture, he was awarded an honorary membership in the Whittington Club and Metropolitan Athenaeum, a club that included men of the magnitude of Dickens among its members.[4] These experiences gave more definite shape to his literary ambitions and a vision of the role he might fill. "He who understands well the history of the colored people, and writes it . . . will be greater than he who leads an army to victorious battle," wrote William J. Wilson in *Frederick Douglass's Paper* in 1855.

In the new climate of the 1850s, following the passage of the Fugitive Slave Law in 1850 and with Dred Scott still to come in 1857, Brown came out in favor of much more militant action than he had heretofore endorsed. After returning from England, he broadened the subject matter of his lectures to include a wide range of literary and historical topics. Fitting his appeal to the tenor of the times, his first published lecture on his return was *St. Domingo: Its Revolutions and Its Patriots*, delivered in Philadelphia in December 1854. In place of the sentimental appeal and emphasis on moral suasion in many of his previous lectures and *Clotel*, Brown provides a new model of revolutionary action that brings to the surface the threatening (for whites) image of the bloody revolution of Santo Domingo. His purpose is to challenge the long-held view of the revolution as simply chaos come again; the revolution he presents to his audience is one of heroic, purposeful action—the achievement of liberty at great odds and with great sacrifice. No longer the passive slave kneeling in chains awaiting his deliverance, Brown puts the force of his thought into his epigraph for the lecture, from Byron's *Childe Harold*: "Hereditary bondsmen! know ye not / Who would be free, themselves must strike the blow?"

The blacks in Haiti are the true heirs of the French Revolution, striking out for liberty against the forces of inherited privilege and oppression. Brown makes clear that the link between the citizens of France and the slaves and dis-possessed mulattoes of Haiti was consciously recognized; as he writes, "the news of the oath of the Tennis Court and the taking of the Bastille was received with wildest enthusiasm by the mulattoes of Hayti." The justness of the cause of the blacks and mulattoes (though separated at first) was recognized by the great-est of the French patriots such as Gregoire and Barnave: "[Gregoire] well knew that the crime for which Oge [one of the Haitian deputies to the new govern-ment] and his friends had suffered in Hayti, had constituted the glory of Mira-beau and Lafayette at Paris."[5] The contrast between the true republican spirit of the blacks and the opportunistic calculations of the planters is made clear when the Assembly (controlled by whites) seeks protection from the English, leav-ing the blacks to adopt the French standard as their ensign: "By this movement the blacks became the government troops, and the planters the insurgents" (11).

The undeniable violence of the revolution is for Brown a testament to the wrath stored up by the planters, just as the excesses of the French Revolution testified to the power of the underlying principles. In the epigram he will use re-peatedly in later years, Brown writes, "Right is the most dangerous of weapons,—woe to him who leaves it to his enemies" (6). The violence in Santo Domingo was different in degree, not in kind, from that in France itself: "The strifes of political and religious partisanship, which had raged in the clubs and streets of Paris, and had caused the guillotine to send its two hundred souls every day for two weeks, unprepared, to eternity, were transplanted to St. Domingo, where they raged with all the heat of a tropical clime, and the animosities of a civil war. Truly did the flames of the French Revolution at Paris, and the ignorance and self-will of the planters, set the island of St. Domingo on fire" (15). Much as David Walker, Frederick Douglass, Brown, and others would use the rhetoric of the American Revolution to position blacks as the true heirs of revolutionary principles, Brown here makes the black patriots of Santo Domingo the fullest expression of the spirit of the revolution in France; what went awfully awry in France would find its fulfillment in these obscure islands among a despised people. As Eric Sund-quist writes, "Brown's historical works . . . argued for the place of blacks in the revolutionary and intellectual traditions that Euro-Americans considered their sole prerogative" (305).

Like William Gilmore Simms and other romantic historians who would seek out the great men in the historical record, men who were capable of imposing form on a threatened chaos, making a time of destruction an opportunity for

the creation of new forms, Brown finds his guiding spirits in the black and mulatto leadership, with the grand figure of Toussaint L'Ouverture looming over
them all. His introduction of Toussaint as the looked-for leader follows a section dealing with the enormous barbarity of the civil war, as Brown presents the
mass killings by the white planters being responded to by the blacks: "This example set by the whites taught the men of color that the struggle was for liberty or death. Crime was repaid with crime, and vengeance followed vengeance.
The educated, refined, and civilized whites degraded themselves even more than
the barbarous and ignorant slaves" (12). In such a time, when civilization is but
a mask for power, the true force of civilization must be carried within, as it had
been with Simms's partisan warriors: "All appeared to look with hope to the rising up of a black chief, who should prove himself adequate to the emergency. . . .
In the midst of the disorders that threatened on all sides, the negro chief made
his appearance in the form of an old slave named Toussaint" (12). Toussaint is
the grandson of an African king and physically, although of average height, is "a
man of prepossessing appearance" and "an iron frame." The power of his vision
and his inner conviction allows him to be a force for moderation and order, as
reflected in his visage: "His dignified, calm, and unaffected features, and broad
and well-developed forehead would cause him to be selected, in any company
of men, as one who was born for a leader" (12). His mind is shaped by reading of
Raynal and other French patriots, but his deep religiosity (which Brown compares to Cromwell's) and humanity provide a stay against the excesses of revolutionary thought. Most important is his grasp of principle and capacity for imaginative vision: "It might be said that an inward and prophetic genius revealed to
him the omnipotence of a firm and unwearied adherence to a principle" (13).

Arrayed around Toussaint are other figures who fully illustrate a range of
types found in any great struggle. Brown responds to the prevailing monolithic
view of the African capable of only savagery or the simplest of virtues—either
beast or faithful servant—by heightening the differences among the black and
mulatto leaders. They range from such men as André Rigaud, the leader of the
mulattoes, a graduate of military school in Paris, and a student of Voltaire and
Rousseau, who "confounded liberty with infidelity," to the black general (and future emperor) Jean-Jacques Dessalines. A native African and a ferocious fighter,
Dessalines is the sum of all white fears: "The furrows and incisions on the face,
neck, and arms of this man pointed out the coast of Africa as his birthplace. He
was a bold, turbulent, and ferocious spirit, whose barbarous eloquence lay in

expressive signs rather than in words. Hunger, thirst, fatigue, and loss of sleep, he seemed made to endure, as if by peculiarity of constitution. He had a fierce and sanguinary look, beneath which was concealed an impenetrable dissimulation" (21). In short, to put it in terms of Melville's "Benito Cereno," if Toussaint is the noble African recognized by all, Dessalines is the terrifying Babo who lurks on the edges of white consciousness, waiting to spring upon the blind Delano. Between these extremes are arrayed the other figures: the black general Henri Christophe is a lesser Toussaint, cut from the same dignified cloth; the other mulattoes such as Alexandre Petion and Jean Pierre Boyer are from the same mold as Rigaud and, like him, capable of the noblest deeds but limited by their haughty self-regard and arrogance toward the blacks. Even Brown's inclusion of the "barbarous and wild blacks" newly arrived and escaped to the mountains only heightens the civilized character of the others. This range of figures and their deeds makes clear that blacks not only are capable of autonomy, in both self and nation, but possess the full range of character and temperament found in any culture and civilization. Their struggle is fully worthy of the respect and study of the historian.

As Brown presents it, the revolution in Santo Domingo, waged against the greatest military power of the day, surpasses anything in the annals of republican struggle. Toussaint's address to the people of Haiti after refusing the demands of the French commander Charles LeClerc captures the spirit of the struggle: "You are going to fight against enemies who have neither faith, law, nor religion; they promise you liberty—they intend your servitude. Why have so many ships traversed the ocean, if not to throw you again into chains? During the last ten years what have you not endured for liberty? The French do not come here to fight for their country, or for liberty, but for slavery" (24). Much like the Latin women fighting the invaders in the *Aeneid* or the models of republican womanhood celebrated in the writing of the early Republic of the United States, the black women of Haiti present a model of sacrifice for liberty contrasting with the corrupted state of the white women. After the bloodhounds sent for from France arrive, Brown juxtaposes the two groups:

Even the women, wives of the planters, went to the sea-side, met the animals, and put garlands about their necks, and some kissed and caressed the dogs. Such was the degradation of human nature. While white women were cheering on the French, who had imported blood-hounds

as their auxiliaries, the black women were using all their powers of persuasion to rouse the blacks to the combat. Many of these women walked
from camp to camp, and from battalion to battalion, exhibiting their naked
bodies, showing their lacerated and scourged persons;—these were the
marks of slavery, made many years before, but now used for the cause of
human freedom. (29–30)

Knowing slavery in one's own person provides the basis for a true understanding
of liberty, an understanding Brown sees lacking in both the French and, more
important for him, the American founders. We see this most strikingly in the
contrast of Toussaint with Washington, which Brown places at the end of the
work after the comparison with Napoleon: "Each was the leader of an oppressed
and outraged people, each had a powerful enemy to contend with and each succeeded in founding a government in the New World. Toussaint's government
made liberty its watchword, incorporated it in its constitution, abolished the
slave-trade, and made freedom universal amongst the people. Washington's government incorporated slavery and the slave-trade, and enacted laws by which
chains were fastened upon the limbs of millions of people" (37). Brown is more
concerned with a prophetic vision of blacks as the agents of liberty than with
a thorough dealing with the historical record; indeed, in good Romantic fashion, the spirit of the history and its underlying form are more important than
the complicating facts on its surface. For example, Dessalines is championed in
spite of his cruelty and his quick assumption of the title of emperor during his
reign; Christophe, who is praised for discarding "the pompous title of emperor,"
took, as we are told only as an afterthought, the title of king for the last years of
his reign. Brown works hard, in spite of the incessant civil war, the naked ambitions of power, and the lack of stable rule, to make Haiti the model of revolutionary action.

Brown does not shy away from the costs of acting on principle any more than
the patriots of Haiti, and the underlying threat to the South runs as an undercurrent throughout the speech. At several points, he makes explicit the parallel
of Santo Domingo and the revolutionary potential of an outraged slave population in the South. Speaking of Toussaint as he fires a city before the French
occupy it, Brown writes, "Like Nat Turner, the Spartacus of the Southampton
revolt, who fled with his brave band to the Virginia swamps, Toussaint and his
generals took to the mountains" (23). More striking, after treating the spectacle

of the massacre of white children by Dessalines at length, Brown adds, "Let the slave-holders in our Southern States tremble when they shall call to mind these events" (25). This threat is made more explicit toward the end of the work when Brown raises the question that has been implicit all along: "Who knows but that a Toussaint, a Christophe, a Rigaud, a Clervaux, and a Dessalines, may some day appear in the Southern States of this Union? That they are there, no one will doubt. That their souls are thirsting for liberty, all will admit. The spirit that caused the blacks to take up arms, and to shed their blood in the American revolutionary war, is still amongst the slaves in the south; and, if we are not mistaken, the day is not far distant when the revolution of St. Domingo will be reenacted in South Carolina and Louisiana" (32). In fact, the end of his address deals not with Santo Domingo but with the South and the specter of racial conflict in the Unites States. He quotes from Jefferson's Query XIII of his *Notes from the State of Virginia* and then moves to his close: "And, should such as contest take place, the God of Justice will be on the side of the oppressed blacks. The exasperated genius of Africa would rise from the depths of the ocean, and show its threatening form; and war against the tyrants would be the rallying cry. The indignation of the slaves of the south would kindle a fire so hot that it would melt their chains, drop by drop, until not a single link would remain; and then revolution that was commenced in 1776 would then be finished, and the glorious sentiments of the Declaration of Independence . . . would be realized" (38).

It was Brown's first full-length historical collection, *The Black Man: His Antecedents, His Genius, and His Achievements* (1863), published during the Civil War, that established him as a leading African American historical authority. Lincoln's developing moral vision of the war had moved to the war to free the blacks by 1863, with the Emancipation Proclamation (however limited) coming in January. Brown, however delighted he was with the prospect of a war against the South, shared the suspicion of many black leaders of the motives for the war and actually spoke against the movement to enlist blacks in the Union army. At a meeting at the Twelfth Baptist Church in Boston in 1861, Brown held that "self-respect should keep Negroes from begging the government for opportunities to defend it" (Farrison 332). His concern was that blacks would not be able to enlist on equal terms and would simply be relegated to menial positions. Like many of his contemporaries, including Martin Delany, Henry Highland Garnett, and even Frederick Douglass, Brown had moved to a more separationist position of blacks doing for themselves, even to the extent of briefly supporting Haitian immigration in the early 1860s. The redefinition of the nature of the war, as a moral crusade against slavery, in late 1862 to 1863 provided Brown and other leaders with the opportunity to reenter the national debate from a stronger position. As spokesmen for African Americans, they could provide a voice for the black people ostensibly at the center of the conflict and make the case (providing the strongest evidence in their own persons and work) that blacks were indeed worthy of liberation and ready to assume the responsibilities of citizenship. *The Black Man*, which included a brief history of black contributions and a collection of biographical sketches of notable people of African descent, would make the case for freedom precisely at the time when freedom was in the offing. Encouraged by the signs, Brown ceased speaking on Haitian immigration in the summer of 1862 as he began to work on the manuscript, writing to noted abolitionist Gerrit Smith, "We think . . . that it is just the work needed for the hour, to place the Negro in a right position before the country, especially the working classes" (Farrison 366).

In his preface, Brown takes the combative tone of one challenging ingrained prejudice, not as an author simply presenting new evidence. He opens by identifying the source of the false images of blacks, saying that the "calumniators and traducers of the Negro" can be divided into the two classes of the slaveholders and the ignorant.[6] As Brown knew from his abolitionist activities (particularly in the 1830s), prejudice was much more ingrained in the North than his classification implies, but his rhetorical strategy allows the members of his audience to place themselves on the side of the angels, those open to enlightenment, in direct opposition to the slaveholder. Brown sets out "to meet and refute these misrepresentations, and to supply a deficiency, long felt in the community, of a work containing sketches of individuals who, by their own genius, capacity, and intellectual development, have surmounted the many obstacles which slavery and prejudice have thrown in their way, and raised themselves to positions of honor and influence" (6). This effort is intended to "aid in vindicating the Negro's character, and show that he is endowed with those intellectual and amiable qualities which adorn and dignify human nature." Brown then includes a thirty-page autobiographical sketch, making his own life the first (and most extensive) exhibit in this effort at vindication.

Brown opens the work proper with a general essay, "The Black Man and His Antecedents," designed to turn the tables on notions of civilization and barbarity and to place the black man both at the fount of civilization and in the future stages of development. After his frank recognition that the "condition of [his] race, whether considered in a mental, moral, or intellectual point of view . . . cannot compare favorably with the Anglo-Saxon," Brown argues that the true potential of the race for development cannot be judged by the slavery-created present but must be judged in light of history, when the rise and fall of civilizations and the development and degradation of peoples become evident (32). In a set piece of African American popular historiography, Brown juxtaposes the savagery in ancient Britain with the accomplishments of ancient Egypt. Egypt and Ethiopia were the source of civilization; as Brown writes, "To the learning and science derived from them we must ascribe those wonderful monuments which still exist to attest the power and skill of the ancient Egyptians" (32). More to the point, they were black civilizations, and seeing black people against the backdrop of this ancient achievements places them in a very different light indeed: "The image of the negro is engraved upon the monuments of Egypt, not as a bondsman, but as the master of art." Minerva, Atlas, and Jupiter Ammon, Brown claims, all have their origins in Africa, and some of the acknowledged masters of Western literature and thought, such as Tertullian and Saint Augustine, contrary to received opinion, were black. Identifying with the monumental history of ancient Egypt allows Brown, and American blacks generally, to radically reorient themselves in relation to history. Brown describes having seen the obelisk of Luxor during his time in Europe. Seeing the tribute to the African general Sesostris, "who drew kings at his chariot wheels," Brown felt a change within himself: "I felt proud of my antecedents, proud of the glorious past, which no amount of hate and prejudice could wipe from history's page, while I had to mourn over the fall and degradation of my race" (35). Set against this glorious past are the descriptions—by notables from Macaulay and Hume to Cicero and Julius Caesar—of the ancient Britons (whom Brown conflates with the Anglo-Saxons), a "rude and barbarous people" with the (for Brown) darkness of a pagan religion and vassalage under the Romans, a people, as he quotes Macaulay saying, "little superior to the Sandwich Islanders" (33). Brown concludes his comparison by saying, "Ancestry is something which the white American should not speak of, unless with his lips to the dust" (35).

Brown makes clear that, in spite of the overwhelming obstacles blacks have faced, they have demonstrated a great potential for development. Far from simply being a permanent victim class in need of white benevolence, blacks are limited only by the conditions in which they have been placed; in Brown's historical vision, nothing is in any race, all is in the conditions and historical trends: "There is nothing in race or blood, in color or features, that imparts susceptibility of improvement to one race over another. The mind left to itself from infancy, without culture, remains a blank. Knowledge is not innate. Development makes the man" (36). The presumption of inferiority is itself the bar to progress, for black and white alike; groundless prejudice prevents the unified effort necessary to national progress. To illustrate this point, Brown provides an anecdote from his seemingly bottomless supply, comparing Lincoln's comment to a black visitor— "But for your race there would not be a war" —to that of a white passenger who fell off the top of a carriage after refusing to ride inside with Brown and promptly blamed him for his injury: "If you had not been black, I should not have left my seat inside" (37). He finds the best example of the potential for progress through emancipation and equality in the British West Indies. Contrary to those people who see only general ruin there and attribute it to emancipation, Brown points out the historical pattern of mismanagement and abuse under slavery and argues that, in reality, the effects of emancipation have been positive for black and white alike: "The principles of freedom triumphed; not a drop of blood was shed by the enfranchised blacks; the colonies have arisen from the blight which they labored under in the time of slavery; the land has increased in value; and, above all, that which is more valuable than cotton, sugar, or rice—the moral and intellectual condition of both blacks and whites is in a better state now than ever before" (39).

From the triumphant example of the West Indies, Brown turns to the more important question of the readiness of slaves in the United States for emancipation and the preparation of blacks generally for the responsible exercise of citizenship. He writes, "One of the most formidable [obstacles to emancipation] has been the series of objections urged against it upon what has been supposed to the slave's want of appreciation of liberty, and his ability to provide for himself in a state of freedom; and now that slavery seems to be near its end, these objections are multiplying, and the cry is heard all over the land, 'What shall be done with the slave if freed?'"(40). To answer this question, Brown asserts the "prosperous condition of the large free colored population of the Southern States," their acquisition of considerable property, and their notable traits: "this industry, this sobriety, this intelligence" (42). The truly dependent class in the South, Brown claims, is not the slave or the free black but the planter class: "He [the slave] is the bone and sinew of the south; he is the producer, while the master is nothing but a consumer, and a very poor consumer at that" (46). Indeed, a better question would be, "What shall we do with the slaveholders if the slaves are freed?" (46). The frequently floated idea of expatriating the emancipated slaves shows the folly of political expediency; it overlooks the dependence of the South and the nation on the labor force provided by blacks and, in good capitalist terms, the promise of four million new consumers in the economy (46).

Part of the problem, as Brown presents it, has been the tendency, springing from prejudice, to treat blacks as a mass problem requiring a mass solution; the lives exemplifying black achievement shift the focus to the individual needing only the opportunity to make the fullest use of his or her gifts. "Why, every man," Brown writes, "must make equality for himself. No society, no government, can make this equality. I do not expect the slave of the south to jump into equality; all I claim for him is that he be allowed to jump into liberty, and let him make equality for himself" (47). The true historical record, with black contributions to the American project and stories of black success included in the larger American narrative, will leave no doubt that African Americans have not only the potential but also the record of accomplishment to claim their rightful place in American life. "From the fall of Attucks," Brown writes, "the first martyr of the American revolution in 1770, down to the present day, the colored people have shown themselves worthy of any confidence that the nation can place in its citizens in the time that tries men's souls" (49). Brown then cites some examples of black sacrifice for the country and, neglecting to mention that he had been more frequently an opponent of efforts to enlist blacks in the Union cause than an advocate, states, "Whenever the rights of the nation have been assailed, the negro has always responded to his country's call, at once, and with every pulsation of his heart beating for freedom" (49).

The bulk of *The Black Man* is made up of material in the dominant mode for popular African American historiography: composite biography, the collection of exemplary race heroes from a wide range of endeavor.[7] Given the context of the war years and the need to establish the potential of blacks for active participation in revolution and patriotic sacrifice, Brown emphasizes figures of military heroism and revolutionary action. Fourteen of Brown's original fifty-four figures—and sixteen of the fifty-six in the expanded edition—fall into this category, encompassing lives of several great Haitian revolutionaries, black patriots in the American Revolution, slaves who aided the Union during the Civil War, and leaders of slave insurrections in the United States. In keeping with Brown's belief, as expressed in a lecture titled "The Heroes of Insurrection" given shortly after John Brown's raid in 1859, that there is a common effort by "the heroes of the pen, the platform, and the sword," Brown places even greater emphasis on the first two: sixteen orators, writers of polemic, and editors of the black press, including major figures such as Douglass, Charles Lenox Remond, and Henry Highland Garnett, as well as less well known figures such as J. Theodore Holly and the westerner John Mercer Langston. If one adds the novelists and poets, such as Alexandre Dumas, Phillis Wheatley, and Charlotte Forten, to the total, then Brown clearly gives the palm to the pen and platform over the sword. The vast majority of the individuals celebrated are activists of one sort or another, but there are others whose achievement has simply been exceptional work in various fields against overwhelming odds. Included are men who have distinguished themselves in scholarship, such James W. C. Pennington, who received a doctorate from Heidelberg, and three other professors; great craftsmen, such as the organ maker James Lawson; actors and painters (most notably Edwin Bannister); and of course the foremost example of black achievement in the American vein, the scientist, mathematician, and almanac maker Benjamin Banneker.

The Black Man, from the time of its publication, has been criticized for its apparent lack of any governing principle of arrangement, but the lack of such a clear principle does not mean that there are no significant patterns. Farrison, for instance, is here as always the sternest critic of Brown as historian, and he rightly faults Brown for indiscriminately inserting sketches as he was able to write them (or, in some cases, receive them from correspondents) and for a lack of proportion in the relative sizes of the sketches (368). The sketch of the actor Ira Aldridge, for instance, is larger than that of Frederick Douglass and other important figures; in another instance, the sketches of the great Haitians, because Brown had the text ready to hand, occupy the greatest number of pages. In a letter to the *Weekly Anglo-African* of August 8, 1863, Brown justified his method "to make a book for the *present crisis*," claiming "sketches of individuals are seldom, if ever, put in alphabetical form; and as for date or merit, the first cannot always be found, and the latter must be decided by the reader" (Farrison 374). In other words, because it is difficult or arbitrary to impose a system on a collection of sketches, he chose to use none at all.

However, regardless of Brown's conscious plan or lack of one, there is a definite effect in the selection and arrangement as the book stands; simply put, *The Black Man* prevents any easy separation of black achievement from revolutionary energies. Consider the placement of the three lives—Crispus Attucks, Benjamin Banneker, and Phillis Wheatley—that are popular starting points for a catalog of prominent African Americans. Instead of beginning with these three together, as in other popular histories, Brown begins with Banneker but then moves to Nat Turner and Madison Washington, two leaders of slave revolts; Attucks, the first American patriot to die in the Revolution, is placed after Toussaint, the father of the Haitian Revolution; and Wheatley, the most seemingly noncontroversial life, is placed between Henri Christophe and Denmark Vesey, a Haitian revolutionary and the leader of the aborted South Carolina slave revolt. What is clear is that this is not another attempt simply to integrate the African American story into the dominant American narrative. Brown, in a time of war and questioning of black people's readiness for freedom, makes that struggle, even in its most threatening forms, central to African American identity; it is an identity in keeping with the underlying theme of American history that blood must be paid for freedom, but at the same time it is deeply disruptive to the existing American order founded on the injustice of slavery and caste. Instead of placing the rebels of Santo Domingo—that nightmare of the white world—in their own section (or eliminating them altogether), Brown spreads them throughout the first half of the lives, a constant reminder that the human longing for liberty cannot be suppressed but at a terrible cost to the slaveholder; similarly, the leaders of slave revolts in the United States are distributed throughout the first half. Brown may give us the story of Ira Aldridge, a native of Senegal who left the United States for a successful career on the London stage as a Shakespearean actor, but he places him between the lives of the cruel Dessalines and Joseph Cinque, the African leader of the revolt on the *Amistad*. Fully half the lives of the first half of the collection are revolutionaries of one sort or another; by this placement, Brown makes clear that the achievements in the more peaceful arts Brown emphasizes in the second half are intertwined with a history of armed struggle.

Brown strikes a balance in his treatment of the revolutionaries between, on the one hand, their nobility, courage, and humanity and, on the other, their audacity and ruthlessness in pursuit of liberty. With Madison Washington, the leader of a slave revolt on the brig *Creole*, for example, he paints a romanticized portrait of the noble hero: "His commanding attitude and daring orders, now that he was free, and his perfect preparation for the grand alternative of liberty or death which stood before him, are splendid exemplifications of the truly heroic" (84). When the others move to take revenge on their former captors after the brig is seized, Washington offers himself to defend them, and Brown writes, "This act of humanity raised the uncouth son of Africa far above his Anglo-Saxon oppressors" (85). But this sort of treatment never completely replaces the darker, threatening element found in the tortured heart of the slave. Brown, after providing the sketch of Nat Turner (largely quoted from Gray's account), draws the threatening moral: "The slaveholder should understand that he lives upon a volcano, which may burst forth at any moment, and give freedom to his victim" (73). Further, Brown claims that the tide of public opinion has turned since 1831 and the duty of revolt in the face of injustice is accepted: "This is a new era, and we are in the midst of the most important crisis that our country has yet witnessed. And in the crisis the negro is an important item. Every eye is now turned toward the south, looking for another Nat Turner" (75).

This emphasis on the militant action of the heroic individual complements and informs the emphasis throughout on the African American as the self-made man or woman. When he writes of Henry Bibb, who escaped from slavery to Canada and established a successful journal, he sketches a life that follows the pattern of the slave narrative (and of course Brown's own story): "From an ignorant slave, he became an educated free man, by his own powers, and left a name that will not soon fade away" (87). This emphasis runs throughout because "among our young readers there is more than one who will exclaim with ardor, and with a firm resolution to fulfill his promise, *I, too, shall make a name*" (87–88).

Brown was busy in the war years following the publication of *The Black Man*. In the wake of the Emancipation Proclamation on January 1, 1863 (its effective date), he played a prominent role in the celebrations and gave himself wholeheartedly to supporting the war effort. With the promise of full participation on an equal footing, Brown began supporting the enlistment of black troops. After the initial, largely ineffective efforts to raise black regiments for the war with the blessing of the secretary of war, George L. Stearns was given permission to supervise recruiting; he promptly employed several of the most prominent African Americans as recruiting agents, including Brown, Delany, Douglass, Garnett, Remond, and others, giving rise to the Fifth Regiment of Massachusetts Volunteer Infantry. During three months of the summer of 1863, Brown used his lectures to highlight the contributions of black soldiers in the war effort, including the attack on Port Hudson, Louisiana, in May and the famous assault on Fort Wagner, South Carolina, in July (Farrison 381–83).

Brown's former reservations about blacks in the war effort returned, however, with the administration's failure to move toward a general emancipation, frequent attacks on black soldiers in the press, unequal pay and conditions in the ranks, and the Democrats pushing for a negotiated peace instead of final victory over the slaveholder. At a meeting in Boston's Twelfth Baptist Church on August 4, 1864, called to address precisely these concerns, Brown spoke against a black minister who supported enlistment of blacks in spite of the difficulties. Overstating his early support for black enlistment, Brown said: "Mr. White's God is bloodthirsty! I worship a different kind of God. My God is a God of peace and goodwill to men. At first I desired that colored men should go to the war, to convince this God-forsaken nation that black men are as valiant as other men. But our people have been so cheated, robbed, deceived, and outraged everywhere, that I cannot urge them to go. . . . I am almost discouraged."[8]

After the war, Brown continued to work to inscribe African Americans into the national narrative. He became general agent for a group, the Freedmen's National Memorial Monument Association, attempting to erect a freedmen's monument on the U.S. Capitol grounds in memory of Lincoln and published the first historical account of black service in the war, *The Negro in the American Rebellion*, in 1867. Although the great betrayal of the African American people with the end of Reconstruction had not yet come to pass, Brown and other prominent black activists were already detecting signs that the meaning of the war as the fulfillment of the Revolution's promise was in danger of being lost. Brown desired to preserve the contribution of black fighting men in the war, as he writes in the preface to *The Negro in the American Rebellion*: "Feeling anxious to preserve for future reference an account of the part which the Negro took in suppressing the Slaveholders' Rebellion, I have been induced to write this work."[9]

Brown clearly sets out to connect the sacrifices and heroism of the black volunteers with the struggle of the Revolution and its continuation in black rebellions against the injustice of slavery. His Civil War is a fundamentally different war from the accounts focusing on the eastern battlefields and the titanic presence of Grant and Sherman on the one hand, Lee, Jackson, and Longstreet on the other. His war is a heroic struggle for black freedom through arms, conducted on the periphery of the other accounts, in the western theater and on the southern coast, at places like Milliken's Bend, Port Hudson, Fort Wagner, Olustee, and Honey Hill. It is a war that accomplished much, most important the final demonstration of the courage and competence of the black man, but it is one that does not end at Appomattox. Final Union victory will come only with enforced universal suffrage for African Americans, else all is squandered.

Brown opens his work with an introduction to black contributions to American independence and the resistance to any recognition of that role or the place in American society it justified. As he writes in the opening:

> The Declaration of American Independence, made July 4, 1776, had scarcely been enunciated, and an organization of the government commenced, ere the people found themselves surrounded by new and trying difficulties, which, for a time, threatened to wreck the ship of state.
>
> The forty-five slaves landed on the banks of the James River, in the colony of Virginia, from the coast of Africa, in 1620, had multiplied to several thousands, and were influencing the political, social, and religious institutions of the country. (1–2)

The troubles Brown had in mind are not primarily those of external threats but the internal moral decay due to the institution of slavery: "The institution bred in the master insulting arrogance, deteriorating sloth, pampered the loathsome lust it inflamed, until licentious luxury sapped the strength and rottened the virtue of the slave-owners in the South. Never were the institutions of a people, or the principles of liberty, put to such a severe test as those of the American Republic" (2). The slaveholders acted from the first, in Brown's account, to ensure that the government would move to suppress the slaves "if they should imitate their masters in striking a blow for freedom." Black volunteers demonstrated precisely that love of freedom in the struggle for independence, and Brown here emphasizes (as he did in *The Black Man*) the place of the mulatto slave Crispus Attucks as the first casualty of the war, the heroism of Peter Salem and others at Bunker Hill, and the conduct of Colonel Christopher Greene's black troops at the Battle of Rhode Island in 1778. The primary note here is one of faithful allegiance, most clearly demonstrated by Brown's gloss on the death of Colonel Greene, whose body was reached only "over the dead bodies of his faithful negroes" (8).

The note shifts in the next three chapters, in which Brown deals not with fidelity but just rebellion against injustice. In three chapters, he again recounts the rebellions of Denmark Vesey, Nat Turner, and Madison Washington, leading off with the proclamation that "human bondage is ever fruitful of insurrection, wherever it exists, and under whatever circumstances it may be found." Brown's intent is clear: the work of black troops in the Civil War is simply an extension of the work of the black patriots who rebelled against the slave power. The struggle of the earlier rebels is raised to legitimate warfare, and the participation of the black troops in the war is connected to a revolutionary impulse toward freedom. This conflation of the rebel and the soldier is heightened by the inclusion of black 'irregulars' among the heroes of the war itself, such as James Lawson, who gathered intelligence behind Confederate lines, and William Tillman, a steward who recaptured the schooner *S. J. Waring* after it had been captured by a Confederate privateer. For Brown, the rightness of the act is not determined by its accordance with law; the legitimacy of the law and the existing order is determined by right. The struggle transcends recognized states of war and peace, and Brown repeats a passage from his work on Santo Domingo to drive home the point: "Every iniquity that society allows to subsist for the benefit of the oppressor is a sword with which she herself arms the oppressed. Right is the most dangerous of weapons: woe to him who leaves it to his enemies" (36).

In Brown's vision of the war, the first two years were simply a time of preparation for the entrance of black troops in 1863, a period in which America stumbled toward rejoining history and the larger struggle for liberation. During the period in which blacks were waiting their time, the northern leadership was divided between individuals who, in Brown's view, correctly understood the nature of the struggle and those who did not. The proslavery, Democratic Union generals, most notably McClellan, were marked by a failure of vision and irresolution that extended far beyond the battlefield. In contrast, antislavery generals such as John Fremont and David Hunter understood that there could be no compromise with slavery and moved quickly in their respective departments (the West and portions of Georgia, Florida, and South Carolina) to issue proclamations immediately emancipating the slaves. General Nathaniel Banks, on taking command after the fall of New Orleans, experienced a conversion of sorts on the slavery question and took steps to suppress the white "rowdies" (as Brown calls them) and brought the black militia (the Native Guards) into Union service. Lincoln's administration, fearing backlash from the Copperhead Democrats and the border states, quickly overruled Fremont and Hunter, but their visionary precedent had been set. On the most important precedent, however, Lincoln overruled objections; the abolition of slavery in the District of Columbia in 1862 provided the strongest evidence, in Brown's eyes, giving the lie to the fearmongering of northern Democrats on the results of emancipation. Brown quotes one contemporary press account to make the point: "There has been no negro saturnalia, no violent outbreak of social disorder, no attempt to invade those barriers of social distinction that must forever exist between the African and Anglo-Saxon" (96). Only with the Emancipation Proclamation, however, would the nation return to the forward edge of history and blacks have a chance to don the uniform of their country in the name of their own freedom.

For Brown, it is the Emancipation Proclamation, not Gettysburg or the ascension of Grant, that is the turning point of the war. The proclamation met with fierce resistance in the North, particularly in the Copperhead press, which simply gave voice to the corrupted moral sense of the North generally. Brown writes: "The toleration of a great social wrong in any country is ever accompanied by blindness of vision, hardness of heart, and cowardice of mind, as well as moral deterioration and industrial impoverishment" (109). With Lincoln's action, the country has the opportunity to recover its moral grounding and prosecute the struggle with the South in the name of right. After sketching "rejoicing meetings" at the end of December in several different cities, Brown turns his attention to a contraband camp in Washington, D.C., on the eve of emancipation for the remainder of the chapter.

In his account, he skillfully moves from the rough dialect of the slave speakers to the more polished song of an "intelligent contraband" and finally to the text of the Emancipation Proclamation itself, making them all part of the same song of freedom. His dialect transcription of the slave speaker runs, "Now, no more dat! no more dat! no more dat! Wid my hands agin my breast I was gwine to my work, when the overseer used to whip me along. Now, no more dat! no more dat! no more dat!" The "intelligent contraband" breaks out in the following "strain": "The first of January next, eighteen sixty-three,— / So says the Proclamation,—the slaves will all be free! / To every kindly heart 'twill be the day of jubilee." Other voices join in the song, "which made the welkin ring," and Brown, having joined folk speech to the flights of the conventionally literary, then passes to the text of the proclamation, making it rise, as it were, out of the multivocal black chorus rather than simply descending as a distant white man's proclamation to lift the poor untutored black folk. The effect of the proclamation, as Brown presents it, was striking and immediate: "The proclamation gave new life and vigor to our men on the battle-field. The bondmen everywhere caught up the magic word, and went with it from farm to farm, and from town to town. Black men flocked to recruiting stations, and offered themselves for the war. Everybody saw light in the distance" (122). Blacks, heretofore limited to irregular roles, were soon to join the war, and the war, through them, was joined to an overriding moral purpose.

Brown establishes, in two successive chapters, the suitability of blacks to military service through the authority of two white commanders of black troops, Thomas Wentworth Higginson and Captain M. M. Miller. Higginson's public stature as a man of letters made his decision to take command of the First South Carolina an influential one. Brown uses his testimony to establish the zeal and capacity of the black volunteers; they learned quickly, and "every thing was done 'for God and country.'" The long letter he reprints from Higginson to a newspaper is sympathetic toward blacks but condescending. In one example, Higginson writes, "Their memories are a vast bewildered chaos of Jewish history and biography; and most of the great events of the past, down to the period of the American Revolution, they instinctively attribute to Moses." Brown, having prepared the ground, then goes on in the next chapter to the far more serious portrayal of the Battle of Milliken's Bend in Louisiana, "the first regular battle . . . fought between blacks and whites in the valley of the Mississippi." Here, for Brown, the arrogance of planters in the Deep South (though most of the rebels were actually Texas troops) would be tested against even the lowliest, "most ignorant" of the slave population. Here the black troops, although driven back and saved by the aid of gunboats, held their ground better than the white troops against far superior numbers in savage close-quarters fighting. After recounting the wounds and gallantry of his men, Captain Miller declared, "I never more wish to hear the expression, 'The niggers won't fight.' Come with me, a hundred yards from where I sit, and I can show you the wounds that cover the bodies of sixteen as brave, loyal, and patriotic soldiers as ever drew bead on a rebel" (139). "This battle," Brown writes, "satisfied the slave-masters of the South that their charm was gone; and that the negro, as a slave, was lost forever" (141).

It is not simply a matter of the service of black troops being acceptable to whites, however; in the next chapter, Brown turns to the difficult question of the reluctance of many blacks to serve in the Union cause when they faced daily prejudice and injustice in the North. Here he writes from his own concerns as expressed at several points during the war years; given the manifest injustices, "Why should we fight?" was a legitimate question. "In every State north of Mason and Dixon's Line, except Massachusetts and Rhode Island, . . . the blacks are disenfranchised, excluded from the jury box, and in most of them from the public schools. The iron hand of prejudice in the Northern States is as circumscribing and unyielding upon him as the manacles that fettered the slave of the South" (142). Lest the northerners pride themselves on their enlightened views of human freedom, Brown reminds them "that the sin of withholding that freedom is not vastly greater than withholding the rights to which he who enjoys it is entitled" (143).

Having established the capacity of the black soldier, Brown then proceeds to the twin high points—east and west—of his history: Port Hudson and Fort Wagner. He uses the raising of the famed Fifty-fourth Massachusetts, heroes of Fort Wagner, to signal the shift in his history, and the war. The soldiers of the Fifty-fourth, "though drawn from a race not hitherto connected with the fortunes of war" (149), in the words of Governor John Andrew at a farewell parade, "have given them an opportunity, which, while it is personal to themselves, is still an opportunity for a whole race of men" (150). The significance of the Fifty-fourth, marching from the birthplace of abolitionism and the land of the Puritan forefathers, is not simply the demonstration of competence on the battlefield but the change in the entire moral tenor of the war. With the marching of these troops, conflict becomes crusade. Brown notes that one of the regimental standards bore the cross and the ancient motto *In Hoc Signo Vinces*, and he comments, *"This is the first Christian banner that has gone into our war.* By a strange, and yet not strange, providence, God has made this despised race the bearers of his standard. They are thus the real leaders of the nation" (156). America, for the moment, has righted itself and taken into its ranks those individuals who would fight for freedom, the spiritual heirs of Denmark Vesey, Nat Turner, Madison Washington, and the others who were forced into the role of rebel.

The first major movement in the rising crescendo that will end on the ramparts of Fort Wagner is the account of the neglected, but crucial, Battle of Port Hudson on the Mississippi. Brown focuses on the heroism of the First Louisiana Native Guard, soldiers under black line officers who would suffer greatly in the assault on the ramparts. The dominant figure in the account, largely because Brown already had written a sketch for a later edition of *The Black Man*, is Captain André Cailloux. With no admixture of white to account for his culture and daring, "he prided himself on being the blackest man in the Crescent City" (169). Cailloux is a Creole figure who would not be out of place in Brown's history of

Santo Domingo: "Finely educated, polished in his manners, a splendid horse-man, a good boxer, bold, athletic, and daring, he never lacked admirers. His men were ready at any time to follow him to the cannon's mouth; and he was as ready to lead them" (169). After charge after charge against the ramparts ordered by General William Dwight, whom Brown accuses of being careless with black lives, we have a final tableau of the heroic Creole: "At this juncture, Capt. Cal-lioux [*sic*] was seen with this left arm dangling by his side,—for a ball had broken it above the elbow,—while his right hand held his unsheathed sword gleaming in the rays of the sun; and his hoarse, faint voice was heard cheering on his men. A moment more, and the brave and generous Callioux was struck by a shell, and fell far in advance of his company" (171). Here is a hero fully equal, in the roman-tic conventions of the day, with Joshua Lawrence Chamberlain on the Union side or John Pelham on the Confederate; in his death, the participation of black troops comes into its maturity. Port Hudson would fall the next day, but Brown portrays the first, unsuccessful assaults as containing the true significance of the battle, the creation of "a new chapter in American history for the colored man": "Many Persians were slain at Thermopylae; but history records only the fall of Leonidas and his four hundred companions. So in the future, when we shall have passed away from the stage, and rising generations shall speak of the conflict at Port Hudson, and the celebrated charge of the negro brigade, they will forget all others in their admiration for André Callioux and his colored associates" (172). In the short term, however, the laurels for the black troops would be withheld. Brown points to the decisions of General Banks in Louisiana, who denied black regiments a "Port Hudson" inscription on unit banners. Banks's actions notwith-standing, Cailloux received a hero's burial in New Orleans, and Brown details it in a chapter that closes his consideration of Port Hudson.

Brown's depiction of the assault on Fort Wagner is rather anticlimactic in comparison, as it is much more of a paean to Colonel Shaw than a tribute to the heroism of the black troops involved. Black heroism there certainly is, but the purpose of this sketch is to emphasize the gallant death of a white leader who suffered and died with his soldiers, not as black subordinates, but as men. The assault of the Fifty-fourth on Fort Wagner was a failure in the moment but an en-during success in its legacy, shaped by the hand of the historian. Brown focuses on the moment of the repulse from the ramparts, with Sergeant Major Lewis H. Douglass, the son of Frederick Douglass, springing up behind Shaw and shout-ing, "Come, boys, come, let's fight for God and Governor Andrew." After the repulse, Sergeant William H. Carney picked up the colors and carried them from the ramparts despite his wounds. Only then does Brown turn to his real subject, the legacy of the Fifty-fourth and Colonel Shaw. The southerners attempted to disgrace Shaw by answering an inquiry concerning his remains with "We have buried him with his niggers!" Brown turns the outrage to eulogy: "No more fitting burial-place, no grander obsequies, could have been given to him who cried, as he led that splendid charge, 'On, my brave boys!' than to give to him and to them one common grave" (202). A curious note enters into the final section, as Brown praises a white paternalism as particularly suited to leading blacks, a note that is at odds with much of his other writing: "Most gentle tempered, genial as a warm winter's sun, sympathetic, full of kindliness, unselfish, unobtrusive, and gifted with a manly beauty and a noble bearing, he was sure to win the love, in a very marked degree, of men of a race peculiarly susceptible to influence from such traits of character as these" (203). Brown's intent, clearly, is to contrast the true benevolence of Shaw with the false, despotic benevolence of the planters, but the passage demonstrates the continued appeal of white paternalism not only to Brown's audience but to Brown himself. This strain is found elsewhere, such as the account of the faithfulness of a body servant to his dead master, Lieutenant Palmer, in a later chapter: "Upon the advance of our line, that faithful servant was found by the side of his dead master,—faithful in life, and faithful amid all the horrors of the battle-field, even in the jaws of death" (311).

Shaw is the greatest of a type that includes Lincoln, Fremont, Banks, Higginson, and others: the white champions of black liberty. Opposed to them are not just the southerners but northern whites who oppose black emancipation and equality at every turn. These include General Banks in New Orleans, General McClellan, the Copperheads, and, as the great traitor and foil to Lincoln, Andrew Johnson. Repeatedly, the specter of the mob makes an appearance as the threat to liberty and ordered rule—a role assigned by many white writers of the time to the blacks. For instance, in Brown's account of the New York draft riots, he tells us that the "mob was composed of the lowest and most degraded of the foreign population (mainly Irish), raked from the filthy cellars and dens of the city, steeped in crimes of the deepest dye, and ready for any act, no matter how dark and damnable" (193). His aim is not simply to discredit Democratic opposition to the war but to align the blacks with native defenders against an alien threat. Though he opposes the dominant nationalist history of the time, he does not subvert its conventions so much as turn them to his own advantage.

Brown uses the war to mark the moral progress of the nation, but the ascent is marred by the failure of Andrew Johnson to consolidate Lincoln's gains. Brown's excoriation of Johnson sets the tone for the final chapters of the work, which deal with the condition of blacks (particularly in the South) after the war. Johnson, for Brown, is the promising Moses who turned Judas to curry favor with the planters and the northern Democrats. His rise and the antislavery sentiments that marked it are tainted by the deep-seated resentment of the southern poor whites against blacks and a concomitant need for acceptance by the planter class. Johnson rose "springing from the highest circles of the lowest class of whites in the South . . . coming up over a tailor's board, and all the obstacles that slaveholding society places between an humbly-born man and social and political elevation" (328). Brown uses one anecdote to explain Johnson's character and inability to hold to a higher course. As the young Johnson was passing along a Tennessee street, he was shouldered aside by a black man and threw mud from the street at the man, who responded, "You better mind what you 'bout, you low white clodhopper, poor white trash!" (332). His birth and its attendant resentments, in Brown's eyes, would ultimately overwhelm his ideals and his duty to his country, causing him as president to turn aside the just appeals of the blacks and listen to the flattery of the former slaveholders.

Brown makes a parable of American race relations from the story of Johnson that sets the stage for his final section, which constitutes a protest against losing the war after it has been won. The South has emerged, in Brown's view, unchanged by the war—it is still "haughty and scornful," and "the Southerners appear determined to reduce the blacks to a state of serfdom if they cannot have them as slaves" (345). Without the enforcement of law by judges and police, the civil rights bill is a "dead letter," and the unjust postbellum labor laws keep blacks as tightly constrained as before, making a terrible mockery of freedom. This situation, for Brown, is one more battle in an unfinished war. Having rewritten the history of the war, Brown now draws its lessons: "The negro must be placed in a position to protect himself. How shall that be done? We answer, the only thing to save him is the ballot. Liberty without equality is no boon. Talk not of civil without political emancipation! It is the technical pleading of the lawyer: it is not the enlarged view of the statesman. If a man has no vote for the men and measures which tax himself, his family, and his property, and all which determine his reputation, that man is still a slave" (356). He ends by attempting, in his final chapter, to recast the obstacle as that of caste, not of any unalterable characteristic of race or nation. Prejudice, for Brown, is always because of condition, not the person. Not without some irony, given his treatment of the Irish and southern poor whites, he argues against the arbitrary distinctions of color and birth. Caste can be overcome through moral progress and strong enforcement of just law, though it sometimes seems that Brown is arguing not for the obliteration of caste but the redrawing of the boundaries in a way that includes him and other blacks of talent, education, and discipline in the upper echelons.

After the war, in addition to his shaping of the conflict in history, Brown had to reshape himself to succeed in an altered landscape. The age of the orators and the professional antislavery activists was drawing to a close, and the ever adaptable Brown anticipated the shift by refashioning himself as a doctor, first writing "M.D." after his name in late 1864 or early 1865 (Farrison 400). He delivered a lecture at Davis's Hall in Plymouth, Massachusetts, on March 29, 1865, entitled "The Rebellion and the Black Man"; with this lecture, Farrison notes, "his career as an antislavery lecturer and agent for almost twenty-two years may be said to have ended" (396). He published the last version of his novel, now titled *Clotelle; or, the Colored Heroine. A Tale of the Southern States,* in 1867, the same year he published *The Negro in the American Rebellion.* With the shift from debates concerning slavery per se, Brown's focus would broaden to include a range of issues confronting freed slaves and American society at large, including temperance, rights for women, and education, but his role as the leading black historian would continue. In the wake of the war, much was yet to be determined about the place of blacks in the new order, and Brown would do his best to ensure that people of African descent could enter into the public space on an equal footing in terms of historical dignity and contributions to American life. His primary effort along this line is his fourth and best historical work: *The Rising Son; or, The Antecedents and Advancement of the Colored Race* (1874).

From the outset of *The Rising Son,* it is clear that Brown has become a grand old man of the movement. Alonzo Moore writes in his foreword to that work that his first recollection of Brown is of his coming to his house more than thirty years before, when Moore was eight years old: "I sat upon his knee while he told me the story of his life and escape from the South."[10] He recounts the familiar facts of his life and the entertaining anecdotes (dearly loved by Brown) that are part of Brown's self-created legend, such as his barely escaping a lynching in Kentucky, then going on to treat one of the mob for delirium tremens. There is a retrospective cast to the whole work, the effort of an aging man to pass on something of the nature of the struggle of the older generation. The certainties (as seen in memory) of the old fights have given way to a need for justification and, more interesting, a reconsideration of some of those certainties themselves, particularly as concerns the ambiguous record of the Caribbean revolutions and even Reconstruction itself.

The Rising Son has a much larger sweep than Brown's previous works. It begins with ancient Egypt and Ethiopia and ends with an expanded set of biographical sketches. The consideration of Egypt and Ethiopia is familiar enough. They are the cradle of civilization, from which sprang the civilization of Greece and Rome. Brown invokes the standard litany of names from Herodotus to Hannibal and praises the civilizations of ancient Thebes, Meroe, and Carthage as existing in a kind of golden age. For example, he writes of the last, "By the wisdom of its laws, Carthage had been able to avoid the opposite evils of aristocracy on the one hand, and democracy on the other"[11]; it was a civilization superior to Athens, Sparta, and Rome. But the greatness of African civilization recalls inevitably the decline with which Brown concludes: "Meroe, the chief city and fountainhead of the Ethiopians, was already fast declining, when Carthage fell, and from that time forward, the destiny of this people appeared to be downward" (64).

The most interesting portion of *The Rising Son*, because the least clichéd, concerns the remainder of Africa. His third chapter presents both the unspoiled vestiges of a native African civilization and the barbarism resulting from the slave trade; we ascend to the Mountains of the Moon before descending to the degradation of Guinea. The Galla nations on the mountain plains to the east provide his starting point: "They are nomadic tribes, vast in numbers, indefinable in the extent of their territory, full of fire and energy, wealthy in flocks and herds, dark-skinned, wooly-haired, and thick-lipped" (65). These are the barbarous yet noble tribesmen, but Brown soon passes on to central Africa, where one finds not darkness but light: "Here is a great family of nations, some but just emerging out of barbarism, some formed into prosperous communities, preserving the forms of social justice and of a more enlightened worship, practicing agriculture, and exhibiting the pleasing results of peaceful and productive industry" (66). On the northern plateaus at the end of the Mountains of the Moon, Brown tells us, dwell the Mandingoes, "one of the most powerful and intelligent of the African tribes. . . . They are made up of shrewd merchants and industrious agriculturalists; kind, hospitable, enterprising, with generous disposition, and open and gentle manners" (67).

The corrupting influence of slavery, of course, plays a large role in Brown's treatment of Africa. If one finds in Guinea "the Negro in his worst state of degradation," the cause is not to be sought in Africa itself. Brown writes, "Such are the passions stimulated by Christian gold, and such the state of society produced by contact with Christian nations. These people, degraded and unhumanized by the slaver, are the progenitors of the black population of the Southern States of the American Union" (68). Such had long been the standard line of the abolitionists, but Brown goes well beyond the normal reach of the degradation thesis when, for instance, he deals with the Hottentots in the south: "He inhabits the desert, lives in caves, subsists on roots or raw flesh, has no religious ideas, and is considered by the Europeans as too wretched a being to be converted into a slave" (70). The Europeans, however, have made the Hottentots what they are.

But slavery is not Brown's sole way of accounting for the backwardness of portions of Africa; at times, he sounds precisely like a white geographer of the nineteenth century in using theories of environmental determinism. Such determinism was nothing new in modern times; the Greeks and later Romans had used it to account for the superiority of peoples from temperate latitudes. In more recent times, however, it had come to be associated with people arguing for the superiority of European cultures over those of the tropics and elsewhere. Brown devotes an entire chapter to the "causes of color" and argues it to be completely the result of climate. The different features of the Africans, he writes later, is due to the "hot climate, which causes them to sleep, more or less, with their mouths open. This fact alone is enough to account for the large, wide mouth and flat nose; common sense teaching us that with the open mouth, the features must fall." Perhaps more surprising, Brown at times even looks to the indigenous animism of African tribes as the source of physiognomic "inferiority." He praises the worship of ancient Egypt and Ethiopia but then can turn to theories that would be at home in *The Pro-Slavery Argument* when dealing with the primitive, as opposed to ancient, cultures in Africa: "Religious superstition and the worship of idols have done much towards changing the features of the Negro from the original Ethiopian of Meroe, to the present inhabitants of the shores of the Zambesi. . . . The farther the human mind strays from the ever-living God as a spirit, the nearer it approximates the beasts; and as the mental controls the physical, so ignorance and brutality are depicted on the countenance" (85). Of course, he does compare this primitivism, and its effects, to that of the ancient

Britons and Germanic tribes, and he is equally harsh on the degrading effects of the alternative Christianity, Roman Catholicism, the rituals of which "would be thought equally idolatrous with those formerly held on the same spot by the descendants of Mumbo Jumbo" (93).

Brown's great counterexample to the existing bias against the possibility of civilization in Africa is not really African at all but the success of the Europeanized Africans who returned from the United States to found Liberia. Brown praises the promise of this new republic in terms that would delight its white proponents of the Federalist period, writing that "it has brought within its elevating influence at least two hundred thousand of the native inhabitants, who are gradually acquiring the arts, comforts, and conveniences of civilized life" (129). But there is something deeper than merely the spread of Western enlightenment; Brown sounds the redemptionist theme that places African Americans on the vanguard of historical progress. The republic founded by the sons of slaves will be superior to the republic founded on slavery; it will be "an asylum free from political oppression, and from all the disabilities of an unholy prejudice" (131). The contradictions and moral stain of slavery that have tainted both Europe and the United States can be transcended only by the chosen people who have suffered as a result. It is Liberia, more than any other place, that will be a light to the nations: "That moral wilderness is yet to blossom with the noblest fruits of civilization and the sweetest flowers of religion. She will yet have her literature, her historians and her poets. Splendid cities will rise where now there are nothing but dark jungles" (134). This redemptionism, as Wilson Jeremiah Moses observes, provides the basis for a progressive theory of history: "African American leaders who were most committed to the redemption of Africa were dedicated to the replacement of 'pagan' and 'primitive' African cultures with a new bourgeois Christianity that was to be based on scientific and industrial progress" (26). "African redemptionists," he writes, "attempted to reconcile the slogan Africa for the Africans with the modernizing formula of the so-called three C's, Christianity, Commerce, and Civilization" (26). Thus Brown's "ironic opportunism": "Torn between two strategies, [he] was uncertain whether he should concentrate on celebrating the African origins of civilization or apologizing for Africa's late entry into progressive history. . . . Africa's late entry into the march of civilization could be a source of embarrassment, but it could also be viewed in terms of a teleology of progress" (64).

Brown's treatment of Santo Domingo and the wider Caribbean is markedly different in tone and conclusions from his earlier work. The advent of Radical Reconstruction after the failures of Johnson had caused Brown to shift his focus from the burgeoning black republics of the Caribbean to the promise of a new order in the South and the United States. He repeats much of his earlier work on Santo Domingo, but the story is now one of tyranny and ultimate failure, not of promise with temporary aberrations. With the noble exceptions of Toussaint and the mulattoes (particularly the later President Geffrard), it is a dark picture indeed. The heroism of the revolution and the noble structure of the constitution (which Brown notes might serve as a model for Europe and the United States) give way to unending bloodshed, tyranny, and turmoil. Dessalines is a "ferocious man . . . stained with innocent blood" (174), and Christophe is a "tyrant by nature" and "the Caligula of the blacks" (216, 222). Brown still finds progress and things to praise, but the praise is now the exception, overshadowed by the tyranny, sometimes with darkly comic results unintended by Brown. For instance, when he writes of the legacy of Christophe, we find: "Many hundreds of lives were sacrificed in the building of Sans Souci, and grading its grounds. The schools put in operation in his time, surpassed anything of the kind ever introduced in that part of the Island before or since" (228). The conclusions Brown draws on Haiti are stark and in keeping with the worst doubts that proslavery advocates (and later Jim Crow proponents) would use in dealing with the emancipated population in the United States. "It may be set down as a truism," Brown writes, "that slavery, proscription, and oppression are poor schools in which to train independent, self-respecting freemen. . . . The bent of the slavery-disciplined mind is either too low or too high. It cannot remain in equilibrium. It either cringes with all the dastard servility of the slave, or assumes the lordly airs of a cruel and imperious despot" (238). Brown finds much to hope for in Jamaica, Cuba, and Brazil, but he deals with them briefly and then returns to the question of Santo Domingo and its earlier hope. His conclusion is that it will need the aid of more 'enlightened' powers, presumably the power of a United States grown beyond the failures of Johnson: "Both Hayti and Santo Domingo will doubtless, at no distant day, fall into the hands of some more civilized nation or nations, for both are on the decline, especially as regards self-defence" (264).

There seems to be an inverse relationship between Brown's hopes for Santo Domingo and those for a more just racial order in the United States. During the period of slavery and then during the Johnson administration, Brown held out Santo Domingo and other burgeoning black republics as exemplars for the

United States; with the advent of Radical Reconstruction, however, it is Santo Domingo that is the troubled failure, and the future is with the newly ascendant blacks in the United States. Most of Brown's treatment of black history in America is unchanged from his previous efforts. He still emphasizes the nobility and justice of revolutionary action and treats Nat Turner, Madison Washington, and other rebel leaders as patriots; there is none of the backpedaling or qualification that enters into his revision of the history of Santo Domingo. But when he deals with abolitionism, his approach has changed from writing of heroes in a present crisis to memorializing the contributions of the previous generation. Brown praises the courage and audacity of the abolitionists, white and black, during the years of "The Iron Age," "when it cost something to be an abolitionist." In *The Rising Son*, it is clear that Brown is no longer exclusively focused on the distinctive contributions of African Americans but rather tracing the larger arc of racial progress in America, about which he is rather sanguine at the time of writing.

The culmination of the first part of the book is a chapter entitled "The New Era," dealing with the hope of Radical Reconstruction. The regression under Andrew Johnson scarcely merits a mention in the picture Brown paints of racial affairs in America. "The close of the Rebellion opened to the Negro a new era in his history," Brown writes. "The chains of slavery had been severed; and although he had not been clothed with all the powers of the citizen, the black man was, nevertheless, sure of all his rights being granted, for revolutions seldom go backward" (413). With the reassertion of congressional power, "Congress . . . settled the question, and clothed the blacks with the powers of citizenship; and with their white fellow-citizens they entered the reconstruction conventions, and commenced the work of bringing their states back into the Union" (413). Brown carefully glosses over the tensions involved in Radical Reconstruction to craft a picture of racial amity, common purpose, and civic duty. Once the last vestiges of the slaveholding power have been eradicated, the revolution is on its way to inevitable completion, or so it seems. South Carolina, ironically enough, becomes the great model in Brown's account: "Her Senate hall, designed to echo the eloquence of the Calhouns, the McDuffies, the Hammonds, the Hamptons, and the Rhetts, has since resounded with the speeches of men who were once her bond slaves." "South Carolina," in Brown's telling, "quietly submitted to her destiny" (415). The only hint he gives of problematic aspects to Reconstruction comes later in his sketch of Francis L. Cardozo, a former slave become secretary of state in South Carolina. Unlike Cardozo, some of the black men rising to prominence and power after Reconstruction, Brown writes, "like their white brethren, are mere adventurers, without ability, native or acquired, and owe their elevated position more to circumstances than to any gifts or virtues of their own" (463).

The bulk of the work, however, is another collection of short biographies of notable black figures. It differs from *The Black Man* in being entirely composed of blacks in the United States, which is a sign of Brown's increasing hope for the nation as a beacon of racial progress in the world, rather than the pan-Africanism of his earlier work. The other notable difference, and perhaps the more significant, is the absence of military leaders and armed revolutionaries. These are replaced by a much larger inclusion of civic leaders, educators, businessmen, and clergy. It is a catalog suited to a time of national reconciliation, a time of reform and the belief that moral progress will follow economic expansion and industrious activity. Although the traditional greats are still present—Attucks, Wheatley, Banneker, Douglass, Garnett, Bannister, and others—they are overshadowed by the number of words devoted to a different sort of leader, such as Charles B. Ray, D.D. Of Ray and many others like him, Brown writes, "Blameless in his family relations, guided by the highest moral rectitude, a true friend to everything that tends to better the moral, social, religious, and political condition of man, Dr. Ray may be looked upon as one of the foremost of the leading men of his race" (473). The most often repeated epithet in the biographies is "self-made man," those men (and women) who rise when opportunity presents itself and who require no other assistance than the removal of arbitrary barriers to their ascent.

In short, at the end of his career Brown, ever adaptable and alert to changes in the marketplace, became a black writer suited to the Gilded Age and the promises of bourgeois individualism and prosperity. His final work would be *My Southern Home; Or, The South and Its People* (1880). The work is largely a reworking and softening of material found in his earlier books, both fiction and nonfiction, recounting his early life and the character of the antebellum South. Though he is certainly no Thomas Nelson Page in his treatment of the plantation, he does cast a much mellower light on the institution of slavery. When he turns to his travels in the South after the war, he laments the absolute reversal of the gains of Reconstruction but takes contemporary accounts at face value in treating the excesses of the Reconstruction legislatures as part of the problem. Brown, as befits the age, is more interested in moral reform and "rational" religion and is so far from his old calls to revolutionary action that he refers to one of his old-time heroes, Nat Turner, as insane. But Brown had done his part in his earlier works, bringing the history of American blacks to the page and offering models of heroism and action. It would remain to the more skilled and subtly ironic black writers to follow, such as Charles Chesnutt and the later writers of the Harlem Renaissance, to exploit the potential of the narrative for subversion.

4

"A DISTURBING AND ALIEN MEMORY"

Allen Tate, Modernism, and the Use of the Past

It comes as no surprise that Thomas Nelson Page turned to writing history—he grew up among people steeped in nostalgia for the Old South, which had only recently passed from the stage. But what of the writers two generations after Page, who came of age in the time of his dotage and for whom the pressing concerns of modernity and crises in the nation and on the world stage were of much greater import than any memory of a now distant war? If we find, as Louis Rubin does, "the invocation for the modern resurgence of southern letters" in the formation of the Fugitive group, a group noted for the cosmopolitanism it brought to southern poetry and letters, then how are we to account for the fact that the first published volumes of two of the foremost Fugitive poets, Allen Tate and Robert Penn Warren, were not books of poetry or cosmopolitan criticism but biographies of Civil War figures—that most backward-looking of all southern subjects?[1]

The answer, in brief, is that their very cosmopolitanism, their detachment from the smothering culture of nostalgia and their immersion in the emerging atmosphere of modernism, led to a crisis of identity—an awareness of the costs involved in the shift that had given them their detachment and its attendant literary power—and that crisis in turn led to a need to relocate themselves in the way southerners will, in relation to their native place and its history. The four biographies of Tate, Warren, and their younger associate Andrew Nelson Lytle were all written when the authors were outside the South, in the distant confines of Paris, Oxford, and New York, and the clearest lesson of their sojourns was the price of deracination, for an individual or a culture. Their engagement with southern history was part of a larger movement to mount a coherent, reasoned defense of their native tradition, a defense that would find expression in the Agrarian symposium *I'll Take My Stand* (1930). Thus far, we have a summary of an argument that has been made before, but I am more concerned in this chapter with the significance of historiography for these three writers.[2] The biographies brought an identification with their region because history is different in kind from the novel or poetry; through a more public form these writers could assume an authoritative role of mediator between past and present, forgoing for the time their artistic prerogative of alienation and subjective vision. But, in the wake of modernism, they could not completely shed their self-consciousness, their awareness of fragmentation and the disjunction between past and present. Theirs is an identification made through force of will, unlike the identification bred in the bone of Page, and their historical works reveal the tensions involved in this act.

Allen Tate, the most committed modernist of the Fugitive-Agrarians, was painfully aware of the distance between himself and the organic, traditional order he attributed to the Old South. However much Tate desired a viable tradition out of which to write, he knew the intellectual violence necessary to bridge that gap for polemical or artistic purposes; unlike Donald Davidson, he was aware that the tradition could not be inherited but had to be refashioned through artifice. In his two Civil War biographies of the 1920s, *Stonewall Jackson: The Good Soldier* (1928) and *Jefferson Davis: His Rise and Fall* (1929), Tate attempts to craft an adequate model of heroism and to anatomize the Old South. Both works bear the marks of Tate's encounter with modernism and his ambivalence about the southern tradition. Far from being a traditional heroic narrative, Tate's *Stonewall* is a work fraught with disjunction; Tate uses the multiple voices and modes characteristic of modernism in an effort to make the heroic available to himself and his age. But the hero he constructs is in many ways antithetical to the Agrarian ideals Tate would champion, and this tension between historical image and ideal is present in *Jefferson Davis* as well. The Davis biography is a study in the failure of mind in the Old South, but Tate attributes the fault to the southern leadership's unwillingness to recognize the nature of the South, not to the nature of the society itself. In several respects, however, the work reveals Tate's suppressed awareness of the inadequacy of the antebellum South as a model of order suited to the crisis of modernity. While Tate would never renounce his Agrarian principles, he would come to recognize the dangers inherent in looking to the past to redeem the present and would insist on a clear distinction between the City of Man and the City of God.

In Allen Tate, all the contradictions and complexities of the Fugitive-Agrarians' path to ardent traditionalism and sectional apology come to the fore. As Singal claims, "Tate may stand as the epitome of the Agrarian mentality" in his search for fixed faith with complete self-awareness, his balancing act between cosmopolitanism and commitment (232). He would end the decade at Benfolly, a plantation house in West Tennessee, but his route there would take him through the metropolises of New York and Paris. Tate had been planning a move to New York for several years before he finally succeeded in making the jump in 1924. Life in the highly literate circles of New York promised the possibility of making a living as a writer and finding a truly cosmopolitan identity not available in the provincial capital of Nashville. In a submission letter to the *Double Dealer* in 1922, Tate confessed that he was twenty-two and lived in Nashville, "of which two facts . . . the latter is perhaps the more damning."[3] New York offered escape and recognition of his capacities. He reveled in the company of such young lions as Hart Crane, Malcolm Cowley, and Kenneth Burke, and though work at *Telling Tales*, a confessional pulp magazine, would hardly seem to qualify, he made his living largely by his pen and gained an international literary reputation with the publication of his first volumes of verse. To gauge his apparent distance from the South and concern with things southern, one might note that his first participation in a symposium was not in *I'll Take My Stand* but *Aesthete, 1925*—a collaborative effort by Tate's New York circle responding to the jibes of Ernest Boyd in "Aesthete, Model 1924." Tate was always at his best on the counterstroke, but here he was responding to an attack not on the South but on the New York literati (though still coming from Mencken's *American Mercury*). As Andrew Lytle found when first meeting Tate at his New York apartment, Tate seemed to have "a mask that kept the world at a distance" and an attitude that demanded "that the profession of letters be accepted as a profession" (qtd. in Squires 58). Outwardly, at least, Tate seemed to have found everything he might have wished in the metropolis.

But being among New York literati was not enough for Tate. Beneath the glittering surface of the New York literary scene, he sensed the lingering threat of disorder, and he turned to an examination of the southern past, the resources of tradition. The freedom and energy of literary modernism came as a response to cultural disorder, but these resources offered Tate an answer only for writing, not for life, and as Rubin points out, the "state of the literary cosmos as made manifest in the metropolis was not without its relevance for the state of American society as a whole" (*Wary Fugitives* 100). Squires offers a succinct portrait of Tate's troubles after his move with Caroline Gordon outside the city to a farmhouse in Patterson:

> Patterson gave promise of stretches of uninterrupted time and, more importantly, relief from the pleasurable but erosive social life in Manhattan. He had arrived at an intellectual and spiritual crisis, and he needed time and serenity to discover his way. For, if he had come to New York to escape the fiefdom of Tennessee, he soon discovered that the literary coteries of Manhattan were no less provincial in their way than had been the circle in Nashville. In addition, since many of the intellectuals in New York centered their faith in "society," rather than "culture," in economics rather than spirit, in political idealism rather than in life, Tate found that the interior life of the individual counted for less than his instinct insisted it must. (59–60)

Tate found himself separated from the New York milieu by temperament and custom and troubled by its lack of any adequate answer to the Waste Land, and he redoubled his efforts to find a source of orientation in the history and culture of the South.

Two central problems haunted Tate's exploration of the southern past during this period: the inadequacy of the southern tradition and, more important, its inaccessibility to an individual estranged in the present. Tate was painfully aware that the problems of consciousness in the modern age were not to be solved easily. Scientific naturalism, secularism, capitalism, industrialism, and ideological forces had done their work too well; the unified sensibility of a truly traditional mind was simply no longer available. Such was the predicament of the narrator in Tate's "Ode to the Confederate Dead," which he began writing at the Patterson farmhouse in the winter of 1925–26. The speaker stands outside the graveyard gate, trapped by his own consciousness and a purely naturalistic landscape, contemplating the deeds of the men who lie there and the gulf that lies between him and them. However much desire and imaginative effort can conjure up their heroism and the brilliance of their defining moment of action, identification is impossible, and the speaker remains trapped: "You hear the shout, the crazy hemlocks point / With troubled fingers to the silence which / Smothers you, a mummy, in time." No proud Lady here for repentant sons to rally to, but only the "murmur of [the soldiers'] chivalry" and "The hound bitch / Toothless and dying, in a musty cellar." The speaker then turns to the alternatives for the alienated self faced with the fact of death and the impossibility of communion with the dead:

> What shall we say who have knowledge
> Carried to the heart? Shall we take the act
> To the grave? Shall we, more hopeful, set up the grave
> In the house? The ravenous grave?[4]

Such is the quandary: to explore the possibility of a viable tradition without setting up the grave in the house—without the identification with the historical image being an association with death, the "verdurous anonymity" of the corpse, rather than life. The vision is bleak but not without possibility; as Squires points out, the serpent in the final lines recalls not only the old adversary in the garden, the death bringer, but the serpent who crawls from the stones as Aeneas honors his dead father, promising the blessing of the pious son and the new birth of Ilium in Rome (82).

And these sons were quickly growing pious as they realized that their southernness somehow set them apart outside the South, that that ineffable something in the southern blood had not been adequately named and it was in danger of being lost before it could be brought to bear on the civilizational crisis at hand. Sometime in 1927, two letters between Tate and Ransom crossed in the mail concerning the need to "do something about the South."[5] Tate picked up certain affectations, such as signing off in his letters to Davidson with "Stars & Bars Forever!" and playing the part of the southerner with self-conscious gusto. But a more serious effort was under way as Tate explored his relationship to the southern tradition by delving into the South's history at the time of its greatest crisis. While in New York, he had been at work on two biographical projects, one of Stonewall Jackson and the other on Jefferson Davis, and his efforts took him into archives and on trips to retrace Jackson's routes and the primary battlefields. Though *Mr. Pope and Other Poems* would come out later the same year, 1928 would see a work of history as Allen Tate's first book: *Stonewall Jackson: The Good Soldier.* Donald Davidson noted the strangeness of the fact in his review of the biography: "Nobody would have dreamed that Allen Tate's first volume would be a narrative about Stonewall Jackson. One would think him more concerned about the French Symbolists, say, than the Battle of Chancellorsville."[6]

Scholars have approached the seeming anomaly of Tate's first book in a number of different ways. The most obvious (and reductionist) route is to point to the sales figures for biographies as compared with those for fiction and poetry, and certainly Minton Balch was offering a fair day's pay for an honest day's work. Then there is Tate's combative temperament, which is undeniable. Rubin combines both of these factors in his assessment of the motives behind the biography: "It was an exercise, done to earn bread and to shock the Brahmins—a game played for the fun of it" (*Wary Fugitives* 98). The crucial aspect of the project, however, is that it was a public one in a way that Tate's other works from this period, such as *Mr. Pope and Other Poems*, were not. Biographies paid well, but they sold because they were aimed at a broader readership than the elite literati who read the reviews and bought the slim poetry volumes. The modernists defined themselves against the dominant values of the time and the fiction and poetry produced for mass consumption. The biographical series allowed Tate—and Warren and Lytle as well—to assume a different role in relation to the public; their aesthetics would not allow them to assume the mantle of public poet (Tate explicitly ruled this route out in his response to his former housemate Hart Crane's Whitmanesque effort in *The Bridge*), but they could speak to a broader public in the guise of amateur historian. Rubin rightly points out the irony of Tate's titling his most famous poem an ode "because neither classical Pindaric ode nor the seventeenth-century imitation of it would have permitted a purely subjective meditation, a lone man standing by a gate, rather than a public celebration" (105). Tate could, however, connect with the public in the biography of a hero in which he could give "a stirring partisan account of the Revolution," as he said in a letter to Donald Davidson.[7] Davidson had asked about the Ode, "Where, O Allen Tate, are the dead?" Tate might have answered that they were to be found in the biography.

Tate provides the full heroic treatment for Jackson, the man of action who might have saved the Confederacy but for interference from Davis and the fatal accident at Chancellorsville. The book is something of a gage thrown at the feet of the northern intelligentsia (and most of the southern as well, for that matter). As Thomas Landess writes in his preface to the most recent edition: "Tate's biography of Stonewall Jackson . . . was the first assault in a war to regain Southern self-respect, the literary equivalent of firing on Fort Sumter. It was bold, aggressive, and merciless—not unlike Stonewall Jackson himself, who ordered his men to fire at the bravest Yankee officers and to shoot Confederate stragglers."[8] More important, Tate presents a heroic counterimage to his young seeker at the gate in the Ode. Jackson, from a respectable yeoman background in Virginia, is perfectly self-possessed—suffering no separation of thought and feeling, of intellect and will—deeply religious, disciplined, fearless, and utterly committed to his cause. Tate at one and the same time is revising the accepted accounts of the war in a provocative way and offering a very different ideal of southern character—one more suited to the crisis of his age than are the genteel heroes of Thomas Nelson Page.

The greatest question surrounding this book is the anomaly of the style throughout much of it, particularly the early portions; it is like nothing else Tate wrote before or after. Reading the opening portion of it, one can scarcely believe that the same author penned this prose and the highly wrought verse of the same period. Speaking of Jackson's childhood world at his uncle's place, Jackson's Mills, Tate writes, "It was a little world to itself, cut off from the old civilization of the seaboard. Tom Jackson was happy there. His Uncle Cummins was a kind man."[9] This passage is a fair sample of the prose in the opening chapter. The clearest clue to what Tate is about here comes in an early paragraph in which young Tom is lying beside the river and perusing a book by Parson Weems:

> The boy had been reading *Francis Marion* by Mason Weems, a man known to fame in his time as the Parson. This Parson had written books about patriots of the first American Revolution; Tom had heard of the others but had never seen them; so he read about the Swamp Fox again and again. . . . The book lying in the grass was the Bible. He read a little in the one, then a little in the other. They were about all he had to read. He liked to read about soldiers. Parson Weems somehow made them seem very luminous, very far away and heroic. Young Jackson's ancestors had lived and fought when the Parson's heroes lived and fought. His ancestors were noble men. How good it would be to be like them . . . (4; ellipsis in original)

"How good it would be to be like them" indeed! And how good for young southerners to remember the works and deeds of Jackson, Pickett, Forrest, and the rest when faced with the onslaught of social planners, industrialism, capitalism, and scientism. But Tate's game is deeper than shaping the minds of young southerners; the aim of his style is a parody of the schoolbook truths propagated by the North in the wake of the war. The struggle, in Tate's mind, is over the meaning of the second American revolution and the new order it produced.

Tate, in not-so-subtle fashion, retains the smug assurance and gospel simplicity while completely reversing the scale of values: northerners become the aggressors in a revolutionary action, rebels against the constitutional order. Here is his introduction of the abolitionists in the midst of the story of Tom's young manhood: "Already there were rumors and some evidence of a powerful revolutionary party growing up in the North. This party as yet had no name of its own, but a great many people shared in a general feeling that would soon require a name. There were people in New England who wanted to destroy democracy and civil liberties in America by freeing the slaves. They were not very intelligent people; so they didn't know precisely what they wanted to destroy. They thought God had told them what to do. A Southern man knew better than this" (25). Tate made this same argument in all seriousness in other places, even within *Stonewall Jackson*, but here he is clearly enjoying the role of agitator, mocking the earnest hyperbole and assumed superiority of the North. Such is the remaining use of the Parson Weems style in the wake of modernist disillusionment: the straightforward narrative of the hero's virtue and nobility is not available for Tate as it had been for Page, but, steeped in irony, it can serve to demolish a few of the opponent's shibboleths.

Radcliffe Squires points us in the direction of another function of this style in his suggestion that Tate might have been attempting to use something of Hemingway's style in these passages, and this suggestion can be profitably followed up in terms of Tate's evocation of a compact sensibility and immediate experience. One qualifier is necessary at the outset, however: had Tate set out to imitate Hemingway's style, he could have come much closer than he does. If there is a connection, it is that what Hemingway's Nick Adams, and Hemingway himself, set out to recover—immediate experience, psychological wholeness, deliberate action—is Jackson's possession by birth. Tate uses a series of simple impressions from Jackson's boyhood at Jackson's Mills to identify him with the culture from which he sprang, in which character was concretely associated with land and shaped by the surrounding community. In the most important instance, Tate uses the grove of sugar maples across the Monongahela to bridge the influences of Jackson's childhood with his last words, after he had proved himself in a larger sphere of action: "When the sap began running it was Tom's business, every year, to draw it off. Uncle Robinson helped him. But in the spring it was hard to get across the river. . . . At high water the only ford in the river at Jackson's Mills was over a boy's head. It was hard to get across the river to the maples. And the sap ran when the spring thaw came on and the stream reached the flood" (9). This passage is followed later by the closing image of the chapter on Jackson's boyhood: "The day's work being over, perhaps Tom . . . went down to the mill pond to read a little, or just to lie on the bank by the dug-out boat and gaze absently across the river at the maple grove. Perhaps Tom or one of the boys, growing restless, said: 'Let's cross over the river and rest in the shade of the trees'" (13). What is Jackson's by birth, though, is not ours, and when the Weems voice crops up in later portions of the narrative (though it does so less and less frequently), it usually involves a sort of strange juxtaposition of commonplaces with a jarring effect. Tate sometimes borders briefly on absurdity as though driving home the point that the simple narrative of heroism is no longer possible, as he does here when describing General Ewell: "General Ewell had convinced himself that he had a bad stomach; he ate only wheat cereals. Ewell was a fine soldier" (135).

From the time young Jackson leaves Virginia for West Point (by way of Washington to gain his appointment), the Parson Weems voice is largely replaced by two others: a modernist voice that anatomizes the character of Jackson, sketches novelistic vignettes to punctuate the basic narrative of action, and dispassionately re-creates the experience of war through concrete images; and a voice of the young polemicist, holding forth in high rhetoric on the failures of southern leadership, the causes of the war and its prosecution, and larger cultural differences between North and South. The Weems voice still surfaces from time to time, and there is a basic narrative line—the voice of the historian, strictly conceived—detailing the movements of the armies and the progress of battles. Each of these voices does its own distinct work. The Weems voice parodies and undermines the cultural mythology (northern and southern) surrounding the meaning of the war in the life of the nation, somewhat in the manner of an artillery barrage preceding an infantry assault. The modernist voice renders the past present, establishing a concrete stratum of experience detached from any debate over its meaning. The polemical voice is as much at odds with the modernist sensibility as the first voice, but it builds upon the concrete rendering of the past to argue for its use; it recognizes the unbridgeable gap separating past and present, lamenting through sarcasm rather than eulogy, but nevertheless is the voice of commitment to an image of the past as a guide for present action. It argues for the use of the past not as it was but as it has been remade through modernist artifice.

No one deals with this work without dwelling on the polemical aspect of it, but we need to keep it in the context of the whole. The polemical here is only one voice and mode among several, and its place is limited. The voice picks up abruptly where the boyhood narrative leaves us, after Jackson has gone to West Point and entered his adult life. It then dominates the fifth chapter, on the Mexican War, in recounting the growing sectional struggle and, in turn, the seventh chapter, which deals with the nomination of Lincoln and the immediate foreground of the war. This amounts to only two chapters out of nineteen, both of which are in the first third of the book; in the latter two hundred pages, Tate does not embark on any polemical tangents but focuses on the character and acts of Jackson and the doomed progress of the war. It follows on the parodic work of the Weems voice, which raises the question of the work and validity of cultural myths, with a direct assault on the received account of the war and its causes.

Tate portrays the war as the matter of a choice between two types of civilization, but again he inverts the scale of values. Tate uses the Mexican War and President Polk's notion that expansion might provide a way of balancing the power of North and South to highlight the sagacity and realism of Calhoun, who foresaw that any such hope was vain. He highlights the hostility of the West to the East and centers his assessment on Andrew Jackson, with his challenge to established institutions: "It is just possible to see Calhoun and Andrew Jackson as the Christ and Antichrist of political order in the United States" (38). With the West bent on breaking the power of the East generally and the North seeking to consolidate its gains over the South, the Mexican War would become "the first campaign of the Northern revolutionists," who "would never permit American society to expand in terms of the Constitution" (38–39). Opposed to their vision stands Calhoun, with his vision of a conservative, hierarchical social and political order: "The institution of slavery was a positive good only in the sense that Calhoun had argued that it was; it had become a necessary element in a stable society. He had argued justly that only in a society of fixed classes can men be free" (39). In other words, the struggle was not over slavery but over a traditional, European perspective versus a revolutionary view of society. In the North, where "the historical sense had atrophied," the concept of responsible freedom became untenable and the destruction of traditional society the object: "They had come to believe in abstract right. Where abstract right supplants obligation, interest begins to supplant loyalty. Revolution may follow. When such a revolution triumphs, society becomes a chaos of self-interest. Its freedom is the freedom to do wrong" (39–40). This sort of revolution also renders the freedom gained illusory for the majority: with capitalism regnant, we find, Tate argues, that "commerce and industry required a different kind of slave. He would be a better slave; he would have the illusion of freedom" (59). Such is the way Tate reverses the poles of constitutionalism and radicalism in sketching the background for the Civil War, but once the struggle is joined, the polemical voice no longer plays a significant role in the narrative.

The modernist voice surfaces primarily in some of the depictions of battle, novelistic touches in the narrative, and in the portrayal of Jackson himself. Most of the first instances simply provide a novelistic counterbalance to the predominant historical summary—troop movements, decisions by commanders, the progress of battle. These instances of confusion and carnage are usually of the kind to be found in good histories of modern war generally, as in this moment at Manassas, when Jackson forms his line and waits to engage the enemy: "In the struggle that came on for the possession of the Henry House Hill, this batter was taken and retaken three times. The carcasses of horses, the splintered caissons stood as a challenge to both armies. On the bare plateau, between the fighting lines, men lay face down, motionless, sprawled in ungraceful postures; so casually prone that they might rise at any moment to rejoin the yelling devils a hundred yards away. Where Jackson's men waited the thick smoke and dust eddied into the pines. A salty sweet stink filled the air. Shells burst over their heads." Other times the moments stand more completely apart from the main narrative of action, and the mark of the modernist is more pronounced in the dispassionate tone capturing an experience so extreme that it deadens the sensibilities. We see this during one portion of the Seven Days, as the various divisions await a delayed flank attack by Jackson to free the river crossings: "Hill's men still waited. The head of his column looked up. A shrill whine rose in the air and flew to the rear. Suddenly a man, standing in the ranks, became headless; his body quivered a fraction of a second, and collapsed in a heap. The soldiers nearby shuffled their feet; then looked seriously ahead" (171). In such passages, Tate portrays the *experience* of radical civilizational change, rather than simply providing commentary on it. The war as Tate deals with it is the path to modernity, and through its textual re-creation he provides the bridge between his deadened modern at the cemetery gate and the dead heroes within. The modernist voice in the narrative works against the polemical voice, to a large extent, in that it demonstrates implicitly that it was not the Union victory in the war that led to the present crisis but the nature of the war itself. Tate's dilemma as a modern is linked with a crisis of consciousness in the war itself, and Stonewall Jackson's heroism lies in his ability to surmount it.

As Tate presents him, Jackson is not, in any sense, the romantic hero; Tate gives us a portrait of a creature of will, acting in a time of cultural disorder. The juxtaposition with Lee, the romantic icon, is made explicit in Tate's portrayal of the two commanders at Sharpsburg. Tate sketches Lee in clearly iconic terms: "Lee had mounted a large limestone rock, and he was calmly surveying the whole field. He held his field-glass to his eyes, and his tall gray figure was like a monument to some hero of the old time" (241). But Lee is not Tate's concern; he shifts our view immediately to Jackson, who, "below the Dunkard Church, was still lost in thought, and, sucking his lemon, seemed perfectly self-possessed" (241). And self-possession is the defining characteristic of Tate's hero, not the gallant self-possession of a Bayard or a Marion but that of the automaton that lacks the troubling problems of consciousness. Tate tells us early, "He was a humorless, unimaginative man, exact as the multiplication table" (64). To some extent, Tate here is giving us something of the public perception of Jackson before First Manassas—the eccentric professor—but the description is in keeping with the elements of Jackson's character emphasized by Tate throughout. Through the one scene in which Jackson is shown with children (Page surely would have included a half dozen more), Tate, rather than relieving the stark discipline of Jackson's temperament, simply heightens it by contrast: "His justice was often tempered by mercy, but his mercy was hardly ever made human by mirth" (104). Jackson is a creature of will—the perfect leader for an army Tate repeatedly describes as a precise machine. Even his faith is an intellectual act, an adjunct to his powerful will (and thus puritanical, as Tate conceives the term). He is the man who early had written in his list of maxims, "You may be whatever you resolve to be," and who had said to his cousin, "I can do anything I will to do" (34). Jackson is a "moral Procrustes": his "moral character was, with respect to will, overdeveloped" (194). But it is this very flaw that rendered Jackson so perfectly suited to the conditions of modern warfare and made for his superiority to his commanders, the vacillating Davis and even the gallant Lee: "Lee saw intellectually the object of the war more clearly than his statesmen. Like every complex sensibility, he was subject to intuitions that disturbed his vision of this object. Up to certain limits he could pursue it with a single purpose. But his character, unlike his great subordinate's, was not in any respect overdeveloped. He saw everything. He was probably the greatest soldier of all time, but his greatness as a man kept him from being a completely successful soldier. He could not bring himself to seize every means to the proposed end. Jackson, who saw one object only, could use them all" (273). This single-mindedness, this possession by a single great idea, was the key to his greatness as a soldier, a greatness limited only by the interference of others. Jackson had proposed a night attack at Fredericksburg to drive the host of the federals into the Rappahannock at the point of the bayonet, a strategy more "like massacre than war," and Lee had balked at it. Asked by his surgeon how he would deal with the overwhelming numbers of the enemy, Jackson answered, "Kill them, sir! Kill every man" (274). Tate's portrayal of his hero demonstrates the extent to which the Agrarians' response to modernity was shaped by the very cultural forces they set themselves against. In fact, Tate makes a statement on Jackson's ambition that is essentially the same as the most damning claim Warren would later make about Old John Brown: "The will to power sometimes becomes the will of God" (10).

Tate, then, gives us a hero for the crisis, whose greatness—far from being a moral greatness—lies in force of will and intellectual power. Jackson's famed reveries—one hand lifted to his eyes, palm outward, gaze in the distance—are not occasions for Tate to dwell on the romantic possibilities of Jackson's vision, as they would have been for Page. Early on in the narrative, Tate tells us, "The power of concentration, of self-forgetfulness, he had developed instinctively since his childhood. It lacked an object then and it was only revery. Now he was learning to control it and it had become an intellectual power of a high order" (32). As he states toward the end of the work, Jackson had developed "his visual, his quantitative imagination into a powerful instrument. The hosts of his enemies he held in the hollow of his hand. Every movement they made he visualized: the whole theatre of war stood immediately present, at every moment of concentration, in his mind. He played against his enemies as if they were pawns in a game of chess. But there was a difference: the pawns of war had will and feeling. From the conduct of a hostile cavalry regiment, thirty miles from the main army, he could infer the Federal general's plan and state of mind" (281). Put simply, Jackson thinks in potent abstract terms without falling prey to abstraction—a feat indeed, and a task that Tate and the other soon-to-be Agrarians had set for themselves (though they might have quarreled with this formulation). He is a supreme commander in the first modern war because, in many respects, he shares much with the makers of modernity without suffering any of its psychic consequences.

As such, he is a rather strange hero for one in Tate's position, and the choice is better explained by Tate's modernist proclivities than by his pieties. According to the litany of virtues the Agrarians would later extol in the Old South, Jackson is sadly lacking. He is a creature of will rather than manner or custom; we see almost no connection after the early portion of the narrative with any extended network of clan or culture; he is as dominated by the single idea as the financier Jay Gould or William Lloyd Garrison; and he has none of the complex moral sensibility, determined by a complex of allegiances and perceptions, that we see in Robert E. Lee. Commentators have insisted on seeing Tate's Jackson as the perfect Agrarian hero because of his small farmer background, his origin in western Virginia rather than the Tidewater, and his religiosity, but this view completely misses the dominant thrust in Tate's study. These aspects are so many details of the foreground; the scene is dominated by a man who is more like Faulkner's Thomas Sutpen than John Donald Wade's Cousin Lucius or one of Davidson's Tall Men.[10] The parallel with Faulkner's Sutpen is far from exact, but the similarity is there nonetheless. We have a man intent on restoring the greatness of a family line (where Sutpen was bent on creating one), a man whose dominant trait is a powerful will determined on a single idea, who is ruthless in the pursuit of his aims. Faulkner challenged the plantation legend by creating a different sort of planter archetype, one who enters the wilderness seeking to will an embodiment of an idea into existence in the midst of wilderness, and Tate makes an observation at one point late in the work that points in the same direction—one made all the more striking in that he is writing of Tidewater Virginia rather than Mississippi: "The country gave out a damp heat that penetrated the very eyes of a man. Great tangled woods stretched off far as sight could go. Thick oaks and pines and luxurious blossoms grew up to the river's edge on both sides, forming a green roof over the water. Swamps lay everywhere. The roads were crooked and uncharted. Here and there, far apart and hidden in the jungle, stood the manor houses of the planters. Tidewater Virginia after two hundred fifty years of European culture was a desolate wilderness" (171). My point here is that Tate's portrayal of Jackson is modernist rather than romantic; the ideal he offers is not the historical image the Agrarians would champion but a model of will and action necessary to champion it, the model of a sensibility that shuts out moral ambiguity and focuses on a single aim.

If one pays attention to the different voices and modes in this work, the claim that it is a simple, youthful exercise in hero worship becomes untenable. It is a work of modernism, with all the unresolved tensions and ambiguities implied in the term, though not a very successful one. Its failure, however, does not mean that we can dismiss the effort Tate makes here and the importance of the text as evidence of his position, as high modernist and newly pious Southron, in relation to the past. Landess claims that Tate attempts an *Aeneid* in the biography, an epic account of the hero's battles, and Rubin and Squires both hold that Tate attempted to do what he had shown couldn't be done in the Ode—establish a direct connection to the heroism of a past age. But Tate is no more writing an *Aeneid* than Joyce was writing the *Odyssey*—if, that is, we mean repeating the performance of the epic poet in the modern age. Though obviously not a work to stand beside Joyce's, Tate's *Stonewall* nonetheless shares with it a multiplicity of voices, and Tate shares with its author a profound recognition of the impossibility of any simple identification with the past. Although both authors recognize the difficulties, the problems of consciousness and identity in the modern age are reflected in the narrative form rather than being commented on. For more direct exposition, we have to turn to Tate's biography of Davis, a less ambitious but more successful work.

The work on Jackson gave Tate the basis to approach history in the coming years of the Agrarian activity; essentially, it provided him with an ethos, the radical partisan whose use of the critical faculty does not undermine in the least his exercise of will and pursuit of a single object. Singal's claim that *Stonewall Jackson* was "a psychological portrait of the sort of man Tate secretly wished he could be" is right in one crucial sense (though wrong in many others): Tate creates in his Jackson a model for resisting the disorder of the age. As Singal says elsewhere, "What at bottom distinguishes the Agrarians from other southern intellectuals of their generation, then, is this attempt to overcome the anguish of cultural transition by *fiat*—to reconcile their conflicting beliefs by an act of sheer will" (201). In fact, one of the striking things about his portrait of Jackson is that he deliberately erases any trace of a historical sense in Jackson. Early on, he tells us of Jackson's home in western Virginia, "It was a new land, taken up only a generation ago. Tom must have thought it old. The past seemed far away;

he must not have heard it mentioned very often" (5). Jackson is concerned with the defense of the present South by any means necessary and stands in contrast to both Davis and Lee, both of whom are hamstrung by the historical sense (i.e., Davis's belief in the old constitutional order and Lee's understanding of his ancestral burden and gentlemanly code). The task the Agrarians set for themselves required an act of will, and Tate more than any of the others was conscious of this requirement, as evident in his remark about his suppression of his Jeffersonian sympathies in the interest of a polemic devoted to hierarchy and aristocracy, one that looks toward "a centralization of a different and better kind": "Emotionally this [suppression of individuality] does me considerable violence because I am, emotionally, a Jeffersonian. That is what I mean by discipline."[11] Tate's Jackson is a traditional man who adapts to modern circumstances and modern means, whereas Tate is a profoundly modern man seeking to find a means in tradition, but both are marked by a powerful will.

In *Jefferson Davis: His Rise and Fall*, Tate would use the basis he had gained through the writing of *Stonewall Jackson* to launch a more cogent, coherent civilizational critique. His purpose, contrary to the views of some critics, is not merely apologetics and a defense of the Old South but a two-pronged assault on the dominant direction of American civilization and the failure of mind in the Old South. Tate worked on the two biographies simultaneously in New York (much of the research obviously would serve both purposes), completed the first, and then left for France to complete the Davis biography. Singal captures the moment well: "In late September, 1928, with his father's gold-headed cane in one hand and Jefferson Davis's two-volume history of the Confederacy under the other, Tate boarded ship with his family for a prolonged stay in Europe courtesy of the Guggenheim Foundation during which he was to complete his work on Davis" (242). Singal's sketch illustrates the nature of Tate's journey; he was marked as the cosmopolitan, recipient of a Guggenheim and established poet with the publication of *Mr. Pope and Other Poems* and bound for the Paris of Hemingway, Fitzgerald, and Stein, but he carried with him the marks of the provincial and the burden of his fathers. His experience of Paris followed much the same trajectory as his time in New York: initially, he was excited about returning to the source of his literary and intellectual heritage and inspired by the proximity and friendship of the foremost literati of the day, visiting in Stein's famous salon and Sylvia Beach's bookstore and taking to the velodrome with Hemingway. But he found himself discontented and disoriented, marked by his manners and temperament as the southerner, as illustrated by his first encounter with Fitzgerald. The midwesterner began rather abruptly, asking, "Do you enjoy making love?"—something of a challenge, a test perhaps, but nevertheless an invitation to the freedom of discourse and hedonistic indulgence of the Paris set. Tate responded, "It's none of your damn business," and one wonders whether Tate held his grandfather's cane at the time (qtd. in Squires 88).

Two poems written in Paris show the tensions in Tate's mind in this period. "Mother and Son" and "Message from Abroad" both explore the problematic relationship with the ancestral past, but, unlike the Ode, they portray a raw, intimidating past that draws one of necessity rather than the heroic past one might seek. "Mother and Son" portrays a man on a sickbed attended by his mother. The son seeks the peace of withdrawal and oblivion—"Now all day long the man who is not dead / Hastens the dark with inattentive eyes"—but the mother stands by in her "importunate womanhood" insisting by her presence on his recognition of the past: "Her hand of death laid upon the living bed, / So lives the fierce compositor of the blood."[12] He lies upon the bed in which she gave birth to him—"She waits; he lies upon the bed of sin / Where greed, avarice, anger writhed and slept / Till to their silence they were gathered in"—and demands his filial recognition:

> The falcon mother cannot will her hand
> Up to the bed, nor break the manacle
> His exile sets upon her harsh command
> That he should say the time is beautiful—
> Transfigured by her own possessing light:
> The sick man craves the impalpable night. (34)

The next stanza brings the image of the "swimming beams / Of memory, blind school of cuttlefish" rising and plunging—the cuttlefish chosen, as Tate later wrote, because it "blinds its prey by squirting a black fluid into the water, in which it hides" as "a man in emotional danger withdraws into his private mind where not even maternal love can follow him and where he becomes very mysterious and menacing" (qtd. in Squires 90). The cultural past holds no greater hope of peace, as it did for Davidson, and in "Message from Abroad" we see the speaker reaching back in vain from his deracinated state in Europe to touch his southern ancestors. The poem opens with the past fragmented, though not in so radical a form as in Tate's earlier ode: "What years of the other times, what centuries / Broken, divided up and claimed?" The larger cultural inheritance of Europe, rather than serving as a refuge, serves only to heighten the sense of alienation from his own immediate heritage of "the man red-faced and tall." Unlike Davidson's Tall Men, Tate evokes the specter of race through metaphor to suggest what rendered the failure of the South, and his own condition, inevitable: "His shadow gliding, a long nigger / Gliding at his feet." The poem ends at an impasse, and the speaker shifts to ironic comment : "I cannot see you / The incorruptibles . . . Your anger is out of date—/ What did you say mornings? / Evenings, what?" Realizing that he has only a reified image of the past and not a connection to a living tradition, the speaker ends: "The man red-faced and tall / Will cast no shadow / From the province of the drowned."[13] As M. E. Bradford notes, the alternatives of the poem are clear, if ultimately unsatisfactory. Having tested the detached aestheticism of Europe—the way of the expatriate—and found it wanting, the speaker must return to America: "Drifting the cold sea and (spiritual) drowning or the greater emasculating perils of . . . aestheticism are the alternatives."[14]

Tate was drawn by compulsion back to the South, as the only answer to his sense of dislocation and disorientation in France, but the combination of need, anger, and fear that haunts the poems would complicate his approach to his region. He felt deeply the inadequacy of the South, Old and present, and at the same time his need for it; he channeled the resulting frustrations into polemic, as he wrote to John Gould Fletcher in 1927, "The stupidity of our people turns me in rage against them, and I wheel in greater rage against their enemies. In this state of mind it is hard to be coherent" (qtd. in Singal 240). Writing the Davis biography allowed Tate to focus his frustration and anger on a single figure—not simply to assess the correctness and efficacy of his actions but to anatomize his mind. As Simms and Page had recognized to a lesser degree, there was a failure of mind in the South, far more important than any failure in the Congress or on the battlefield, and the man of letters is bound up with it in a crucial sense. Tate's identity was bound up with the failure of the South, not because of what had been done to it so much as the way its own contradictions and weakness rendered it vulnerable.

The story of Jefferson Davis is no story of a hero, as that of Jackson had been; Tate's concern is with a moment of crisis and the mind of the man most responsible for responding to it. He places us at the heart of the crisis from the first page, beginning in medias res with Jefferson Davis preparing to take his leave of the U.S. Senate, and everything Tate will claim about the character, mind, and temperament of Davis, and the failure of the southern leadership generally, is given to us through the novelistic treatment of the first chapter, "The Man and the Hour." The remainder is simply the inexorable progress of the Greek tragedy that Tate explicitly invokes in the later portions of the work. Tate begins by evoking the atmosphere of the day, January 21, 1861, and the accusations of treason swirling around Davis as he prepared to cast his lot with the South and withdraw from the Senate, preparing for "the astonishing spectacle of the deeply conservative party accepting the part of revolutionists."[15] Davis and his counterparts were the moderates of their party, standing in contrast to the fire-eating secessionists such as Robert Barnwell Rhett, and the agony of their decision resulted from the fact that they were "emotionally bound to the Union"; Davis, "but not he alone of the Southern leaders, has a disturbing and alien memory to look back to; a kind of Sodom, if you will, that he came to hate, but to which he was still drawn, the vision of which was to turn him into a pillar of salt!" (5–6). The defining moment for Davis, at Tate portrays him, is not his speech accepting the presidency of the Confederacy but his farewell to the Senate.

Tate, in his most extended portrait, captures Davis as he is about to rise and speak and sets out the defining traits that would prove the ruin of his cause: a powerful will, overweening pride of intellect, and a marked separation of thought and feeling. Davis's "deep-set gray eyes looked out with a kind of unseeing intensity" (7), and one might read the fate of the South through a glance at the man who would lead it:

A glance at this man would have revealed his possession of absolute self-mastery. Looked at more closely, he might have seemed less harmonized than self-conquered; as if he suppressed a certain instability of temperament by will alone, and then ignored it. One would have supposed that the man could understand people intellectually, by a comparison of their ideas with his own; but not emotionally. He seemed to lack emotional subtlety; while of every logical and intellectual subtlety he was the master. His gaunt ascetic face and withdrawn eyes betrayed a haughty and impatient pride; he would expect ideas to settle in the course of events, and not quite grasp the necessity of cajoling men into sharing his desires. A great statesman, perhaps the most distinguished statesman in American history, he seemed too remote and uncompromising to be a politician. As he stood at his desk about to speak, he must have struck the detached observer with a certain inflexibility of pose. (8)

Davis ends by sitting, taking his head in his hands, and weeping out of an emotional attachment to the old Union and an inability to govern his feelings. "He was emotionally underdeveloped," Tate tells us, "and for that reason he could not altogether get at the motives of men" (12). Jackson was the opposite, and where his Procrustean bed had been emotional, Davis's was intellectual. Torn as he was, he still held out hope in his speech that a "better understanding of theory" might resolve differences and split the logical hairs of nullification and secession in the best tradition of Calhoun. He could not understand that the North was "bent on domination" and that "conflicts are not decided by citations of the law, or by the results of discussion: the intellectual habits of the secluded, theoretical student had not been altered by his years of politics; they had been transformed into the habits of the parliamentary committeeman" (12). With Davis's exit from the Senate, "the old Constitutional Republic came—though Davis could not see it—to a dramatic end. There would no longer be a Union in the exact sense of the word; there would be a uniformity; for one of the two types of American civilization must prevail" (14). Ironically, as Tate presents it, Jackson, possessed of a premodern mind, was equipped to deal with a profoundly modern crisis because he understood the stakes and saw only the single object of victory; Davis, in contrast, suffered the dissociation of sensibility defining modernity for Tate as it had for Eliot, and he profoundly misjudged the crisis.

At the opposite end of the spectrum from Davis stands the fire-eating Rhett, and, far from blaming Rhett and the others for heightening the crisis and making compromise impossible, Tate eulogizes him for recognizing the nature of the struggle. Rhett, for Tate, is the "most completely vindicated" great man in American history:

the prophet of secession, who, from the dingy office of the Charleston *Mercury*, had thundered against half-measures in the South for more than twenty years: the South was destroyed, and the American nation became what he said it would become. He saw the weakness of the Southern faith in mere political action—its futility against the extra-legal procedure of the North, whose most clamorous and radical leaders were driven by irrational, fixed ideas that recognized no Constitutional authority whatever. The slow, temporizing Southern intelligence could not cope with such a force, for which the body politic was no longer a reality. The North was, at that time, the most advanced modern state, in which government, and men as political entities, were instrumental to the superior ends of commerce and trade. It was the ironic distinction of the elder Rhett merely to have *seen*. (14)

The failure of Davis, Stephens, and the majority of the members of the Constitutional Convention was that they sought to preserve their identity as Americans under the democratic, republican ideals of the old constitutional order—the nation had changed, not they. The collection of men gathered in Montgomery to write the new constitution "were there to enact their own extinction, to write the obituary of their race." They were a peculiar, and relatively new, southern type developed in the Lower South—aristocratic and profoundly antidemocratic—but they failed to recognize it. Their philosophy of action was "inarticulate" outside political forms, and they could generate no "fresh vision of their own society." The fire-eaters—Rhett, Tombs, and Yancey—were repudiated in the leadership in favor of men like Davis who were known as moderates and compromisers, but in reality the extremists were "more typical of the powerful lower South aristocracy." Of Davis and the other men chosen, Tate writes, "Their political genius only hastened their downfall; it was not a time for politics; it was the hour for a man of great conviction who could act without precedent or fear, who saw through the outworn political machinery into the real motives of the Lower South. New and expansive, unbound by strong local tradition, the Lower South was gradually pushing towards an empire, agricultural, slave-owning, aristocratic" (19). The failure of the Confederacy and of the Old South in Tate's mind was precisely this: that the leaders of the South were unwilling to recognize what sort of society it was becoming and to act on that knowledge. In his second chapter, "King Cotton," Tate moves to an exploration of the civilization that arose in the Lower South after the invention of the cotton gin.

Far from the rather static vision of Page's Virginia, with its great families and aristocratic tradition, Tate's focus is on the dynamism of the Lower South and the rise of the cotton aristocracy in a single generation. The draw of the Lower South was precisely an escape from the stratification of the seaboard; it was a society coming into a new form: "The Lower South, which has been sentimentalized over more than any other section of the country as the stronghold of chivalry and the abode of true romance, is thus seen to have been largely a society of *nouveaux riches*. But like *nouveaux riches* everywhere they speedily took on the customs and manners of the local *haute noblesse*" (33). The soon-to-be great planters were men like Samuel Davis, Jefferson's father, who worked side by side with his slaves and lived in a two-room log shotgun house—Jefferson was in fact born in this sort of house, rather than the grandiose manor. Tate's purpose, however, is not to emphasize democratic, frontier origins but to reset the standards of judgment to an aspiring aristocracy. He follows William Dodd, for example, in claiming that the Old South "did not make a bad showing in education" if we understand the aim was educating individuals to their station and take into account the patronage of higher education by a "higher minority" than in the North. Similarly, Tate argues that we need to view the institution of slavery in terms of the needs of a burgeoning aristocracy. Though he makes clear that slavery cannot be called good simply for the fact that it is slavery, he argues that it was generally a benevolent institution in the South and suited to the aristocratic order. The horrors Tate reserves to the terrors of capture by native operators, the inhumanity of the Middle Passage, and the practice of traders (Nathan Bedford Forrest graciously excepted). Tate emphasizes the distinctions among slaves that paralleled those of the whites—"On every plantation a hierarchy of rank, privilege, and esteem was rigidly observed" (41)—and the crucial role of many a black overseer and house servant in the plantation order. "On the whole," Tate argues, "it may be said that out of the great evil of slavery had come a certain good: the master and the slave were forever bound by ties of association and affection that exceeded all considerations of interest. The injustice of the system consisted in two things: the first was the humiliation of the name—slavery; the other was that it gave the talented individual little chance to rise" (43). There is almost no trace of graciousness or beauty in the passages depicting the Old South and the rise of the Lower South aristocracy (Tate leaves that to the Romanticists); his purpose is to make clear the nature of the Old South and to set forth the very facts its leadership failed to realize about its civilization.

Tate's aim in these early portions of the narrative is to emphasize the nature of the civilizational contest on the horizon, to take a position from which to assault the dominant American line of development by recourse to the only alternative (as he sees it) in our nation's experience—that of the agrarian South. Singal calls the Davis biography Tate's "most comprehensive statement of his

Agrarian view of Southern history" (243), and it is so not because of his treatment of Davis himself but because of his treatment of the society of which he was a part. Searching for a historical image to set against the dominant ethos of the society he found himself dissatisfied with, he turns to the landed aristocracy that had set itself athwart the path of American progress: "This identification of power and responsibility is the best basis for a society; in the Lower South it produced a genuine ruling class. Men were bound by their responsibility to a definite physical legacy—land and slaves—which more and more, as Southern society tended to become stable after 1850, checked the desire for wealth and power. Men are everywhere the same, and it is only the social system that imposes a check upon the acquisitive instinct, accidentally and as the condition of a certain prosperity, that in the end makes for stability and creates the close ties which distinguished a civilization from a mere social machine. Only the agricultural order in the past has achieved this" (56). According to Tate, antebellum southerners had held a largely correct notion of themselves and their society, but they had been unwilling to accept its implications: "Southerners believed that they stood for 'Christianity and Civilization' and, seen in the light of the main traditions of Europe, the assertion was literally true: theirs was the last stand, they were the forlorn hope, of conservative Fundamentalist Christianity and civilization, based on agrarian, class rule, in the European sense. Europe was already being Americanized—which means Northernized, industrialized—and the South by 1850 was more European than Europe" (87).[16] The philosophical Thomas R. Dew had stood by "whispering the new philosophy of inequality that the Lower South stood waiting for" (44), but Davis and others were too wedded to the American notions of equality, democracy, progress, and science to face the fundamental incompatibility of these ideas with their civilization. They had been unwilling to "go the whole hog of reaction," to borrow Tate's words to Davidson concerning the Agrarian movement.

Tate, aligning himself with the fire-eaters, repeatedly contrasts the reality (as he sees it) of the antebellum South not with an abstract ideal of the good society but with the fruits of the northern victory. Having set forth the problematic good of slavery as he does above, for example, he proceeds to contrast the good achieved in the plantation order with that of the industrial:

Only in these two respects [ostensible freedom and the hypothetical chance for advancement] is the modern industrial laborer better off than the Negro slave: as a class he has no more than the slave's chance to better himself. He has feeling, which the Negro lacked, of not belonging to an institution or a class—a void that he fills with cheap luxuries, cheap automobiles, cheap radios, cheap literatures; so that, because he is the major consumer of mass production, the production is diluted to his wants, and the higher values of all society are degraded. For society as a whole the modern system is probably inferior to that of slavery; the classes are not so closely knit; and the employer feels responsible to no law but his own desire. Industrialism comes in the end to absentee landlordism on a grand scale; this was comparatively rare in the Old South. (41–42)

As the contemporary references in this passage indicate, Tate's concern is not with the theoretical merits of North and South in the years leading up to the Civil War but with a vision of the Old South that affords him a perspective on the crisis of his own day, which he experienced within himself. Rubin points to this aspect of Tate's thought: "However much Tate's imagination was stirred by the aesthetic possibilities of the antebellum, aristocratic South, it was never really a recoverable object for him. Rather, it afforded him a point of view, and an instrument of strategy in his transactions with the life, values, and attitudes of his own day. . . . The Old South reference, then, represented the discovery on Tate's part of a way of ordering his response to the modernism within himself and all around him. It was, to repeat, a strategy, not an end in itself" (*Wary Fugitives* 96–97). We see this strategy in his concern with consumerism, the deadening of sensibility and discernment, and the disintegration of the social order in the passage above. In perhaps the clearest instance, though, we see the concern of the poet with the decay of language. Speaking of the conversation that had filled The Hurricane (the Davis plantation) and others like it, Tate writes, "The great Southern art of conversation—which left no county records and is lost to the documentary historian—was, in the end, the medium through which the people profoundly understood one another, and were made civilized. Contrasted with this, the conversation of modern Americans is a collection of primitive signs, by means of which even educated people express only a sense of animal existence . . . broken sentences . . . half phrases . . . repetitions . . ." (75–76; ellipses in original). Tate, like Eliot and Joyce, was deeply aware of the decay of language as both symptom and cause of civilizational decline, and Tate's poetry, like the work of his greater counterparts, was geared toward finding a new model of coherence to stem the tide. In his historical work, he was concerned with finding a historical counterimage to the disorder of his own age; the antebellum South provided an image of order, but on the whole it was an inadequate one, for the South, in Tate's view, had failed to realize its potential, to act in accordance with its nature.

The failure of the South in this regard is exemplified in the failure of Jefferson Davis. Tate turns to explore Davis's background only after setting the larger context in the chapter "King Cotton," and he portrays Davis as the product of an archetypal Lower South plantation family. As he tells us early in the chapter titled "Davis and the Lower South," "The transformation of the Davis family in one generation from insecure small farmers into great planters, and the growth of the patriarchal ideal, whereby Samuel Davis, a plain man, became the symbol of knightly grace—and the fountainhead of wisdom to his children . . . this process of expansion in one family is the story of the rise of the Lower South" (51). Samuel Davis, Jefferson's father, had been of frontier stock—deeply religious, plainspoken, hardworking, and unaristocratic—but he had been one of the many who had laid the foundations for a genuine aristocracy to arise: "he was a man of fine character—well fitted to sire the leader of a great society—all the great leaders of which came from much the same stock" (56).

Jefferson, however, was bookish and withdrawn and early made the choice to follow intellectual pursuits over the hard labor of the plantation life. Schooled for a time at Transylvania University in Kentucky, he imbibed not the developing sectionalism of the lower Mississippi basin but the "most truly national" atmosphere of all the colleges in America. Then proceeding to West Point, he gained a faith in trained soldiers (the "West Pointism" that would draw the ire of instinctive soldiers such as Forrest), a "haughty pride," and "a belief in education as the remedy for all ills," in addition to the smattering of political theory and constitutional law that would lay the basis of secession (65). His service in the Northwest as an Indian-fighter gave him the added stature of a hero and confirmed in him a fatal belief in his own military prowess. Confirmed as the "studious, neurotic egoist," he was set to embark on a political career in which he was to stand for the interests of the aristocratic, agrarian South, but he was, in many ways, divorced from the realities necessary to maintaining that society. Davis returned to Mississippi after his military service to a plantation that had been given him by his brother. Tate writes, "Jefferson Davis's life up to 1835 had been a miracle of good fortune, but he had learned almost nothing for he had suffered

no checks to his easy career" (67). As Tate presents him, he was profoundly un-
equipped to deal with the crisis ahead: "He had not gained any discipline over his
feelings, for this comes by adversity or by long training to a traditional ideal; nor
did he understand that moral and political convictions are the complex product
of feeling; for he supposed these to be matters of reason. Before he entered politics he was convinced that people who disagreed with him were insincere" (68).
Davis went on to win a seat in the U.S. Senate on the strength of his war record
and then became secretary of war under Pierce. He was in a position to see the
approaching struggle, but, as Tate makes clear in his opening chapter, he was unable to judge its nature.

Tate returns us to Davis's farewell speech and ascension to the Confederate
presidency at the end of his third chapter; with all his primary claims about the
society, the struggle between two opposing ideas of civilization, and the character of Davis in place, we are left with a much more straightforward narrative
of events for the remainder of the book. Tate now assumes the role of tragic dra-
matist, laying out the chain of events that proceed inexorably to the defeat of
Davis and the South. Tate writes, "The history of Jefferson Davis during the War
between the States is practically identical with the movements, the failures and
the victories, of the southern armies. He had almost no social life, and his political life was the shadow of this military policy. The vast drama of the war was
in a sense the externalization of the interior drama of Davis's soul" (251). Tate reserves the explicit comparisons to Greek tragedy for the late stages of the war,
from 1864. Earlier, there is a sense that things might have been different, that disaster might have been averted, but the character of Davis determined the events
that set the tragic stage as surely as a certain end would follow from the course
of the war.

Essentially, Tate sees the defeat of the South as largely resulting from three
things, all the direct result of Davis's mind and temperament: his departmental
scheme and commitment to a defensive policy; his obstinate support for Braxton
Bragg; and his inability to understand the political realities that required an appeal to the people at large rather than the letter of the law. The defensive policy
arose from Davis's belief in the abstract rightness of the southern cause and the
departmental system from a belief that the defensive strategy should be carried
out based on the territorial abstractions of a map rather than strategic necessities. "Like Woodrow Wilson at Versailles," Tate writes, "he could not see why
a beautifully arranged program should not succeed" (15), and he waited vainly

through the first two years of the war for a recognition of the Confederacy and intervention from Europe. Apart from the rightness of the cause, European intervention would have to come because of the economic importance of King Cotton, and Davis insisted on holding back the southern stocks from English mills (thus denying the Confederacy an important source of capital): "The technical rightness of the South and of Davis's view of the economic situation were both beside the point; but it is clear that he made of these fantasies a bed of Procrustes upon which, he thought, all difficulties would have to lie," but there were "incalculable forces let loose" that Davis's mind could not grasp. "The passive and dispersive strategy of the South had brought her to the brink of ruin" by the end of 1861, with the fall of Forts Donelson and Henry, challenging the Confederate interior through the Cumberland and Tennessee rivers, the loss of much of the Mississippi River and New Orleans, and the presence of a huge Union force under McClellan on Virginia's Northern Neck. But by the end of February 1862, Davis saw that European intervention would not come in time for the coming campaigns: "He changed his policy. It is by no means easy for a man to unsettle all his confirmed habits of thought and strike out vigorously in a new direction; but Davis did this. And the new policy marks him as a great man" (132). Recognizing the need for a large army, Davis instituted conscription acts, extended terms of service, and postponed discharges, bringing on the ire of Stephens and other states' rightists, who objected to constitutional violations, but "what Stephens and the other martinets failed to see was that the states, at least in the South, had no rights until they were won on the battlefield" (135). Most important, Tate praises Davis for recognizing the genius of Lee and placing him in command of the Army of Northern Virginia, leading to the lifting of the siege of Richmond and driving McClellan back to Washington. In spite of the shift in his policy, he still remained passive, satisfied with temporary gains, obsessed with the protection of Richmond, and never willing to cede territory for the sake of strategic advantage.

Tate depicts his decision to appoint and sustain Bragg as bound up with his pride and his unwillingness to recognize political and military realities. After Johnston had been killed at Shiloh, and following his temporary replacement by the unpopular Beauregard, Davis had appointed Bragg to command of the West, with disastrous results: "His appointment was one of the few great mistakes that Davis made in selecting his generals; indeed it may be said to be his only mistake; for all the others, as we shall see, came out of the complications of this single one" (130). Following his ill-fated invasion of Kentucky, Bragg had utterly lost the confidence of his officers, his men, and the public: "he was capable of energy of the hysterical kind only, and when that failed he invariably found a scapegoat to bear the blame" (146). Davis forbore from responding to the invectives in the press directed at Bragg and supported his general, desiring to transcend the public melee and the crisis in the ranks. Tate writes, "It was to his lasting credit that he wished to display the Christian virtues of charity and forbearance; but what his country needed was the Machiavellian virtue of policy" (148). He supported Bragg much as he supported Lee after his offer to resign his command following Gettysburg, a moment Tate singles out as one of his finest; in both cases, "His attitude toward his generals was thus not analytical, based on a calm inspection of their situations; it was emotional, and it was more akin to loyalty than derived from intelligence" (199). Following Bragg's pseudovictory at Chickamauga, when the outcry was even greater (and no less a soldier than Longstreet argued for Bragg's removal), Davis would not be moved, and Tate finds in the event "a sinister suggestion, in this act of madness, that Davis's sense of reality, seriously shaken in July, was still further deteriorating; the tragedy of the doctrinaire, Procrustean mind is its inability to stretch beyond its own preconception of events" (204). Davis would go even further on his course and appoint Bragg chief of staff of the Confederate armies, and "the public now felt that Davis was indeed a tyrant" (206). He was confirmed in this course by a sense that contempt for the public will (or the ill-couched advice of advisers) was a vindication of principle, and Tate faults him repeatedly for not recognizing that a time of crisis demanded a charismatic leader who could appeal to the people. He had supported Bragg largely because "he would not be dictated to by the mob," and this tendency (in the case of Bragg and others) alienated the public and aided the powerful anti-Davis faction. Supposing "that the Constitution was the source of his power . . . he would impatiently appeal to it, but not to the people themselves" (84).

In a striking series of passages, Tate describes the leader demanded by the situation as nothing short of a demagogue. At times, he gives us a rather moderate estimate of the political realities: "It was Jefferson Davis's mistake to ignore the source of his strength, and to suppose that his official position alone gave him the right to rule. He was, on the whole, a wise ruler: he certainly knew the needs of the country better than, say, a county politician; but his error lay in his failure to pretend that the county politician knew better than he. In this, he contrasted sharply and unhappily with his rival north of the Potomac River" (207). But Tate continues in this vein elsewhere and reaches a much more extreme conclusion: "He constantly forgot that the Confederacy was a political experiment, and that the people were not fixed forces to be called into action by executive order; they needed to be coaxed and coddled; and he deprived them of the kind of public performance that they most loved—oratory from their leaders. In no sense was Davis ever the leader of the Southern people as a whole, and this was due to his complete lack of demagoguery, to his high opinion of the public intelligence" (180). Taking the prescription Tate gives here, we are left with stump speeches and a rather low estimate of the public intelligence, conjuring up the image of a closet Calhoun and a public Vardaman. If we are left with any question as to the seriousness of Tate's claims here, he answers it late in the volume when treating the crisis provoked by Sherman's march: "The need of the hour was a revolutionary leader who would call the people to arms, trample on law and government, and conduct a people's war" (271). We are close here to having Andrew Jackson, the anti-Christ of southern conservatives, riding to the aid of the last vestige of European civilization! That victory, at the price of such a leader, and the nation that would result from it do not enter into Tate's narrative, but clearly that nation would no longer be the South Tate and the Agrarians stood to defend. But Tate the rhetorician, like Jackson the general, is proceeding with one object in mind and does not scruple to dispose of any straggling doubts that might enter the mind. Nothing more clearly indicates than do these passages that the identification with the society of the Old South was an act of will for Tate, providing the rhetorical posture of defiance to allay the inner awareness of defeat and failure in the consciousness, a failure that arose from the society itself as much from any pressure brought against it.

Notwithstanding the rhetorical fireworks, the true identification for Tate is with the failure of Davis and the South. As he wrote to Bishop after completing the Davis biography: "The older I get the more I realize that I set out about ten years ago to live a life of failure, to imitate, in my own life, the history of my people. For it was only in this fashion, considering the circumstances, that I could identify myself with them. We have an instinct—if we are artists particularly—to live at the center of some way of life and to be borne up by its innermost significance. The significance of the Southern way of life in my time is failure. . . . What else is there for me but a complete acceptance of the idea of failure?"[17] It is this identification that earns Davis tragic dignity rather than con-

tempt in the narrative of the events following on 1864. Tate casts him in the role
of Oedipus, that greatest of tragic figures:

> There was Davis, the protagonist, suffering the consequences of his mis-
> takes, but equally the victim of circumstances and fate; never faltering;
> never admitting defeat; but always, in his austere gray cape and wide hat,
> walking along Clay Street, the very image of unbending pride, of that
> vice of the mighty which the Greeks called Hybris. In this last year there
> was in him, perhaps, a little of the madness of pride, a certain tortured re-
> sentment against an adversary too complex for him to understand; and
> yet he felt none of that humility he was later to feel in the face of an in-
> comprehensible fate. He was now Oedipus raging against misfortune,
> but not yet knowing that he was blind. (240)

The denouement follows, "and every event brought to him a harbinger of disaster like the Nuntius of classical drama rushing in again and again to pile woe
after woe upon the breaking protagonist" (262), and Davis, at the head of a government that no longer exists, is left to flee and be captured as a Quixote in his
wife's petticoats. He would learn the wisdom of Oedipus only in the prison of
Fortress Monroe. Tate relieves us of none of the pathos of the closing scenes by
referring to the grand gesture and noble dignity of Lee at Appomattox; we hear
of Lee's surrender only as a report.

Tate returned to the States in 1930, after completing the Davis biography
and his contribution to *I'll Take My Stand*. He and Caroline moved to Benfolly, an
antebellum plantation house in Tennessee overlooking the Cumberland that had
been bought for him by his industrialist brother Ben. In both his work on Davis
and his *I'll Take My Stand* essay, "Remarks on the Southern Religion," he makes essentially the same point: the South had not understood itself. "The form requires
the myth," he writes in the Ode, and these works make it abundantly clear that
the South's mythos was all wrong, a thing of native shreds and alien patches. The
South's tradition had been lost to his generation because it had not been adequately embodied, and his move to Benfolly, as Rubin points out, represented the
recourse he had pointed to in his essay—reclaiming the tradition "by violence"
(*Wary Fugitives* 299–300). His surroundings seemed suited to the effort; he was
now master of a plantation house and had a Confederate flag above the mantel.

In Clarksville he undertook his third biographical effort, a biography of Robert E. Lee.

But the biography of Lee would not be written; he could not complete it without doing more violence than he had bargained for to himself and the subject. Lee appears as a vexed figure for Tate in the earlier biographies because his very virtues constituted a weakness. In a striking passage in *Stonewall Jackson*, he makes his case for why Jackson should have been given overall command: "Jackson alone, as a soldier, was Lee and Longstreet combined; Longstreet alone was—Longstreet; Lee alone, as a soldier and as a man, was almost God. And that is why . . . Lee, one of the great men of all time, should have left the army to Jackson. For Lee, the soldier, was always something more than that. Godlike omniscience, being what it is, puts limits on its own powers" (254). Rubin states the problem well:

> If Tate were to examine Lee, he would be brought up against many of the virtues and attitudes that he most cherished as the hallmark of the self-contained, humane, classically proportioned society that he saw as exemplified in antebellum Virginia life at its best. Did they hold up under scrutiny? If not, then what were they ultimately worth? If these virtues, in the character of the foremost Virginia hero, had caused the war to be lost, when more ruthlessness and greater personal ambition would have achieved a different result, what did that say about the "virtues"? Yet without them, would the winning of the war and the preservation of southern antebellum society have really been worthwhile after all? (*Wary Fugitives* 298)

According to Rubin, Lee presented the challenge of an identification with the hero that the other two subjects did not, and Tate was simply not willing to make it. Taking the identification in either direction was hazardous: identifying himself with Lee would involve him in the difficulties of the passage above, and identifying Lee with himself, to bring the character to life on the page, would make it necessary "to give Lee the kind of self-conscious irony and habit of cerebration that would violate what Tate felt that Lee was and what he represented" (301). Simpson approaches the problem from a slightly different direction by claiming that "Tate's dilemma was that he could not accommodate Lee to the southern culture of failure."[18] The hour demanded a hero who would embody "the innermost significance of the South," and Tate, as Bishop suggested, was troubled by the fact that such an effort led him not into a portrait of the "marble man" but into an identification of Lee with himself. Bishop saw no difficulty in such an identification: "write the life of the Southerner (yourself, myself, all of us) in terms of Lee, so much more will it be than a life of Lee."[19] But, as Simpson writes, "Tate was overwhelmed by his sensitivity to the problem of writing a life of Lee that would be at the same time his own self-biography and, so to speak, an autobiography of the South. His complex awareness of the moral burden his self-conscious quest for his cultural identity as a southerner had placed on him was too much" (*Fable* 34).

The turn from the historical image inward unsettled Tate, pushing him beyond the relatively simple theses of the polemicist and detached modern to the disturbing awareness that the truth of southern history involved him in the darker reality of a modern slave society. As Thomas Underwood writes of this phase of Tate's career, "He was trapped between his growing political convictions and his genealogical obsessions. . . . If ideological assuredness shaped his public identity as a Southern intellectual, spiritual loneliness festered in his artistic imagination."[20] Lewis Simpson gives us the most searching account of Tate's progression to autobiography through his analysis of two fragmentary manuscripts left by Tate: one an attempt to trace the history of the South through the history of a family divided, like his own, between Tidewater and frontier, Virginia and Kentucky; the other an ambitious autobiography that would have been the history of his own mind. He began the first project in the early 1930s, initially tracing his own family's history down to his brother and himself, "who are fairly good types of modern America, absolutely different but motivated by the same blood traits. . . . There will be two chief figures to a generation, about eight in all. Although each new chapter will introduce two new figures, each of them will continue what his father stood for, and I think the continuity will be preserved. The fundamental contrast will be between the Va. tidewater idea— stability land, the establishment—and the pioneer, who frequently of course took on the Va. idea, even in Tenn., but who usually had some energy left over, which has made modern America. My brother and I will show these two types fairly well."[21] Tate, realizing the difficulty of framing the narrative, shifted his plan to a novel, "Ancestors of Exile," that would preserve the tension between the two strains—Scotch-Irish on the frontier and aristocratic English in Tidewater Virginia—but end with a woman in St. Louis: the final chapter would record "the chaotic protest of a woman produced by the union of Tidewater and Scotch-Irish strains—her protest against the aimless life to which she is committed without quite understanding why it is aimless." Tate could thereby present his "judgment upon the modern mind."[22] Tate's new focus, Simpson writes, was "the idea that the sense of exile the modern southerner experiences is inherent in the failure of the exiles who were his forebears to establish a stable culture" (*Fable* 36). But he goes further to claim that Tate's scheme, by "making an equation between blood, self, and mind" and focusing on the mixing of blood lines, "opened his story up to the most sensitive issue in southern culture, that of the blood mixing of blacks and whites" (37). Tate's suppressed awareness that the master-slave relationship, rather than the frontiersman-aristocrat one, was the central dynamic of the antebellum South would inform his novel *The Fathers*, written shortly after he had resigned himself to the failure of "Ancestors of Exile." In *The Fathers* Tate writes purely as the modernist artist rather than the polemicist; turning inward, he presents a vision of history far more complex than that in his biographies.

As we have seen, Tate recognized early on that his connection with the southern past was one not of continuity but of a deliberate, willed seizing of a tradition by an act of intellectual violence; as his career progressed, however, and he moved toward his conversion to Roman Catholicism in 1950, he came to see more clearly that he had replicated the earlier failure of antebellum southerners in positing the Old South as a redemptive history. In his essays "Religion in the Old South" (1930) and "The Profession of Letters in the South" (1935), he anatomized the failure of mind in the Old South—a society that failed to understand itself and that was grounded on slavery. As time went on, he would carry this further, in the understanding that the history of the South, instead of being redemptive, was itself—as all human history—in need of redemption. Mark Malavasi finds in Tate's later understanding "the image of the South as a fallen world, which singularly embodied and reflected the sinfulness of the human condition—a world from which redemption nonetheless remained possible."[23] Not that he (like Ransom) would renounce his Agrarianism; properly understood, as a flawed but vital image of human community, it had much to offer his era. Writing to Donald Davidson in 1953 (after his conversion), he would state his sustained belief in their old project with qualifications: "We were trying to find a religion in the secular, historical experience as such, particularly in the Old South. I would go further than John [Crowe Ransom] and say we were idolaters. But it is better to be an idolater than to worship nothing, and as far as our old religion went I still believe in it."[24] In "The Man of Letters in the Modern World" (1952), Tate echoed many of the old Agrarian themes but stated them in the broader context of Western society since the Renaissance; his concern is with the corruption of language and the role of the man of letters, and the battle, he writes, "is now between the dehumanized society of secularism, which imitates Descartes' mechanized nature, and the eternal society of the communion of the human spirit."[25] He turns, in other words, from the City of Man to the City of God. His early recognition of the failure of the South, and his own involvement with it, led him to a far different relationship to history, from a reliance on the unaided will to force history to conform to the dictates of the self, to a reliance upon grace.

5

"HISTORY IS BLIND, BUT MAN IS NOT"

Robert Penn Warren and the Rebuke of the Past

While Tate found a measure of certainty by turning to Catholic orthodoxy and the long view of the West, his younger counterpart Robert Penn Warren found the essence of history in its very indeterminacy. Having a City of God to set against the City of Man—the realm of history and its attendant decline—allowed Tate some measure of reconciliation to the alienation of the present. Such a solution was unavailable for Warren; like Herman Melville, he could "neither believe nor be comfortable in his unbelief," and his entire career constitutes a search—at times a desperate one—for the meaning possible in the present.[1] He viewed the situation of humankind in essentially existentialist terms, with the individual struggling in the "agony of will" amid the savage flux of history. Existentialism did not allow Warren to escape the burden of the past; rather, it drove him to explore profoundly the meaning of the self in time. Warren's obsession with history goes beyond that of any of the other Fugitive-Agrarians and dominates his best fiction, much of his poetry, and a significant portion of his nonfiction prose. Although his fictional treatments of the encounter with history, particularly *All the King's Men*, are deservedly the most famous of his works, our concern here is with the historical writings in which Warren dons the mantle of historian without the overt mediation of fiction: primarily, in his first work in the polemical fervor of the late 1920s, *John Brown: The Making of a Martyr* (1929), his later meditations on history in *Legacy of the Civil War* (1961), and essays and addresses such as "The Use of the Past."

Unlike Tate, with his mother's visions of a lost legacy in the Old Dominion, Warren was more fully a child of the Dark and Bloody Ground. His forebears on both sides had been in Kentucky (or nearby in Tennessee) since the early nineteenth century. His father was an aristocrat only by very local standards and held that position as a banker rather than a landholder; moreover, he was strangely reticent when talking about the family history.[2] Warren's most imme-diate tie to his ancestral past came not through his father but through his mother, in the person of Gabriel Thomas Penn, his maternal grandfather. Penn was a great storyteller, and Warren spent much of his time in the summers out on his grandfather's farm listening to the old man tell stories, many of which concerned his days as a cavalry officer with Forrest. While his grandfather was certainly a romantic figure to him, some of his stories had a distinctively frontier tinge, as when he told his grandson of hanging a group of bushwhackers who had taken to preying on civilians during the war. As Joseph Blotner notes, many of these stories did not lend themselves to romantic notions of warfare.[3] Current events in Warren's boyhood tempered his romanticization of the past as well. Though he read avidly in books such as Parkman's *The Oregon Trail*, Motley's *Rise of the Dutch Republic*, and Buckle's *The History of Civilization in England*, the residual vio-lence of the frontier was never far away. Apart from the knife fights, brawls, and cockfighting that Warren remembered as part of the fabric of life in Guthrie, there was a strong communal memory of the "Black Patch Tobacco Wars" (in 1905, the year of Warren's birth), which pitted the tobacco growers against the American Tobacco Company and required the intervention of federal troops to stem the violence. All these events, his grandfather's stories and songs, and what he later remembered as his father's peculiar isolation from the past formed his background when he left Guthrie to attend Vanderbilt.

Warren was the youngest of the Fugitive-Agrarians, coming to take part in the Fugitive meetings as something of a young prodigy shortly after his arrival at Vanderbilt in 1921, and he bore a different relationship to the Agrarian project that was later to emerge. The seriousness of his poetic commitment was second to none, and the poetic apprenticeship to Ransom and Tate proved immensely valuable. Though he contributed to both *I'll Take My Stand* and the second sym-posium, *Who Owns America?* (1936), he was less committed to the programmatic aspects of the Agrarian group as it evolved in the late twenties and early thirties. By the time of the Agrarian symposium, Warren had left the South, first for the University of California at Berkeley in 1925, then, following a brief stint at Yale, for Oxford as a Rhodes scholar in 1928, and his central concern with the issues of the day took a somewhat different formulation. Looking back to the time of the symposium at the Fugitives reunion in 1956, Warren identified the ques-tions that provided the fundamental impetus of the Agrarian movement: "one, the sense of the disintegration of the notion of the individual in that society we're living in—it's a common notion, we all know—and the relation of that to democracy."[4] His commitment was decidedly less ideological than that of the others, never giving rise to such efforts as Tate's call for "an academy of Southern *positive* reactionaries," Ransom's immersion in economics and farming techniques, or Davidson's lifelong attempt to forge a usable, distinctively southern mythos from the materials of the Tennessee past. Whatever the contrast, Warren's participation in the Agrarian effort should not be underplayed, for the lasting meaning of the Agrarian movement, as it has emerged in the past sixty years, is consonant with Warren's primary concerns from his earliest work to his latest: the problem of the American self and the relationship of that self to history.

Warren, like the other Agrarians, was entering the public sphere as a man of letters, deliberately putting aside the prerogative of artistic detachment to engage in the ongoing debate over the course and direction of American culture. His contribution to *I'll Take My Stand* would set him apart from the others, and when he followed Tate into writing Civil War biography, his choice of subject was equally distinctive. Instead of treating another of the southern icons, such as Jackson, Davis, or (as Lytle would later) Forrest, Warren turned to a northern one, and a decidedly marginal one at that—John Brown of Pottawatomie and Harpers Ferry fame. Although the choice of subject presented itself to some extent, Warren could certainly have sought out others.[5] Tate and Lytle chose figures who had risen to play a public role of leadership, leading large numbers of people in large designs; Warren turned to a figure of the frontier whose specialty was guerrilla warfare. Though Brown is a partisan warrior of sorts, he is not one of the light-bearers in the wilderness that we saw in Simms; Warren, shaped by Kentucky and childhood stories of the Black Patch Wars, was deeply interested in the often savage manner of self-realization on the frontier. One of the other Agrarians might have taken up Brown only to give him a good debunking, and while Warren would do his share of that, his concerns in the biography are more fundamental and would remain with him throughout his career.

The primary difference from Tate's and Lytle's biographies is that in *John Brown: The Making of a Martyr* Warren analyzes the methods of historical construction as much as he simply attempts to set forth the truth of what happened. His subtitle is significant, as Jonathan Cullick notes: it is "an indication that Warren's objective is to record not only the history of how Brown lived, but the history of how Brown has been historicized. The text is not simply about John Brown. It is concerned with how Brown has been constructed—how he has been 'made'—as an historical figure. Warren set out to write a history about the 'making' of history" (37). On one level, Warren works to debunk the romantic image of Brown popularized by his apologists among the abolitionists, transcendentalists Ralph Waldo Emerson and Henry David Thoreau, and some later historians. This mode, marked by a youthful sarcasm, is similar to that employed by Tate in his biographies. More important, though, Warren explores the question of the individual in relation to history and begins to develop the existential ground of his mature perspective and his lifelong concern with darker manifestations of American idealism, a trait Warren would soon come to see marking northerners and southerners alike.[6] Essentially, Warren shapes the biography into three phases: first, Brown's early life and his self-mythologizing; second, his discovery of the abstract ideal and violence as the path to identity in Kansas; and third, his creation and manipulation of a public image as he moves toward his defining act and eventual apotheosis at Harpers Ferry.

Much of Warren's attention in the early portions of the biography is devoted to identifying the strands of Brown's personal history that have been woven back in as part of a narrative of identity. The most important of these events, of course, are those dealing with Brown's resolution "to declare or swear unremitting war against slavery," and Warren downplays these by situating them rather casually amid the incidents of Brown's boyhood in Ohio. Further, he never treats them as events containing inherent meaning but as incidents, unremarkable in themselves, which gain force only when incorporated into the larger narrative to be constructed later. The first of these, when Brown witnessed the beating of a slave boy when he was away driving his father's cattle, Warren places after a section describing the Brown family's profit from the War of 1812 and John Brown's avoidance of active military service in the conflict ("when he came of age[,] he paid fines like a Quaker to escape the required drilling").[7] With this unvalorous introduction, Warren then continues, "It seems that John acquired another conviction as well as that concerning military affairs . . . eternal war with slavery," as he described it "after he had become the relentless Kansas Captain John Brown" (19). Rather than challenging the incident, Warren speculates on the source of its characterization, of the shape of the historical projection: perhaps Brown had read something of the kind in the "story of Hannibal's infant oath on the altar of Baal? Or in the book he knew best the story of the voice calling at night to the child Samuel?" (19). The other primary incident comes soon after this one in the narrative, as Brown shelters an escaped slave from pursuers "as almost any Northern citizen would have done if the pursuit was not too hot" (21). According to Brown's later account of the incident, he found the slave lying behind a log and, as Brown says, "heard his heart thumping before I reached him" (21). Warren counters the force of the incident, adding sarcastically, "Incidentally, he seized upon the opportunity to again swear eternal enmity against slavery" (21), and going on to note that one of Brown's sons later recounted the incident with the same details but made himself an eyewitness: "Some have professed surprise at the coincidence," Warren notes; "others have professed surprise only at the acoustics of Hudson township, Ohio" (22).

Warren emphasizes Brown's unsuccessful efforts in "worldly affairs" throughout most of the first portion to offset the obscure and as yet inchoate sense of destiny and mission forming in his mind. We see Brown not as the single-minded prophet of popular legend but as something of a projector, moving from failed scheme to failed scheme. Warren uses Brown's activities to set a very different context for them than that set by his apologists. Where they see a calling, Warren sees a man who fails to gain worldly success and seeks to overcome that failure by embracing the pure idea. The most important example of Warren's method comes when Frederick Douglass makes his first visit to Brown's home and Brown describes to him his audacious plan for an attack on Virginia by a small group of men in the mountains who would lead a slave uprising. He makes his declaration: "No political action will ever abolish the system of slavery. It will have to go out in blood. Those men who hold slaves have even forfeited their right to live" (52), and sketches his plan: "Then John Brown rose and took down a map of the United States. He placed the tip of a bony, nervous finger on the border of New York State and ran it along the shadings of the Alleghenies. It rested on the mountains of Virginia" (53). The meeting left its impression on Douglass, and it leaves its impression on the reader, but it is not that of the visionary prophet; it is of a man speaking out of an absolute certainty of self and a prophecy self-fulfilling in every sense. The moment is a powerful one, but Warren shapes our perception of it by situating it in the midst of a larger discussion of Brown's unsuccessful efforts to form the woolen cooperative. With Brown, as with his forebears, "it seems to have been his custom after each failure in business to hunt out some undeveloped region and begin again with his axe and plow" (56). The actual place of the "undeveloped region" would not matter; what mattered was the freedom from contingency, from anything that might impinge on the unsullied purity of the great idea.

In this final period before Brown would leave for Kansas, Warren creates the sense of a convergence of the twain, of Brown and the public image that would finally suit his private certainty of self. As Warren presents it, Kansas provided Brown with precisely what he needed: a potentially bloody conflict over the abstract idea of slavery, and a setting in which the actions of an individual could be of far greater consequence than in the East. "One cannot afford to read the motives that took John Brown to Kansas as being pure and simple," Warren tells us. As one of his daughters later recorded, he went to see "if something would not turn up to his advantage" (106). In the West, Brown found a new territory peculiarly well suited to his character and temperament: a man might found a settlement there and redeem his failures in the East, and the question of slavery pushed men to extremes. Warren spends most of the time in his first chapter on Kansas sketching the background of the territory in the wake of the Kansas-Nebraska Bill of 1854. Motives were most assuredly mixed in all groups concerned, whether pro- or antislavery. The Emigrant Aid Company was "to make money and was to save Kansas for God and freedom," Warren tells us, providing a telling quote from the vice president of the company, Eli Thayer: "When a man does a benevolent deed and makes money at the same time, it merely shows that all his faculties are working in harmony" (90). Brown himself had not even intended to go to Kansas after his sons' departure, but he recognized an opportunity.

Brown finds in Kansas his long-sought opportunity to act on the idea that has been his support in spite of mundane complications, and Warren heightens the context of Brown's action by isolating him in a starkly naturalistic landscape. Earlier, when Brown was on the farm at North Elba, serving as "father to the Negroes at North Elba" and awaiting his opportunity, Warren emphasizes the infertility of the ground and, by extension, the project: "It was real pioneer work, such as the Browns had seen before in Ohio and Pennsylvania, but the land here was more intractable and the climate more harsh" (63). The land had been cleared by slash-and-burn, leaving charred stumps in the fields, "where the plow for years would catch on old roots and stone," and "worse, the winter hung over the region for six months of the year, and snow still clung in deep patches of drift at a time when crops were green in the country the Browns had left" (63). His picture is one of barrenness: "In ordinary times neither corn nor wheat could mature on those hillsides. Rye, oats, potatoes, and vegetables were all that the land would produce, and that only at painful expense of labor and anxiety."

By situating Brown in a bleak landscape suitable only to a very abstract crop indeed, Warren establishes Brown's separation from the traditional order of both culture and agriculture, and these extremes are only heightened when he moves to Kansas. Warren records his disappointment—"he had come to fight and not to settle"—when no violence accompanies the election of the territorial legislature upon his arrival. But the first encounter between the forces at Lawrence had been peaceably resolved, leaving Brown adrift in the harsh, frontier landscape with no vent to his impulse and no way, as Warren says much later, "to put his philanthropy on a paying basis":

> The faculties of old man Brown of Osawatomie were not working in harmony. He had marched off to benevolently strike a blow for Lawrence and freedom, and had marched back after a bloodless victory with boot soles a little thinner and only the fine title—Captain of the Liberty Guards— by way of reward. The dignity of those words—Captain of the Liberty Guards—didn't chink the cabins, or get corn, or pay for leather to mend boots, when there was ice in the river, in the timber, and under the snow eighteen inches thick, or when the level blizzard wind off the prairies drove the snow like dry sand and whipped the smoke back down the unfinished chimney to scatter sparks and burning ash over the rude hearth. (125)

Warren here uses naturalistic detail to highlight Brown's solipsism and tenuous sense of self in this period of waiting. Against this backdrop, Warren undercuts any heroic grounding of Brown's later actions while at the same time humanizing them by connecting the most abstract of needs—for justice, autonomy, and so forth—with the most elemental. Brown's course will be prompted by the same blind need in the self that all people respond to, though its nature will be determined by the dominant idea of his mind.

The first satisfactory manifestation of Brown's self-image would come only with the slaughter of suspected proslavery men along Pottawatomie Creek. Keeping his eye on the "main chance," he waited for the current of events to turn in his favor, and the opening of violence in the territory soon came. Warren paints a stark portrait of the events leading to the violence, the awkward and savage manifestation of higher ideas in the brutal context of the frontier and private quarrels. Warren maintains an even hand throughout the Kansas section, taking both the pro- and antislavery factions to task; apart from his comments on hypocrisy, the evocation of brutality in the name of ideals draws his attention more than any polemical revisiting of the Kansas question. As he writes, "There were murders and reprisals on both sides, with little to choose between them on the score of humanity or justice" (148). After Franklin Pierce's election, federal troops were sent to enforce the laws of the proslavery legislature, and the antislavery factions were preparing for the clash. Brown "knows his moment," envisioning "a spark that could divide the nation" (141), and he withdraws from his command of the militia unit to command a smaller, nonmilitia force suitable to his decidedly off-the-record purposes.

Warren's account of the infamous massacre on Pottawatomie Creek is direct and reportorial. He relates the events as facts in a few pages and then turns to focus on the more important issue: what was done with those facts. He begins with Brown's preparations and care to ensure the secrecy of his raid. He was acting as he preferred to, as a free agent responsible only to himself and his God. The mixed purposes of the raid are marked by the question by which, in Warren's gloss, Brown selected his victims: "Was the man known to be proslavery and did he have good horses?" A negative on either count and the man would be passed over. In each case during the night, the men are taken out of the house and questioned, then either killed or (in one case) returned and the house looted and horses taken. The narrative, as the raid itself, proceeds dispassionately and methodically: "The three victims were hurried a short distance down the road toward Dutch Henry's and there the party halted. John Brown set the example. He presented a revolver to the forehead of old Doyle and fired. It had begun; there was no turning back now. The Brown sons fell on William and Drury Doyle and hacked them down. Drury tried to flee but they pursued and overtook him. In the young grass near a ravine they left his mangled body. The other two lay in a bloody heap by the roadside where they had fallen" (163). The night ends with the final exchange of the stolen, "pro-slavery" horses for northern ones, removing evidence of the crime and ensuring a decent profit for the venture. Initially, under the sheer horror of the facts, "the repudiation of John Brown and all the tribe of Browns was swift and unmistakable," but "party feeling" would soon revive enough to justify the facts under the name of principle. After his presentation of the events, Warren follows the public reaction with more graphic detail of the costs of the raid. He describes the mutilation of the bodies, ending with the starkest image: "Everybody knew by this time how Harris had found the gigantic body of Dutch Bill lying in the creek, whose waters had washed out some of the brains from the clefts in his skull and carried the blood away from the stump of his left arm" (170). His placement of the descriptions is crucial, coming after the rather bare-bones description of the night in question; again, he is concerned not with sensationalizing the facts but with turning attention to what was done with them, with the process that rendered the brutal sublime. The reaction to the deeds was all-important for Brown, for only if the public was willing to receive them in terms of a given narrative of purpose would they serve in his larger plan. The justification came. As Warren writes, "Pottawatomie opened a new life for John Brown; it showed him how one thing might be done as well as another" (177).

This "new life" took form after the public image of John Brown as the hero of Kansas began to take shape; it began to take on the lineaments of Brown's interior self, and the remainder of his life would push toward a perfect identification, until the private self would die so that the public self might live in Brown's martyrdom. Brown had learned the value of words in shaping public perception even before coming to Kansas, when he solicited donations for arms by reading two letters from his eldest son that detailed the evil intentions of the slaveholders: "John Brown Jr. had been right; Eastern people *were* interested in guns for Kansas. When a letter would bring tears it would bring money. Harriet Beecher Stowe knew the trick, for her *Uncle Tom's Cabin* had provided a tidy fortune" (102). Now, in the wake of Pottawatomie and Brown's encounters with proslavery forces elsewhere, the emergence of the public Brown really begins with the intervention of a northern correspondent, James Redpath, who seeks Brown out in hiding; Warren presents him as a "Union-splitter" who "saw John Brown as a possible tool to the desired end of civil war" (180–81). The bloodshed of Pottawatomie, of course, was the key to Brown's notoriety and the power of his name, but Redpath and others would refine and redirect the energy while eliding the event from the record. Redpath needed a hero to consolidate eastern sympathy, and he had found his man: "Old John Brown would do admirably. A grey-haired old man, dirty and poorly dressed, with toes sticking out of broken boots, leaning over a pot and clutching a greasy iron fork" (183).

Brown returns to the East fully confident in his new identity as champion of freedom and aware of the power his association of name and idea has in the northern parlors and meeting halls. He moves under the aegis of Kansas, but his real mark has shifted to the main goal—striking at the South. As Warren writes earlier, when looking ahead to this shift, "It was always the one big *coup* that he wanted—a stake that would wipe out all the miserable score of the past at a single sweep" (129). He gains letters of introduction from prominent figures and turns, as Warren notes, not to the house at North Elba, where his wife is still struggling to get by, but to the "houses of wealthy, prominent men, where the letters would insure consideration and honor" (226). The political climate had shifted in the fifties; where abolition had formerly been out of favor in the interest of protecting markets, now, in the words of Henry Ward Beecher, "that nation is the best customer that is freest" (227). The West was a closed field to Brown now. He met with disapproval on one of his brief return trips for a raid into Missouri, as he found most pointedly when a pastor refused the "thanksgiving" for his success: "The Reverend John Todd was frankly puzzled; the poor man was not quite sure as to the decorum of thanking the good Lord for his success in horse stealing and murder" (307). A bounty was even put on Brown's head, and he was forced to seek sanctuary in the East, and Warren notes, "It is doubtful if he paid for this increased security by the cynical reflection that the farther he got from Kansas the more general the approbation of his services there" (311). But, he tells us, "John Brown never looked back; his past and history were simply an instrument for framing an astounding future" (310). Brown's history meant a far different thing in the East; rather than a record of involvement in questionable and bloody doings from mixed motives, it was his badge of honorable service in the cause. The Massachusetts Emigrant Aid Company had grown suspicious of Brown's actual intentions with the arms and supplies meant for Kansas, but Brown knew his real audience and how to couch his appeal. Warren provides a telling instance of Brown giving a test reading of an address to Theodore Parker's congregation for Mrs. Stearns, the wife of a wealthy Bostonian. The address laments Brown's having to return to Kansas empty handed, not having found benefactors in the wealthy East to support his noble, suffering men. The effect of Brown's words on Mrs. Stearns was immediate and profound—she prodded her husband into writing a check for seven thousand dollars before breakfast— leading Warren to remark: "The two paragraphs of 'Old Brown's Farewell' are one of the highest paid literary productions on record" (241). Separated from specific acts and concrete consequences, Brown's identification with a higher cause makes his name his currency.

But Brown does more than simply shape his public image; more important, for Warren, he continues to refine and expand the magnificent self-conception he carries within himself, defined by the grand gesture that will be the slave revolt beginning at Harpers Ferry. When Brown assembled his men in Tabor, Iowa, he presented an idea whose power lay not in its plausibility but in its audacity and scope. "Confounded and dazzled" by the abstract purity of the idea—well beyond the reach of pragmatic considerations—his men were placed in a realm of the ideal, of noble gestures, heroic acts, and the promise of a new land. When he later assembled his constitutional convention for his new government in Canada, it became clear that the project promised not simply freedom for the slaves but emancipation for the participants—from history: "Being war, and being a righteous war, it vindicated everything. Robbery became, under its terms, confiscation, and murder became execution. And so, a little tardily, the events of Pottawatomie received their definition. . . . The game now involved a generation and a state and not five men and a herd of horses. The comparison almost tricks one into acquiescence: to steal a horse is immoral, but to steal a state is neither moral nor immoral; it simply succeeds or fails" (281). What is forgotten in this, as Warren notes, is "how ghastly would have been the way of its success," just as the howling of the wolves in the prairie night had not been heard by the enraptured men in the camp at Tabor. Brown had created his men anew as adjuncts to his own self, and that self would find a great many to aid its projection onto the world stage.

The basis of Brown's appeal in the North was his seeming purity of motive and record of action in the West, and Warren uses this appeal for a critique of abstract notions of the "higher law." Brown returned to the East and was met with approbation for his certainty and single-minded intensity of purpose. Here was a man unconstrained by history or law. Transcendentalist Bronson Alcott found him "superior to any legal tradition, able to do his own thinking" (313), and he and others like him responded to a recognized kinship: "He was 'superior to any legal tradition'—just as most of these people felt themselves to be—and if he claimed to have a divine commission, they could understand what he meant, for they too were privy to God" (314). Warren contrasts this view with the more concrete, historically grounded view of the South: "The Southerner pointed to the Constitution and said: 'There is the law and the bargain; keep them and give us justice,' Garrison burned the Constitution as a 'covenant with Hell' and many other countrymen of his, if they were not ready to do this, could still call on conscience and the higher law. . . . The disagreement might conceivably have been settled under terms of law, but when it was transposed into terms of theology there was no hope of settlement. There is only one way to conclude a theological argument: bayonets and bullets" (314). But Warren emphasizes repeatedly that such consequences of the absolute idea were not taken into account by those people who chose not to sully themselves in the world of fact, and Brown gained his most important support from the man most capable of rendering the sublimity of the idea without being distracted by fact—Ralph Waldo Emerson. Warren writes, "Emerson possessed a set of ideas which have been given the interesting name of Transcendentalism; he spent his life trying to find something in man or nature which would correspond to the fine ideas and the big words. In John Brown, Emerson thought that he found his man" (245). Emerson needed Brown as the embodiment of an ideal, and Brown would need Emerson's power with language to refine his public identity after the horrific results of acting on the pure idea had come to pass: "They [Emerson and Thoreau] didn't give him money, but in 1859 they gave back to the world his own definition of himself" (245).

While Emerson and the majority of Brown's backers of the Mrs. Stearns variety would be involved with Brown at the level of ideas, both before and after the assault on Harpers Ferry, there were the New England elite who bound themselves to Brown in the event itself. The "Secret Six," as they became known, knew something of Brown's intentions and the scope of his plans, and they recognized in Brown the man to steel himself to the act. Thomas Wentworth Higginson, one of the more radical of their number, recognized in Brown the "best Disunion champion you could find." Although some of the conspirators were doubtful, and even dismayed, at first when told of the plan and presented with the provisional constitution, Brown overcame all objections, as he had much earlier with Douglass, with a repeated assurance of his own certainty. They were drawn into Brown's vision and aided him in his pursuit of self-definition, and Brown served a purpose for them as well: "They maintained something of the detachment of the experimenter; they knew what John Brown intended, they put in the way the money and rifles and pikes, and they waited, with the sense of not being too much involved, for the result of the experiment" (317). Brown allowed them the satisfaction of action and the security of "innocence": "They were entirely in accord with Gerrit Smith's feeling: 'I do not want to know of Captain Brown's plans; I hope he will keep them to himself.' They did not want to be embarrassed by knowledge, and when the telegraph wires hummed with tidings of insurrection and savage fighting at Harper's Ferry, and when the big print of the newspapers announced the lamentable end, they must have fervently thanked God for the foresight which had kept them so innocent, so technically innocent" (288). In many respects, Warren's treatment of the "Secret Six" and their preservation of "technical" innocence is harsher than that of Brown himself; Brown recognized the cost of acting on his vision—"Without the shedding of blood, there is no remission of sins," as his oft repeated favorite scripture has it—but the experimentalists, without whom there could have been no Harpers Ferry, could keep their distance from the deed while embracing the idea.

The figures Warren chooses to provide contrast to the attitude of Brown's co-conspirators are not exclusively southerners; they are the northern and western men who recognized historical cost and human fallibility. Warren singles out Senator Wilson of Massachusetts, whom he presents as prevented from intervention only by the deceptions of Brown's sponsors. Wilson is a champion of the law, seen not as an abstract embodiment of justice but as an imperfect realization of order. Warren presents an encounter between Brown and Wilson to highlight their very different conceptions of law: Wilson tells Brown, "I believe [your course] to be a very great injury to the anti-slavery cause, just as I regard every illegal act, and every imprudent act, as being against it," and Warren notes, "Being a 'higher law man' John Brown could not comprehend such an objection, and so he simply declared that he was right. Not being a 'higher law man' Mr. Wilson had no answer at all to that" (315). Wilson's approach—"let us do what we can with the law"—contrasted markedly with that of Theodore Parker, who quoted Cromwell approvingly, "There is one general grievance, and that is the law!" Warren also appeals to the great pragmatist Abraham Lincoln, whom he describes as "humane, wise, and fallible, but learning from his own failings" (317). Warren's models here are not drawn (as Tate's had been) from the strict constructionist school of Calhoun but simply those people who recognized historical contingency and human imperfection. If some in the South had a superior position, in Warren's view, it was simply in a more accurate assessment of human nature, but those individuals had no corner on the view. Warren's fundamental critique is grounded in the hubris that allows one to identify the will of God with one's own will: "They could not understand the philosophy that one must live in an imperfect world and should try to do what one can with the imperfect institutions devised by other imperfect men; they were so sure they knew the truth" (317–18).

The Harpers Ferry portion begins with a chapter that brings this omission to the fore, as Warren focuses on setting the contrast between Brown's guerrilla band of liberators and the settled, traditional life on the Maryland-Virginia border. This section, with its contrast between the abstract and the concrete, the revolutionary and the traditional, might even have passed muster with Davidson. Warren begins in novelistic fashion with the encounter of Brown and a yeoman farmer, Mr. Unseld, as Brown searches for the house he has in mind to rent: "'Good morning, gentlemen; how do you do?' Mr. Unseld regarded the four men in the road before him with the easy, half-kindly curiosity which greeted all strangers in that neighborhood. One was an old fellow, stooped and bearded, and the other three were young men" (320). Unlike a similar approach in the Kansas section, when Brown's sons encounter a band of men who immediately challenge them "on the goose" (the slavery question), here we are introduced into a region of manners and concrete sensibilities rather than abstractions. Unseld invites the men to his house for supper (they refuse, of course). The farmer fits well with the surrounding landscape, as Warren describes it: "It was a very pleasant place, a fine view; it was a fine country—comfortable but not smug, for the mountains prevented that, and rich but strong and unsuspicious" (321). It is an image of harmony rather than warring extremes, and Warren notes that Unseld points to "a field nearby where a few white men and negroes worked side by side cutting grain" (321).

Only when we reach this section dealing with Maryland and Virginia does Warren begin to sound the familiar notes of the apologist, when dealing with the institution of slavery in its supposedly more benign forms. The contrast between the "strange household" of the Browns (maintaining the pretense of an establishment while gathering arms and supplies) and the settled society around grows as the section proceeds; Brown sees only the image of the South in his head—the South he has come to overthrow—and is blind to the reality of life as it actually proceeds around him. Brown "adopted a course of doubtful" wisdom in choosing Harpers Ferry to incite a slave revolt, Warren claims. He failed to see the difference between the field hands, who might be drawn to extreme action, and the house servants, "whose situation was comfortable and who held to a great degree the confidence of their masters" (331). In Harpers Ferry, there was a preponderance of the latter. Yet the larger problem was not one of calculation but of vision: "John Brown, along with the greater number of Abolitionists, thought of slavery in terms of abstract morality, and never in the more human terms of its practical workings" (331). Warren mounts something of an apology for slavery along traditional lines here; he notes the real abuses under absentee ownership elsewhere but insists on the "exercise of obligation" between master and slave and the economic incentive for good treatment of slaves as "property," but this passage is something of an aside. He returns here as elsewhere to Brown's incapacity to grasp slavery as something other than an abstract relation, capturing it with a later incident when Brown's men confront a Mr. Byrne and demand his slaves: "Mr. Byrne's reply told something about the South's peculiar institution. 'Mr. Cook, if you want my slaves, you will have to do as I do when I want them—hunt for them. They went off Saturday evening and they haven't gotten back yet'" (332). While setting the scene—with Brown the avenging angel of right amid the settled landscape of the practicable—Warren turns his attention briefly to the larger political scene and the increasing division between North and South, when the nation, as Brown, would turn from the idea to the act.

Warren here again juxtaposes the larger currents of thought and events with the private motives of the men who were preparing for the assault on the arsenal. Lincoln, "the shambling Cassandra," had foreseen that people could be driven to extremes of action that many did not think possible, and his vision was shortly to be confirmed by events at Harpers Ferry. Unlike what one might expect in an account of the raid by Thomas Nelson Page or even Tate—an assault by monomaniac zealots on a peaceful people—Warren focuses on the very strangeness of this period for the men involved. They are drawn, like the crew of the Melville's *Pequod*, into an action that makes sense only when seen from the vantage point of their commander, but one that is in some secret sense theirs as well. Warren deflates the heroic only to accentuate the human element in the men's situation. He grants their bravery but notes, "They knew they were taking their lives into their hands—but every robber and bandit knows the same thing. Action in the face of such knowledge does not necessarily constitute heroism, and the risk which these men were taking was not commensurate with the dazzling stake; they intended to steal a state" (348). But earlier he gives a surprisingly sympathetic portrayal of one of Brown's sons, Watson, as he writes to his wife with genuine grief of the plight of the slaves in the neighborhood: "There was a slave near here whose wife was sold off South the other day, and he was found in Thomas Kennedy's orchard, dead, the next morning. Cannot come home so long as such things are done here. . . . I sometimes think perhaps we shall not meet again. If we should not, you have an object to live for,—to be a mother to our little Fred. He is not quite a reality to me yet" (345). Warren includes this genuinely moving portrait of Watson in a paragraph that sets out, with no critical commentary, the daily regimen of life for the men in the days before the assault, but the passage is effective in portraying the strangeness of the situation: the idea of freedom for the slaves, and Brown's mad plan for carrying it off, had somehow become more real than any concrete reality the men knew. Brown consolidates his hold over the men with a swearing-in ceremony under the new constitution, a symbol of the new revolution, and a plan to seize the sword presented to George Washington by Lafayette, a symbol of the first. Under Brown's influence, these symbols provide the outward form for the inward idea. What meaning the men's actions had lay solely in the mind and heart of John Brown, and as Warren shows them marching toward the Ferry "on their way to be shot and bayoneted and hanged," he writes, "It is hard to believe that any of them could have completely answered the question; 'My friend, why are you here?'" (348).

Warren deals with Brown himself in much the same way as his men; rather than emphasizing his responsibility, he treats the inward compulsion driving Brown and its power to seem something other than the needs of the self and the drive of the will. Following a good authority, George Gill, a cabinet member of Brown's provisional government, Warren tells us, "John Brown, according to Gill, might *do* good, but it was not because he *was* good; it was because he was strong. He marched down the road to Harper's Ferry because he could not do otherwise" (349). After his capture, Brown had answered a congressman's question about who sent him by saying, "No man sent me here. . . . It was my own prompting and that of my Maker, or that of the Devil, whichever you please to ascribe to it. I acknowledge no master in human form" (349–50). As with Melville's Ahab, the power of Brown's will was so great that it became, even for him, fate itself: "John Brown was there because it was the will of God—or the will of the Devil; it was his name for the profound compulsion with which his own will was identified. He somehow felt, by reason of its very strength, that it was outside himself, but that he was identified with it and acquiesced in it" (350). Warren recalls Brown's long history of failure and his constant desire for the act that would redeem the past, and he ends the last chapter before the assault with a culminating statement of Brown's need to at last find an adequate expression of his self:

It was all there—the Word, the Law. And his own will and God's will were one. Hypocrisy is too easy a word to use here, and too simple. If

John Brown had no scruple at deception it was because the end justified
the means. The end had justified so much in his life—embezzlement,
theft, lying, cruelty, murder. That end, that goal, which beckoned year
after year, seemed to float and shift and change its shape like some mi-
rage. In other words, John Brown's enormous egotism expressed itself in
one set of terms after another, and after Harper's Ferry there would be a
final transposition of this egotism into new terms. . . . It was necessary to
invoke "Liberty" in Kansas; in Virginia it was almost gratuitous to do so,
for the theft of a state justifies itself. Does man's will need justification beyond the will of God? (350–51)

The book builds more to this chapter than to the one following it, on the assault
itself. Here we have Warren's Brown in his most fully developed terms, as he
moves toward the crisis. The act has greater clarity here in Brown's private vision, having been predestined by his (or God's) will and only awaiting the proper
moment to unfold. Brown had set himself and his men toward an act that would
be self-defining, that would transcend any standard categories for judging good
or evil in historical events—that would, in fact, transcend history itself by taking the form of an act of God.

The most interesting aspect of the Harpers Ferry section is Warren's skill-
ful manipulation of perspectives during the assault. This chapter reveals most
clearly that Warren is a modernist novelist rather than a historian. He is not concerned so much with the events at Harpers Ferry as with the responses of Brown
and his men to those events, and he uses the novelistic tools at his disposal to
convey their radical disorientation as the idea fails to emerge from the sequence
of events. The assault is rendered matter-of-factly, like the Pottawatomie massacre, but here we find a chain of unintended consequences. Although the capture of the armory and the taking of hostages and the various positions in town
proceed methodically and successfully, the bloodshed that accompanies these
events seems purposeless; none of these successes secures any real objective, and
the victims are not the wealthy slaveholders Brown might have designated "de-
serving" victims. In fact, the first victims are a free black named Haywood and
the employer who tries to rescue him. As the plan is carried out, its abstract perfection becomes sullied in the encounter with men, motives, and circumstance.
Brown has suffered his reentry into history and historical contingency.

Warren highlights the experience of Brown's men outside town as they view the Ferry from a distance, evoking a sense of purposelessness—of men cut adrift and left with the fragments of a vision that no longer sustains them. In the early going, Warren captures one of Brown's men sitting with his hostage, Mr. Byrne, by the roadside, and we see the distance between idea and reality as Warren sets the once all-powerful idea in a broader perspective that causes it to shrink into insignificance: "So they sat close under the umbrella, Leeman [one of Brown's men] confident and excited now that action had begun, and Byrne trying hard to keep cheerful before his own apprehensions; the rain dripped from the bare branches, thumped the tight fabric of the umbrella, and, far away, drifted like a slow mist down the valley of the confluent rivers" (363). He isolates the individuals in the larger context of the natural world, as he had done with Brown earlier on the plains of Kansas, but rather than the harsh, naturalistic imagery of the wind, snow, wolves, and cold stars that had dominated that portion, he gives us a settled, peaceful landscape: the range of mountains, the slow rain, the small town viewed from above, and the confluence of the rivers. Warren presents the actors in a scene bereft of the meaning the action had seemed to promise. As another of Brown's men, Cook, hears of the troops surrounding the arsenal, he moves closer to the town to see for himself:

> From a position on the mountainside he could look down on the whole scene. There were the rivers bending down on the whole scene. There were the rivers bending together under Loudon and the Maryland Heights, with the houses of the town on the neck of land between. There were the bridges, the engine house, the neat lawns and flower pots of the armory, the station hotel, and the shining rails of the tracks which splayed out of the dark mouth of the Potomac bridge and disappeared down the valley. It must have looked very small, and unimportant, and complete, laid out at his feet. People below scurried back and forth in the uneven streets of the town, or clustered together at points of cover. And from those points on the long arc swung around the engine house, puffs of smoke, very small and unimportant, burst. The steady sound of rifles echoed between the hills. (371)

In this scene—"very small, and unimportant, and complete"—Warren's focus is certainly not on a polemical purpose but on the human situation of the actors.

The rightness or wrongness of Brown's actions is shunted aside as Warren explores the creation of meaning or the failure of meaning in the present.

Brown's execution represents the final apocalypse of the self, when self is lost in symbol, and Warren turns our attention in the final stages to the nature of that apocalypse and its cost. Brown ended the trial with his final statement—"his last deathless oration"—which removed the raid as far as possible from its horrendous implications; the meaning, however, would not be found in his words but in his death. Brown made the discovery that his strength was in his weakness, and Warren deals at length with the way Brown made his acceptance of final defeat into a triumph of the will: "His will and God's will were one, and that astounding egotism had discovered the last and absolute terms of its expression. He had rejected the world and gained it in that rejection. He was somebody, and his name was in the big print of all the newspapers" (415). In these final sections, we see why Brown fascinated the young Warren and took him beyond the simple polemic he might easily have written. Brown's ultimate assertion of the self takes the form of the greatest abnegation of self in the death of the martyr, but Warren leads us to see that there is a cost to the self in such identity. Brown, in his death, does transcend his own past as he rises to the level of symbol, but he does so at the cost of meaningful selfhood in time. When Warren treats the contemporary debates over the meaning of John Brown and his acts, he argues that Brown the man became lost in Brown the symbol: "John Brown was a cipher, a symbol, in this argument" (432). What sets Warren apart from his Agrarian counterparts even at this early stage of his career is that he is more interested in the problem of self-definition than in the "truth" of history—in fact, for Warren, the struggle for self-definition is the only truth history has to offer.

While Warren was completing *John Brown* in Oxford, he was also working on a short story, "Prime Leaf" (1931), which would develop into his first novel, *Night Rider* (1939); the deeper resonance of John Brown's story would soon be evident as Warren turned his focus to the question of Kentucky and the South. As Joseph Blotner writes, "John Brown's life had made Warren look back at his own origins and his homeland" (103). The connection was not that of North and South (defining each other by contrast) but the essential situation of the self in America, the terms of which were clarified in the context of the frontier. Here, whether in Brown's Kansas or the dark and bloody ground of Kentucky, individuals sought the promise of liberty and freedom, but the very absence of the constraints of traditional society unleashed darker impulses as well—one thing, indeed, might be done as well as another. The situation on the frontier, along with the naturalistic world it invokes—the cold, distant stars, the wind howling over vast distances, and the isolation of the self—is no special case but the human situation. William Bedford Clark points to the "dominant thematic tension that informs the whole range of his writing": "How do we assume the threatening burden of our liberty? In a society based on self-actualization, but subject itself to the exigencies of history and happenstance, how do we become ourselves?"[8] Warren's work on *John Brown* had its limitations, largely because of its polemical strain, but nonetheless it helped him begin to formulate his dominant concerns. Looking back on his work in the 1970s, Warren said in an interview, "The book was shot through with Southern defensiveness, and in my ignorance the psychological picture was presented too schematically. But even so, the work on the book was my real introduction into some awareness of the dark and tangled problem of motives and values."[9]

John Brown had finally avoided responsibility for his acts in his translation to the martyr, and Warren would continue to explore the issues of guilt and responsibility within history during his entire career. In *Night Rider* Warren turned to the recent past of Kentucky—the Black Patch Wars of 1905—and presents a protagonist, Percy Munn, caught up in the "just cause" of a tobacco growers' association as the work of that group moves from political and economic action to violence and bloodshed. Although John Brown's transfiguration in the public mind through the intercession of Emerson and the outcome of the Civil War prevented a real reckoning with the cost of his aims, the final brutality of the actors in *Night Rider* remains at the fore: "A failed revolution cannot conceal the darker forces it has unleashed, forces a successful revolutionary enterprise sublimates into acts of heroism and martyrdom" (Clark 79). Characters in *At Heaven's Gate* (1943) move in a world of modern media images—of false selves—as Warren continues to explore the split between public and private selves he had engaged in *John Brown*. The clearest parallel with Brown, however, comes with the story of Jeremiah Beaumont in *World Enough and Time* (1950). Beaumont, like Brown, holds to the purity of the idea and ends up driven to the murder of the all-too-human Colonel Fort in the name of his idealized beloved. Like Brown, he believes he has found the "act to redeem the world," but unlike Old Osawatomie, he is brought to recognize his complicity in the corruption he sought to transcend. Having escaped to the West, he makes the return so important in Warren's work and comes East again to "kiss the hangman's hand" in his acceptance of his guilt, rather than a translation into martyrdom (as with Brown). The pervasive theme of Warren's earliest volume of poetry, *Eleven Poems on the Same Theme* (1942), deals with the question of guilt as well, as figures are haunted by the specter of guilt, the "shadow self" in Victor Strandberg's Jungian terms that demands recognition.[10] This acceptance of guilt finds its greatest expression, of course, in Warren's masterwork, *All the King's Men* (1946), as Jack Burden comes to his recognition through the story of Cass Mastern at the book's core: "He learned that the world is like an enormous spider web and if you touch it, however lightly, at any point, the vibration ripples to the remotest perimeter and the drowsy spider feels the tinge and is drowsy no more but springs out to fling the gossamer coils about you who have touched the web and then inject the black numbing poison under your hide. It does not matter whether you meant to brush the web of things. Your happy foot or gay wing may have brushed it ever so lightly, but what happens always happens and there is the spider bearded black and with his great faceted eyes glittering like mirrors in the sun, or like God's eye, and the fangs dripping."[11] Burden only comes late (after the chain of deaths he unwittingly set in motion) to recognize the implications of Mastern's story for himself. In all of Warren's work, consequence rarely matches intention, and effects are always far reaching in a way the actor cannot conceive; the present is never free of the past and hence the future never free of the present. However one may try to escape it, there is an inevitable involvement with guilt. The only choice is the response of the actor to recognition of the fact; denial, for Warren, is tantamount to a death of the self.

Yet the imperative remains, for Warren, to act for self-definition, in spite of the cost. In the tension between the fact and the idea that runs throughout his work, he makes it clear that neither pole can be neglected. James Justus opens his study of Warren with an assessment of Warren's vision: "Put simply, that vision is an orthodox Christianity chastened and challenged by the secular faiths peculiar to the twentieth century: naturalism . . . and existentialism" (1). People must act for self-definition, and the individual's striving for identity through action in the "ruck of event" constitutes the human drama. That drama is not that of history itself, which Warren conceives to be the result of large forces converging in a pattern in itself devoid of objective meaning, but rather the drama of the self amid the blind forces of history. In *All the King's Men*, Jack refers to this condition as the "agony of will," which Justus glosses as "the human imperative to act in a world that apparently resists human shaping" (7). The forces impinging on people include the forces of both human history (war, economic change, and so on) and nonhuman history (such as floods and droughts); history in this sense, as L. Hugh Moore tells us in *Robert Penn Warren and History*, "is at best amoral and at worst destructive and evil; in itself it offers no redemption to man."[12] Though this judgment raises the specter of determinism, Warren's works constantly offer the reminder that, in Hugh Miller's words from *All the King's Men*, "history is blind, but man is not" (436). In what he considers the proper sense of the human lot, stated in the introduction to his edition of Melville's poems, "man must try to comprehend the density and equivocalness of experience, but at the same time he must not forfeit the ability to act" (25). The only meaning in history comes through action, though it inevitably carries the costs exacted by historical contingency; to gain this meaning "one must oppose one's will to the mechanical process of history" (Moore 66).

If we are faced with the strivings of the self in a history devoid of larger meaning, the question should be asked: Why turn to history at all? Why did Warren not move to a more purely existentialist position that could well render history irrelevant? Warren provides a dramatic answer repeatedly in his novels and poems: the self has its own history that is inextricably linked to human history. In *All the King's Men*, Jack Burden refers frequently to the various selves he has encountered, as when he prefaces a remark with "This Jack Burden (of whom the present Jack Burden, *Me*, is a legal, biological, and perhaps even metaphysical continuator)" (159) or suggests more humorously: "You might have a family reunion with barbecue under the trees. It would be interesting to know what they would say to each other" (129). Clearly summarizing the relationship for Warren between history and the self, Moore writes: "If history is a cosmic net, if all times are one time, if the future as well as the past exists in the present, then the individual self exists as a continuum of selves. Just as the future cannot be radically different than the past, new innocence is impossible. One must frame the future self by an understanding and acceptance of all the past selves, and this idea has a corollary that one must accept one's father, family, and heritage" (96). History serves as a reminder that the self is itself a historical entity, and it should serve as a rebuke (to use Warren's often repeated term) by reminding people in the present of the costs of self-definition, or the costs of the failure to attempt it. The past is "always a rebuke to the present," Warren said at the Fugitive's reunion at Vanderbilt in 1956: "It's a better rebuke than any dream of the future. It's a better rebuke because you can see what some of the costs were, what frail virtues were achieved in the past by frail men. And it's there, and you can see it, and see what it cost them, and how they had to go at it. . . . The drama of the past that corrects us in the drama of our struggles to be human, or our struggles to define the values of our forbears in the face of their difficulties" (Purdy 210). History, Warren holds, "keeps alive the human sense. . . . It's man's long effort to be human."[13]

Through his work on *John Brown*, Warren assumed the role of historian coming to terms with the effort of a historical figure to achieve self-definition. As Clark notes, "The youthful Warren studies Brown's 'texts' in a way that looks forward to Jack Burden's puzzling over the narrative of Cass Mastern . . . and the nameless historian-narrator's presentation of the journal of Jeremiah Beaumont in *World Enough and Time*" (38). The narrators in these novels, as well as the persona R. P. W. in Warren's book-length poem *Brother to Dragons* (1953), actively participate in the reconstruction of event, motive, and responsibility, and the historical effort itself becomes part of their self-definition. If the narrator maintains the cynical detachment of the modern (which is maintained in *John Brown*), he in effect refuses to recognize his kinship with the subject and shares in the error of characters like Brown, Jeremiah Beaumont, or Thomas Jefferson. Of *World Enough and Time*, Clark writes, "As the story of Jeremiah Beaumont unfolds, two powerful streams, the historical past and the lived present, converge and move inexorably toward a revelation and rebirth that is the equivalent of a religious conversion in which the 'sick soul' of a representative modern man, alienated, skeptical, and vulnerable, is made whole" (93). In *Brother to Dragons*, Thomas Jefferson is brought to recognize his share in human evil, but in the larger movement of the poem, R. P. W. "must struggle with the possibility of human virtue."[14] This movement—the reconciliation of fact and idea, naturalism and idealism— allows the possibility of joy: "Of some faith past our consistent failure / And the filth we strew." As Jefferson says, "We are condemned to some hope," a line Justus rightly claims could serve as a gloss on Warren's entire corpus.

Warren specifically addressed the question of the "use" of the past, the proper function of history, and the role of the artist in a series of lectures published as "The Use of the Past." He opens by pointing out the characteristic American "contempt for the past" and claims that "it can be argued that the lesson of the American past is that the past has no lesson and that the burden of American history is that history is, indeed, bunk."[15] The dynamics of the American relation to the past were established early on by the movement to the mythic West: the "movement westward was a perpetual baptism into a new innocence. . . . The dimension of space redeemed man from the dimension of time" (32). Our contempt for the past brings not liberation but a loss of selfhood and an inability to act meaningfully in the present, as Warren argued at the opening of *Democracy and Poetry*: "The contempt for the past means that the self we have is more and more a fictive self . . . for any true self is not only the result of a vital relation with a community but is also a development in time, and if there is no past there can be no self."[16] Further, this illusion of innocence has the potential to turn destructive in the life of the nation, as it does for Warren's individual protagonists. We have the illusion of being able to overcome evil, in the heart and in society, by an act of will and the application of knowledge: "The thread runs true from Emerson's drip-dry Christianity, with no Blood of the Lamb required, to B. F. Skinner's *Walden II*" (33).

The potential consequences of this illusory innocence, in the context of the Cold War and America's emergence as a superpower, are enormous indeed, and Warren draws on Reinhold Niebuhr's treatment of "the illusion of our innocence, virtue, and omnipotence" that covers even our most questionable actions on the world stage, from the Philippines in the Spanish-American War to Vietnam.[17] Warren uses a quotation from *John Brown* to illustrate this tendency to justification in the name of absolute right: "And if somebody points out that one hand is indeed in the cookie jar, we are likely to claim that that's clearly what God intended—as a reward for our righteousness. As Eli Thayer . . . put it in the 1850s: 'If a man does a good deed and makes money at the same time, it merely proves that his faculties are working in harmony'" (35). This identification of God's will with our own is precisely the fatal error of the idealist, and Warren takes the occasion of the Bicentennial to ask, "Are we ready to face that we may not, after all, be the Chosen People? . . . For what was once our future has now become our past—and that is the deepest irony of all, and the irony hardest for the child-mind to grapple with" (36).

As a corrective, Warren offers his vision of history as a rebuke to the present, a vision that allows individuals to emerge in their full humanity. The founders detached themselves from the immediate past but sought a continuity with the ancient past of Greece and Rome, and Warren asks: "When there is no vision, the people perish, and in that Edenic hour long ago, what would the vision of our future have been without the dynamism of our vision of the past?" (36). If we restrict our study of people, whether in history or the present, to the realm of mere fact, the province of the social scientist, Warren argues, "the idea of pondering the story of men as men, whether noble or vicious, will be replaced by the study of statistics of nonideographic units of an infinite series, and computers will dictate how such units, which strangely enough do breathe and move and rejoice and suffer, can best be manipulated for their own good" (37). Even if not in this radically reductionist form, there remains the dominant impulse to assert freedom from the past through the discovery of its laws, and Warren gives a brief catalog of such efforts to use the past to "break the bank of the future": "This is the perennial dream: to discover in the past the laws that govern human events, just as the scientist, by studying nature, discovers the laws that permit us to predict and control nature" (39). Beginning with the early example of Machiavelli, he mentions Darwin, Marx, and Freud, "great men who, like Machiavelli, tried to see the inner logic of the past—the biological past, the historical past, the psychological past—to look on the nakedness of the past without prurience or shame" (39). The end of this quotation points out the problem for Warren: the assumed detachment from the common lot of people in the name of the pure idea. "Brooding over History, like God" (to use Jack Burden's self-description), the philosophers of history construct their master narratives to control the future: "There have been many since Machiavelli who have sought to define the laws of history and thus break the bank of the future—Vico, Marx, Henry Adams, Buckle, Spengler, Toynbee, and even Yeats. . . . But the bank of the future remains unbroken" (39).

What Warren offers instead of the formulation of laws is at once much simpler and infinitely more complex. "The deepest value of history," he tells us, "keeps alive the sense that men have striven, suffered, achieved, and have been base or generous—have, in short, been men" (37). He draws on historian Arthur Schlesinger Jr.'s assertion that the gain from history is not a set of laws but "historical insight—a sense of the climate in which decisions are made, or what we may call the medium in which action is undertaken" (40). All the claims about history make assumptions, even if implicit, about human nature and the human condition, and Warren emphasizes the complexity of knowing the past or, by extension, the self: "Man's fate is double, an outer and an inner fate, the world that the self is in, and the self that is in the world. And more and more we see, painfully, that the two worlds are indissolubly linked and interpenetrating—mirror facing mirror, as it were" (38). The historian's work, seen in this light, is akin to that of the artist, giving us "an image of the soul confronting its fate" and a second image that is the work itself: "These two kinds of image, in their very doubleness, have a powerful appeal for us, first because we are all (though often unconsciously) inevitably concerned about our fate, and second, because our concern is itself twofold: we confront our fate and we confront ourselves in the act of confronting our fate" (46). The work can serve the same purpose as the materials that draw the narrator-historian of *World Enough and Time* or Jack Burden: "The shifting arcades and perspectives of being and fate, the wilderness of mirrors, the ever unfolding and fluctuating ratio of identity and difference—we need these things in all their increasing complexity if we are to pursue the never-ending task of knowing the self" (46).

Warren's perspective is grounded here, as in most of his work, by a fundamental concern with the loss of a viable selfhood in modern life. His makes the relevance of his message clear, in terms that echo the enduring critique of *I'll Take My Stand* many years before, when he states: "Now here is the point: at the very same time, we see, in the world of technology, the depersonalizing process growing apace, with *the constantly expanding destruction of the very concept of the responsible self*, and we also see the consequences of this process in a general malaise and in frequent eruptions of violence in every sector of life, from slum to university campus. The trouble is that man feels himself devalued, alienated, powerless—in short, he feels that he had been made into a 'thing'" (44; emphasis mine). Reductionist accounts of the self in the world—whether the "nonideographic units of an infinite series" of the social scientist or the self bound by the abstract necessity of historical laws—are particularly destructive in a society that was founded, so Warren argues, on the notion of the responsible self acting in history. Without this basis, the self in America, as well as its larger expression, the United States, becomes prone to acting destructively—because blindly—in the world: "The past makes us ask what we have done with our dazzling achievements—or what they have done with us. It makes us ask whether our very achievements are not ironical counterpoint and contrast to our fundamental failures" (45). What Warren argues for in the later portions of the essay is an adequate myth of the past that strengthens, rather than weakens, the self as responsible actor.

Myth, far from implying a lesser reality to history, is the route to what Warren holds is its only possible meaning. As Moore writes, "Because [Warren] believes . . . that the blind neutrality of history threatens human values, Warren feels that history requires a myth to accommodate it to man" (18). In *Jefferson*

Davis Gets His Citizenship Back (1980), one of his late works, Warren contemplates critically the need the Kentucky monument to Davis fulfills and the way a monument (or monumental history) serves only to distance us from the past it seeks to preserve, and he makes the same sort of point in "The Use of the Past." By recognizing history as myth, we lose the clarity of the simplified image but might recapture the complexity and density of the experience of the individual in history in the effort to "make the lying words stand for the old living truth" (24). In that sense, historical meaning is the True Lie, essential for viable selfhood in the present: "There is no absolute, positive past available to us, no matter how rigorously we strive to determine it—as strive we must. Inevitably, the past, so far as we know it, is an inference, a creation, and this, without being paradoxical, can be said to be its chief value for us. In creating the image of the past, we create ourselves, and without the task of creating the past we might barely be said to exist. Without it, we sink to the level of a protoplasmic swarm" (51). What Warren is arguing for here is not, as indicated above, a history of lessons—or, as it was for Simms, "philosophy teaching by example"—but something that returns us to "the density and equivocalness of experience." As Justus points out, Warren pushes toward "the responsibility to seek meaning in one's own complex nature rather than in the languor of the too easily received myth" (55). Warren, from *John Brown* forward, was only too aware of the mechanisms for self-justification (North, South, and universally) and warns against this sort of use of the past, arguing that it should be "the sovereign tonic for self-pity" (51). While the "past is, in fact, the great pantheon where we can all find the bearers of the values by which we could live. It gives us the image of a community and of a role, an identity, within that community, the image of a self to be achieved" (50); it also, properly approached, serves as the sort of rebuke outlined above. "If the past tells us anything," Warren writes, "it tells us that even the vision must be earned" (52). Through the recognition of the situation of humankind in the "agony of will" and the recognition of complicity, we may grope toward a different vision of ourselves: "Out of discipline, the artist, saint, scientist, and sage earn vision. And the same can be said of any of us who seeks as the highest achievement a vision of the significance of his own life, beyond all self pity" (52).

Warren's mature perspective on the use of the past is best illustrated by *The Legacy of the Civil War: Meditations on the Centennial*, which he gave as a lecture in 1961 and subsequently published as an independent volume. In it, we see the distance Warren had traveled from the polemical work of *John Brown*; the three intervening decades allowed Warren time to test his vision again and again in works of fiction and poetry, and with an "earned vision" of a far more subtle dialectic between history and the self. The observance of the Centennial, coming as it did in the early years of the civil rights movement, was bound up with contemporary political questions and led to much self-congratulation in the North and retrenchment in the South. The decision by state legislatures to incorporate the Confederate battle flag into state flags is only the most visible sign of this dynamic. Further, the 1960s seemed to threaten a repetition of the post-Reconstruction New South synthesis that, as we saw with Page, used the legacy of the Civil War for the consolidation of white supremacy and political control—all in the name of sectional harmony and national destiny. Warren, rather than staking out a position on the meaning of the event, turned instead to a consideration of the "massiveness of the experience" and the distortions of the historical image that allow the individual to evade historical responsibility and maintain the illusion of innocence.

Warren opens with the claim that "before the Civil War we had no history in the deepest and most inward sense," by which he means, as we see by the end, a tragic vision gained from history: "the image in action of the deepest questions of man's fate and man's attitude toward his fate" (270, 308). We had the promise of America from the Revolution, but "the vision had not been finally submitted to the test of history" (270). He prepares for his ultimate focus on the response of the individual to history by sketching some of the dominant issues in the discussion of the Civil War. In the realm of pragmatic history—of happenings—he lays out some of the consequences of the war: our unity as a nation, a change from an agrarian society to one of "Big Technology and Big Business," the unleashing of energies that resulted in expansion and confirmed destiny (most notably in the "winning of the West"), and the supremacy of the federal government. But all these facts veil the more fundamental legacy of the war, as Warren sees it: the individual's vision of him- or herself in history and the loss of the responsible self.

The most salutary effect of the war was the pragmatism that came to dominate American thought and politics after the war. It arose from necessity, with much of the impetus for it coming from the encounter with novel situations in the crisis, in the application of new strategies and technologies. Seen simply as a matter of expediency, pragmatism, for Warren, certainly has its darker side: the "total war" doctrine of the North (and with it the beginnings of modern warfare) and the rules of "Big Technology" and "Big Business" are certainly in keeping with strict focus on consequences in the judgment of right. But Warren has in mind a pragmatist's view of human life and action, a consideration of consequences rather than a strict appeal to abstract principle. As Warren notes, it is "an ethic that demands scrutiny of motive, context, and consequences, particularly the consequences to others. This kind of ethic, laborious, fumbling, running the risk of degenerating into expediency, finds its apotheosis in Lincoln" (281). Warren cites T. Harry Williams's assessment of Lincoln: "One of the keys to his thinking is his statement that few things in this world are wholly good or wholly bad. Consequently the position he took on specific political issues was always a pragmatic one. His personal or inner opinions were based on principle; his public or outer opinions were tempered by empiricism" (276).[18] If it is "a new name for an old way of thinking," it is so because it restores in some measure a sense of human limitation, fallibility, and the need for accommodation in an imperfect world. Pragmatism, Warren argues, was a reaction against two forms of absolutism: "We may call these two opposing absolutes 'higher law' and 'legalism'" (276). These were the tendencies, in both the North and the South, that rendered the sectional divide unbridgeable.

Warren's indictment of the "higher law" mentality remains unchanged from that found in *John Brown*. In fact, Warren draws heavily on his earlier work in the biography for his critique of those individuals who "claimed a corner on the truth by reason of divine revelation"—this is the error of people, like Brown and many of Warren's characters, who identify their own will with God's. "The man who is privy to God's will," Warren writes, "cannot long brook argument, and when one declines the arbitrament of reason, even because one seems to have all the reason and virtue on one's side, one is making ready for the arbitrament of blood" (276–77). Warren draws quotes from Brown, the journalist James Redpath, and Garrison to establish the link between a "higher law" mentality and violence. Warren explicitly acknowledges the justice of the abolitionists' cause (in stronger terms than he had years earlier) but still reaches the same conclusion: "But who can fail to be disturbed and chastened by the picture of the joyful mustering of the darker forces of our nature in that just cause" (278). The larger question Warren raises here is one of "the right relation between intellect and society," or to put it into other terms, between history and the self, since the self in history is bound up with other selves, as Cass Mastern, Jack Burden, Jeremiah Beaumont, and others so painfully discovered. The "higher law" individual "must ultimately, deny the very concept of society" because of its inherent limitation of the self. The intellectuals, "having lost access to power and importance in the world of affairs, . . . repudiated all the institutions in which power is manifested—church, state, family, law, business," and turned instead to the purity of the idea and the beckoning image of the self unbound by history, society, fact, "For all things were equally besmirched and besmirching to the ineffable and quivering purity" (279). The men of letters, seeking a role, sought a solution—an assertion of the word—that would not involve them with the messiness of reform, and slavery presented the possibility of the absolute, uncompromising solution: "One could demand the total solution, the solution of absolute morality; one could achieve the apocalyptic *frisson*" (280). "Conscience without responsibility," Warren writes, "this is truly the last infirmity of a noble mind" (281). Taken on this basis of titanic selfhood abstracted from social and historical context, selfhood becomes a grotesque: "In other words, man as a total abstraction, in the pure blinding light of total isolation, alone with the Alone, narcissism raised to the infinite power" (280).

Thus far we are fairly on the ground of Warren's earlier critique of abolition, but through his career Warren had realized that absolutism and destructive idealism were very American traits with northern and southern variants. Instead of the picture of the Old Dominion plantation society, with its balanced, traditional view of life, as Warren used it in the final portion of *John Brown*, here he characterizes the southern view of life as static, in line with the standard account of the closure of the southern mind. But he extends that critique further by charging that the closure of the southern mind amounted to a denial of life itself. "Southerners," Warren tells us, "did not deny the concept of society. But the version of society which these egregious logicians deduced so logically from their premises denied, instead, the very concept of life. It denied life in its defense, anachronistic and inhuman, of bondage. It denied life also, and in a sense more viciously, in its refusal to allow, through the inductive scrutiny of fact, for change, for the working of the life process through history" (282). Warren here goes well beyond a simple critique of efficacy or adequacy, such as the critiques mounted earlier by Tate; in fact, he is closer to W. J. Cash and his "savage ideal" or to the awareness of the life-denying character of the Old South as expressed by Tate through the consciousness of Lacy Buchan in *The Fathers*.

Pragmatism, for Warren, was the reaction against these two forms of absolutism, but the danger of pragmatism as the dominant ethos of a people is complacency and a tendency toward expediency. Absolutism certainly can be destructive, but human life, as Warren sees it, is a dialectic between the fact and the idea—to ignore the latter is to lose our vision of human possibilities. The ethic of personal absolutism "gives us the heroic, charged images that our hearts and imaginations strenuously demand," and Warren, significantly, uses the example of John Brown on the scaffold as one of his instances of this sort of image: "[Personal absolutism] even gives us the image of John Brown abstracted from his life and from history, standing at the scaffold and drawing a pin from the lapel of his coat and offering it to the executioner to use in adjusting the hood. Such images survive everything—logic, criticism, even fact if fact stands in the way. They generate their own values. For men need symbols for their aspirations" (281). The decline of selfhood in the modern state is perhaps a greater danger to the self than distortions arising from idealism, and Warren raises the question, "Is it possible for the individual, in the great modern industrial state, to retain some sense of responsibility? Is it possible for him to remain an individual?" (287). Here is where history can and must function as a rebuke to the present, and the Civil War, as the primary source of our modern nation: "We sense that one way, however modest, to undertake this mandatory task of our time is to contemplate the Civil War itself, that mystic cloud from which emerged our modernity" (287). History, though, is no panacea because, as Warren sees it, it is not self-interpreting and subject to all manner of distortions, particularly those arising from the "hidden needs" of the self in its desire for justification. Warren finds the primary legacy of the war in two variants of this misuse of history. The victory, as all victories, had its costs, and Warren turns his attention from the those of blood and treasure to "a kind more subtle, pervasive, and continuing, a kind that conditions in a thousand ways the temper of American life today. This cost is psychological, and it is, of course, different for the winner and loser. To give things labels, we may say that the War gave the South the Great Alibi and gave the North the Treasury of Virtue" (289).

In the case of the South, the end of the war meant entrapment in history. As with Simms, history happened to the South with defeat and Reconstruction, but the entrapment came as a result not of the events themselves but of the response of southerners to them. Early on, Warren tells us that though the war undid the Confederacy, it made the South more southern: "The Confederacy became a City of the Soul, beyond the haggling of constitutional lawyers, the ambition of politicians, and the jealousy of localisms" (274). Viewing the Lost Cause as a redemptive history, any act of impiety would be a betrayal of that City of the Soul and the self founded on its myth. "By the Great Alibi," Warren writes,

> the South explains, condones, and transmutes everything. . . . Even now, any common lyncher becomes a defender of the Southern tradition, and any rabble-rouser the gallant leader of a thin gray line of heroes. . . . Pellagra, hookworm, and illiteracy are all explained, or explained away, and mortgages are converted into badges of distinction. Laziness becomes the aesthetic sense, blood-lust rising from a matrix of boredom and resentful misery becomes a high sense of honor, and ignorance becomes divine revelation. By the Great Alibi, the Southerner . . . turns defeat into victory, defects into virtues. Even more pathetically, he turns his great virtues into absurdities—sometimes vicious absurdities. (290)

So far is Warren from writing in the mode of southern apologetics, he establishes a new position here in the line of Walter Hines Page, Mencken, and W. J. Cash, writing of "he" rather than the embattled "we." In this passage, Warren reaches back for a critique of the South that could have been written any time from about, say, 1880 to the present, as though to make it painfully clear (to himself as much as anyone else) that the flesh had indeed been mortified, the old posture of defensiveness put to rest. The guise of the critic firmly in place (and thus the right relation of intellect and society reestablished), Warren brings out the upshot of the legacy of the war for southerners in the 1960s: "As he hears his own lips parroting the sad clichés of 1850, does the Southerner sometimes wonder if the words are his own? . . . Does he ever realize that the events of Tuscaloosa, Little Rock, and New Orleans are nothing more than an obscene parody of the meaning of his history? . . . Can the man howling in the mob imagine General R. E. Lee, CSA, shaking hands with Orval Faubus, Governor of Arkansas?" (290–91). He can even go so far as to echo his Agrarian essay "The Briar Patch," but in the clear context of an earned vision: "Does he ever consider the possibility that whatever degree of dignity and success a Negro achieves actually enriches, in the end, the life of the white man and enlarges his own worth as a human being?" (291).

The northern version of the psychological cost of the war—the Treasury of Virtue—is the more dangerous, as Warren sees it, for being more seemingly innocent and far more pervasive in our national life. "If the Southerner, with his

Great Alibi, feels trapped by history," Warren argues, "the Northerner, with his Treasury of Virtue, feels redeemed by history, automatically redeemed. He has in his pocket . . . an indulgence, a plenary indulgence, for all sins past, present, and future, freely given by the hand of history" (291). This is the dangerous innocence that is Warren's most persistent concern throughout his career, but here it is made all the more dangerous by seeming to have historical confirmation in the outcome of the Civil War. In spite of all the facts that complicate any effort to render the war a "consciously undertaken crusade," the need for justification, for purity, overrides the resistant facts that might offer a rebuke to those in the present: "From the start America has had adequate baggage of self-righteousness and Phariseeism, but with the Civil War came grace abounding, for the least of sinners" (293). The Treasury of Virtue covers the national sins; foremost among these, Warren writes, is the "Big Sell-Out of the Negro" after the war, a particularly grievous sin given the connection of African American freedom to the Treasury of Virtue itself. Regardless of omissions, the conviction of virtue was reinforced by the increasing prosperity of the country, and "prosperity was clearly a reward for virtue. In fact, prosperity *was* virtue" (295). On the international level, this sense of national innocence and confirmed virtue leads to the irony of our historical situation, the disparity between our sense of ourselves and the perception of the United States abroad: "From the first, Americans had a strong tendency to think of their land as the Galahad among the nations, and the Civil War, with its happy marriage of victory and virtue, has converted this tendency into an article of faith nearly as sacrosanct as the Declaration of Independence. . . . But moral narcissism is a particularly unlovely and unlovable trait" (296). This point leads Warren, as it did in *John Brown*, to a consideration of responsibility because the illusion of innocence allows irresponsible action—the righteous actor does not have to consider consequences. As Warren writes, "The American, in his conviction of righteousness, may be, on some occasions, morally unassailable, but for reasons that may also make him politically irresponsible" (297). To render our acts on the world stage commensurate with our story of ourselves, we are forced to lie, "lie to ourselves and transmute the lie into a kind of superior truth" (297). Though Warren does not make the parallel explicit, we are in danger of becoming the John Brown, rather than the Galahad, of the nations—the John Brown of whom one figure in Warren's biography said, "Whether the enterprise of John Brown . . . was wise or foolish, right or wrong . . . John Brown himself is right" (431).

With this awareness of how the use of history can serve the purposes of justification, Warren returns to a consideration of the war and its actors, beyond those needs. "The Great Alibi and the Treasury of Virtue both serve deep needs of poor human nature, and if, without historical realism and self-criticism, we look back on the War, we are merely compounding the old inherited delusions which our weakness craves. We fear, in other words, to lose the comforting automatism of the Great Alibi and the Treasury of Virtue," Warren writes. Susceptible though the war is to reduction, it continues to draw us with a power not explained by the simplified narratives of justification: "The event stands there larger than life, massively symbolic in its inexhaustible and sibylline significance. Significances, rather, for it is an image of life, and as such, is a condensation of many kinds of meanings. There is no one single meaning appropriate to our occasion, and that portentous richness is one of the things that make us stare at the towering event" (299). Drawn by the "need to understand ourselves," we find in the war "a gallery of great human images for our contemplation . . . a dazzling array of figures, noble in proportion yet human, caught out of time as in a frieze, in stances so profoundly touching or powerfully mythic that they move us in a way no mere consideration of 'historical importance' ever could" (300). Far from calling for the simple debunking (or even vilification) that would become popular in revisionist circles after the sixties, Warren presents these figures as answering our need for glory: "That was our Homeric period, and the figures loom up a little less than gods, but even so, we recognize the lineaments and passions of men, and by that recognition of common kinship, share in their grandeur" (300). The Civil War answers our need because we recognize the deep divisions within ourselves in a way we cannot with the Revolution, which (in the "somewhat unhistorical" understanding) "lacks inner drama. We never think, for instance, of Washington or Jefferson caught in the dark inner conflicts such as those of Lincoln or Lee or Stonewall Jackson experienced. If Washington brooded in the night at Valley Forge, his trouble was not of that order" (300). While we tend to read the Revolution in terms of black and white, the Civil War forces upon us the awareness of complexity, division, and turmoil, since, Warren claims, civil war is the "prototype of all war":

> For in the persons of fellow citizens who happen to be the enemy, we
> meet again, with the old ambivalence of love and hate and with all the old
> guilts, the blood brothers of our childhood. In a civil war—especially in

one such as this when the nation shares deep and significant convictions and is not a mere handbasket of factions huddled arbitrarily together by historical happen-so—all the self-divisions of conflicts within individuals become a series of mirrors in which the plight of the country is reflected, and the self-division of the country a great mirror in which the individual may see imaged his own deep conflicts, not only the conflicts of political loyalties, but those more profoundly personal. (300–301)

Only when we are driven back on ourselves and forced to confront images of frail human beings in an "agony of will" can we begin to work toward a more adequate self-definition, by means of a vision of "a strength somehow earned out of inner turmoil" (303).

As Warren reminds us in "The Use of the Past," recognition involves difference as well as similarity, and the differences between ourselves and the actors in the war carry much of the rebuke. Much as these figures shared our modern predicament of internal division and the radical shift in scale that threatens the individual, they did not succumb to acedia, the deadness of soul that leads to the failure of action. Warren writes, "For we must remember that those men, from conflict to conflict, rose to strength. From complication they made the cutting edge of action. They were, in the deepest sense, individuals; that is, by moral awareness they had achieved, in varying degrees, identity. In our age of conformity, of 'other-directedness,' of uniformity and the gray flannel suit, of personality created by the charm school . . . how nostalgically, how romantically, we look back on those powerful and suggestive images of integrity" (303). Warren is not calling here for a simple mimicking of noble actions but rather a recovery of the context of action and the costs of self-definition, to which the twentieth century is too often blind. Instead of seeking the "obscene gratifications of history" in the pursuit of justification or ignoring history altogether, he asks, "What happens if, by the act of historical imagination—the historian's and our own— we are transported into the documented, re-created moment of the past and, in a double vision, see the problems and values of that moment and those of our own, set against each other in mutual criticism and clarification?" (306). Such an act, he argues, might help to determine "the limits of responsibility" in experience and help us "to understand, even to frame, the logic of experience to which we shall submit" (307).

Such an understanding is imperative for Warren at any time, but particularly in the prolonged crisis of the Cold War that provides the context for his address. Confronted at home by questions of social justice and abroad by the problem of the responsible exercise of power on the world stage, we are confronted by one enormous question that is fundamental to our experience: "To what extent is man always—or sometimes—trapped in the great texture of causality, of nature and history? Most of us are not metaphysicians and do not often consider the questions abstractly, but as men, we know that our 'felt' answer to it, the answer in our guts, gives the tone to our living and conditions the range and vigor of our actions" (307). Here is precisely where history, and particularly the Civil War, can be of greatest value, for it "does not bring this question to us abstractly" but in human life and action, in the "unique facts of the irrevocable past" (307). The Cold War raises, as the Civil War did, the most pressing question, "Can differences be resolved by compromise?"—if not, Warren asks, "When do we start shooting?" Recalling Hugh Miller's dictum in *All the King's Men* that "history is blind, but man is not," Warren raises the question of responsible action in the face of the blind forces of history: "Can we, in fact, learn only that we are victims of nature and of history? Or can we learn that we can make, or at least have a hand in the making of, our future?" (307). "We are living," he tells us, "not only in a time of national crisis but in a time of crucial inspection of the nature and role of the individual. And so the Civil War draws us as an oracle, darkly riddled and portentous, of personal, as well as national, fate" (308).

The Civil War, of course, does not provide the answers to these questions, but rightly approached, Warren argues, it can provide the "feel for the medium," as he called it in "The Use of the Past." Instead of historical laws or lessons, the contemplation of history leads us back to the tragic vision of man, which Warren uses "in its deepest significance": "the image in action of the deepest questions of man's fate and man's attitude toward his fate" (308). The Civil War, because of its scope and nature, offers us the possibility of restoring the tragic sense, which modernity has made increasingly difficult to retain: "For the Civil War is, massively, that. It is the story of a crime of monstrous inhumanity, into which almost innocently men stumbled; of consequences which could not be trammeled up, and of men who entangled themselves more and more vindictively and desperately until the powers of reason were twisted and their very virtues perverted; of a climax drenched with blood but with nobility gleaming ironically, and redeemingly, through the murk; of a conclusion in which, for the participants at least, there is a reconciliation by human recognition" (308). Melville had hoped,

Warren tells us, that the war, by the magnitude of the suffering and death it inflicted, might have adequately taught us "pity and terror," in the proper function of tragedy. But Warren responds to Melville's hope with his insistence, shown by the intervening century, that the tragic vision must be won, the story retold in a way that forbids pride or self-pity: "Beyond the satisfaction it may give to rancor, self-righteousness, spite, pride, spiritual pride, vindictiveness, armchair blood lust, and complacency, we can yet see in the Civil War an image of the powerful, painful, grinding process by which an ideal emerges out of history. That should teach us humility beyond the Great Alibi and the Treasury of Virtue, but at the same time, it draws us to the glory of the human effort to win meaning from the complex and confused motives of men and the blind ruck of event" (310). Warren's case is compelling, but he would not be the one to retell the war, though he would approach it in prose meditations and his novel *Wilderness* (1961). Recapturing the massiveness and tragic force of the war would be the work of another artist, a younger Mississippian named Shelby Foote. In fact, at the time of Warren's address, Foote was already one volume into his three-volume narrative of the war, a narrative that would accomplish in prose what Warren could only prescribe.

6

"THE CONFLICT IS BEHIND ME NOW"

Shelby Foote Writes the Civil War

Even early in his career, Shelby Foote did not share the Agrarians' urge to defend the South. Beginning his career as a writer during World War II, he combined Allen Tate's high-modernist devotion to art with Walker Percy's ironic assessment of the southern tradition. As a descendant of an aristocratic Mississippi Delta family long since declined, Foote knew the feeling of dispossession, but he had a chance the young Fugitives lacked to estimate the limitations of the southern tradition, even in one of its finest latter-day incarnations: the household of William Alexander Percy. Whereas the aesthetic confines of the Fugitive coterie were disturbed by the ideological turbulence of the 1930s, Foote, living amid the relative political consensus at midcentury, came of age utterly devoted to art, following after the great models of Joyce, Faulkner, and Proust. The Agrarians had turned aside from art to the realm of history in order to say something about that history and its meaning; Foote, with no polemical urge driving him, remained devoted to modernism as something approaching a religion, accepted his detachment from the past, and was buoyed by a faith in art to create a reality superior to any present. In his great achievement, *The Civil War: A Narrative* (1958–74), this devotion allows Foote to craft not a commentary about the war but a re-creation of it. He uses the means of modernist art to create a medium wherein the war itself can play out in the reader's consciousness. Meaning, in professional history and in the histories and biographies of the Agrarians, still resided in the judgment of the historian about the happenings in the realm of pragmatic history; meaning for Foote resides in the work itself. Form, for Foote and the great modernists, *is* meaning rather than simply an organizing device, and he constructs a highly structured narrative that contains the force of lived experience, bringing the multiple, competing voices and heterogeneous facts of the war into a narrative controlled by a single voice. Where Warren and Tate could find a viable use of the past only by placing southern history in a radically different context—existentialism for Warren and religious orthodoxy for Tate—Foote moves more deeply into it to capture a sense of "how it was." He re-creates the war in words and through the reader's experience allows the catharsis of pity and fear that Warren could only prescribe in his *Legacy*.

Born in Greenville, Mississippi, in 1916, Foote had a lifelong sense of himself as a Deltan combined with a critical detachment from his familial and regional past; he tended toward irony rather than piety. Unlike Faulkner's Gail Hightower—whose inheritance he shared to a certain extent—he could simultaneously see the ridiculous and the sublime in the past and view each with equal eye. Foote's inheritance in the Delta provided him with a clear sense of the old plantation order as a fragile thing: a series of fortunes quickly made and quickly lost rather than an abiding order. His grandfather on one side, Huger Foote, had come to the Delta from the Black Prairie country to the east, sent by his father to manage four newly acquired plantations after the Civil War; he had prospered and bought his favorite of the four places, only to sell it later, move to Greenville, and lose his money at a card table. His maternal grandfather, Morris Rosenstock, was a Viennese Jew who had immigrated to the United States and the Delta and come into a plantation by first working as a bookkeeper for the owner, then marrying his daughter. Foote, born into the middle-class family of a businessman, was well aware of the boom-and-bust history of the Delta; as he later wrote, "Both of my grandfathers were worth close to a million dollars in the course of their lives; they barely had the money to dig the holes to put them in when they died."[1] Foote's isolation from this tradition was heightened by the fact that not only had his father been forced into business (rather than the more patrician alternative of the law), but he died when Foote was only seven. His son had only the remnants and, like Tate, had heard the stories of a lost past and was led to assess the reasons for its failure. But Foote was closer to the reality than was Tate, who was left to visualize the Tidewater from the distance of Kentucky; Foote grew up a generation after him, and he had the Jewish inheritance of his grandfather to provide an additional measure of detachment. More realistic, he was less sparing in his assessment of the old order. Speaking later of Faulkner's lack of knowledge (as a hillman) of the planter aristocracy, he says, "Faulkner knew almost nothing about the planter aristocracy, or any other kind of aristocracy. . . . I come from a long line of planter aristocrats . . . and if that is aristocracy, we are bad off."[2] If the Delta provided, as Foote said on several occasions, the hero of his fiction, the planter provided the villain; however much Foote admired the planters' ambition and discipline, honor and manners, he saw them as maintaining their position and power in the South through a peculiar sleight of hand, saying (in effect) if you follow my lead "someday you will be in my position and you will be allowed to do as I do" (qtd. in White and Sugg 12). What seemed, then, to be achieved through personal merit and noblesse oblige was in reality achieved through an implicit knavery, at least in Foote's eyes.

Foote had ample opportunity to test the validity of his judgment against not only the experience of his own family but also perhaps the finest example of a latter-day planter-aristocrat the Delta had to offer, William Alexander Percy. Not that Percy was typical, but a young man growing up in his presence might have been tempted to use his example as Page had used that of Lee: justifying the civilization or social order simply by pointing to the fact it had produced such a man. Foote returned to Greenville with his mother shortly after the great flood of 1927, a crisis that provided the centerpiece to Percy's memoir *Lanterns on the Levee* (1941), and soon found himself asked to provide companionship to Percy's orphaned cousins, including Walker Percy. Percy's household in Greenville provided a cultural center, filled as it was with artists, journalists, academics, and politicians (though only a touch of the last) at all times of the year. It was as extraordinary as the poet-lawyer-planter-war hero who presided over it, a man Walker Percy later described as "a personage, a presence" and "a fixed point in a confusing world." To know him, Percy claims, "was to encounter a complete, articulated view of the world as tragic as it was noble," and Walker was not given to romantic flights of rhetoric.[3] In *Lanterns*, Percy provided the requiem for a dying order of plantation life in the South, an order of aristocratic responsibility for one's dependents (including sharecroppers) and community, of resistance to race-baiting demagogues and the KKK; of culture, grace, refinement, and personal integrity. More important, he lived as the incarnation of that ideal, however flawed in conception, and provided the model of one response—the Stoic's—to modernity and civilizational change; amid the decline of one's civilization, with the bottom rail (poor whites, for Percy, not blacks) rapidly on its way to the top, one reads Livy and the Emperor and listens to Brahms, acts according to duty, and maintains a strict integrity in the wintry kingdom of the self.[4] Both Foote and Walker Percy had to struggle with the legacy of William Alexander Percy, and both found it powerful but lacking. There was an undeniable integrity in Percy's life, but it failed to offer a viable alternative to the tensions of life in the mid-twentieth century; much as Tate before them, they sought out the seeds of the failure of the plantation order within it, rather than from pressures brought to bear from without. As White and Sugg write: "[Foote] shared with Percy preoccupations with the aristocratic past and could see Percy as an earnest of its reality or at least of its unrealized potential. He, too, registered the dark of modernity. He tended to regard this, however, rather as the legacy of deficiencies in early plantation society rather than as the world of contemporary Yahoos, whose condition was after all part of the legacy" (10). On social questions, Foote tended to side with another figure who participated in the Percy household, Hodding Carter, and indeed he worked for his progressivist newspaper after dropping out of the University of North Carolina in 1938. Not that he shared Carter's reformist zeal by any means, but he knew that the social and economic questions of the age required a hard-nosed realism. Later, Foote would say of his relationship with Percy, "I differ with Mr. Will in almost every view he has of the planter aristocracy, of the rednecks of the hills, and of the position of the blacks—he and I would have fallen out almost certainly if we'd allowed ourselves to overtheorize about society and what's good and what's bad."[5] The primary legacy of William Alexander Percy for Foote, as for Walker Percy, was an acceptance of the contradictions in the southern tradition. Writing to Walker about the futility of attempts to capture what Percy had been in life, he asked, "How could you combine the incidental petulance— mainly a boundless capacity for outrage—with the enormous compassion?"[6] Faced with Percy's undeniable virtues, Foote early had to temper his inclination toward cynicism and gained a valuable lesson in seeing greatness and frailty with equal eye. He could, as Walker had it, come to understand a view of the world "as tragic as it was noble" in human terms, without falling prey to sentimentality or abstraction.

William Alexander Percy also opened a new possibility for Foote, as he did for Walker: the life of a writer. Here was a practicing, well-received poet and man of letters whose house was one of the necessary stopping points on any literary pilgrimage to the South. In addition to the other prominent Greenville artists, such as Hodding Carter, the composer Kenneth Haxton, and his wife, Josephine (Ellen Douglas), any number of other writers, southern and northern alike, came by the house to pay their respects, among them Faulkner, Carl Sandburg, Langston Hughes, and Stark Young. Perhaps Percy's greatest contribution—

by both his own example and the literary household he maintained—to the two young men was simply the sense that one could *be* a writer, wholly and unapologetically. Percy identifies his debt to his elder cousin: "I know what I gained: a vocation and in a real sense a second self; that is, the work and the self which, for better or worse, would not otherwise have been open to me" (55); in Foote's case, this sense of vocation would run much deeper, never being diluted by an aborted medical career. Writing for Foote would be a religion, followed according to the rule of the great modern masters of the order.

Foote's calling was as a priest, not of the order of Melchizedek but of Flaubert, Joyce, Faulkner, Lawrence, and Proust. When he encountered *David Copperfield* at age twelve, Foote "suddenly got aware that there was a world, if anything, more real than the real world," and he would feel himself a citizen of that world from his high school days on, after encountering the great modernists. His mother gave him a set of Proust's *Remembrance of Things Past* when he was seventeen, and Foote recalls that he paid little attention in school afterward, at least in the classroom. Foote's time at Chapel Hill amounted to a private education through reading in the stacks, supplemented by the occasional course in literature and history; he continued writing critical pieces there and began a novel after withdrawing and returning to Greenville in the late thirties, where he worked odd jobs and wrote for Hodding Carter II's *Delta Democrat Times*. He drafted his first novel, *Tournament*, in 1939 and submitted it to Knopf, only to have it rejected, albeit with praise, as overly influenced by Joyce and Wolfe. Upon his return from service in World War II, Foote succeeded in publishing his first story, "Flood Burial," in the *Saturday Evening Post* and began to make enough money from publishing to devote himself to writing full-time, resulting in the publication of *Tournament* in 1949 and a draft of his second novel, *Follow Me Down*, the same year.[7] Foote's letters to Percy during this period reveal his sense of vocation and utter devotion to art, perhaps heightened a bit to contrast with his friend's Catholicism. Writing of artists as the "outriders for the saints; we go beyond (where they won't go)," Foote makes it clear that art for him is a form of piety, but of a peculiarly Promethean sort: "If we burn for that, we'll take pride in our burning, our pain; the triumph wont be God's."[8] Art is "an act of devotion beyond prayer," and its serves its own purposes, not those of the moralist, preacher, or social reformer. Foote's artistic ideals are those of the modernists: attention to form, with art as the "organization of experience"; the communication of sensation rather than the delivery of a message; and, above all, Proust's "quality of vision." As he wrote to Percy in 1950, "I think I know at last what it is that I really want. I want to teach people how to *see*. I want to impart to them a 'quality of vision' (Proust's definition of style)."[9] Foote's view of the artist—of himself as artist—and his place in a later generation served to distance him from polemical warfare (though the turmoil of the civil rights era would soon catch his attention) and to strengthen his belief that his highest purpose was served simply by writing fiction, not by turning aside for a role more in the public forum. "The novel is the one bright book of life," Lawrence wrote in one of Foote's favorite dicta, and Foote saw no need to step down from that higher stratum of experience either to defend the South or to reform it.[10]

Not that he was unconcerned with the South—far from it; his fiction, like Faulkner's, has been concerned from the start with his own "postage stamp" of soil in Washington County, Mississippi (Jordan County in the novels). In his first novel, *Tournament*, the young narrator, Asa Bart, attempts to understand his grandfather, who came, like Huger Foote, to the Delta as a young man.[11] As with Faulkner or Warren, the novel is not a historical novel proper but a treatment of the narrator's attempt to come to terms with the past. In the character of Hugh Bart, Foote explores the belief he would continue to hold that character must create the dramatic situation. Bart's restless ambition and his mistaken object in the forms of the plantation ideal lead ultimately to his downfall, which, while not spectacular, is decisive. The larger implied perspective on the plantation aristocracy in the Delta reveals a respect for the virtues of the plantation order—strength of character, drive, and dignity—but also an awareness of its faults, particularly its tendency to accept ossified forms instead of allowing for growth and change. The more important point here, though, is the distance between a southerner coming of age in the twentieth century and the tradition preceding him; Asa Bart by the end of the novel still has to confess his inability to know his grandfather. The central image of this loss of the past—a failure of cultural memory—is to be found in the novel's central section, which would be published separately as "Flood Burial." Major Barcroft, a Civil War veteran and amateur historian, dies during a Mississippi flood and is buried by Hugh Bart in a trunk containing thousands of ruined manuscript pages of his Civil War history; this section provides, as Phillips notes, "a telling Proustian image of a modern world that has lost touch with its past."[12] *Follow Me Down*, albeit in another form, also centers on the difficulty of ascertaining the truth of a past event—in this case a murder—and uses a more experimental framework, with multiple narrators of varying degrees of knowledge and engagement, but Foote's greatest effort to re-create the past in novel form came with *Shiloh* (1952).

Shiloh was one of three novels Foote planned to write about western battles during the Civil War; he completed it in 1948 (though it would not be published until 1952) and planned a similar work on Brice's Crossroads before moving to a major work on the Vicksburg campaign. Foote took on the Civil War novels largely as a technical challenge—the attempt to capture the totality of a single battle without any overarching narrative voice to provide continuity or coherence—and the experience would serve him well when he came to write his Civil War narrative. The novel has seven sections told in the voice of different combatants—northern and southern, officers and enlisted—and limited to their perspective; it builds in cumulative force as the patterns of the larger battle emerge from the chaotic experience of the individual soldiers. The book is unified not by a narrative line but by common incidents in the various narratives— the same maneuver or event seen from multiple perspectives—the topography and climate all the combatants share, and, most important, the unseen hand that determines the careful structure of the work. As a work of Foote's self-called experimental phase, *Shiloh* provided an opportunity to experiment in recapturing experience by mingling fact and fiction, but the lessons would hold when Foote turned to history proper. In fact, the connection is made explicit when two of Foote's combatants (Union enlisted men) meditate on the writing of history and how to capture the massiveness of the experience of war. One focuses on the inadequacy of traditional battle histories that portray events in a manner far removed from the men doing the fighting; the writers of these histories, in their omniscience and hindsight, miss the confused perspective of the soldiers: "no one but God ever saw it that way." He holds that "a book about war, to be read by men, ought to tell what each . . . of us saw in our own little corner. Then it would be the way it was—not to God but to us." Such is essentially the approach taken by Foote in his novel, and while it is a strength of a novel, another character points out its limitations as history: "Nobody would do it that way. It would be too jumbled. People when they read, and people when they write, want to be looking out of that big Eye in the sky, playing God."[13]

The writing of *Shiloh* proved something of a watershed for Foote. His research had taken him deep into the primary documents concerning the battle, as well as the historical scholarship. He had visited the battlefield several times and consulted park historians to get a better feel for the land, climate, and actual locations of events on the landscape. Foote began to establish himself not simply as a *litterateur* dabbling in historical subject matter but as a historical authority in his own right; the province of the writer extended to historiography as well as fiction, provided one put in the necessary hours of research, and the awareness of this fact would lead him to challenge the separation of the spheres insisted on by many professional historians (and some professional writers, for that matter). In "The Novelist's View of History," Foote would assert the traditional prerogative of the writer as man of letters, one that recalls the words of William Gilmore Simms: "Both [the honest novelist and the honest historian] are seeking the same thing: the truth—not a different truth: the same truth—only they reach it, or try to reach it, by different routes. Whether the event took place in a world now gone to dust, preserved by documents to be evaluated by scholarship, or in the imagination, preserved by memory to be distilled by the creative process, they both want to tell us *how it was:* to recreate it, by their separate methods, and to make it live again in the world around them."[14] There is a "basic difference" in method, of course: "the historian attempts this by communicating facts, whereas the novelist would communicate sensation. The one stresses action, the other *re*-action. And yet the two are not hermetically sealed off from one another." But Foote insists the advantage adheres to the creative writer, particularly on the basic matter of style and handling dramatic structure, provided the writer does not use artistic license to violate the facts; most important, the novelist is disciplined to showing rather than telling.

The turning point of Foote's career came in the early 1950s, when he left the novel and committed himself to the two-decade project of writing the Civil War. He had completed his three-book apprenticeship phase with *Love in a Dry Season* and embarked on an experimental period with the publication of *Shiloh* and work on *Child by Fever.*[15] His confidence reached titanic proportions. By 1951, he was laying plans for his "big book," *Two Gates to the City,* and feeling his powers, proclaiming to Percy in 1952: "Stand by: I'll tell you true—I'm going to be one of the greatest writers who ever lived."[16] But the next month would see Foote in a crisis, following on the heels of his second divorce; he sensed, in Phillips's words, that "the pattern for his life would not fit." Foote wrote at the time, "I touched absolute bottom; then I came back up. Man, it's dark down there."[17] Following one of his great models, Dostoevsky, he learned the value of suffering to the artist and continued to write his great, "black" novel, but fate would intervene and open a distinctly different path to greatness than that followed by the great modern novelists. Preparations for the Civil War Centennial were gearing up, and publishers were preparing to feed the public appetite with hundreds of books concerning the conflict. J. Bennett Cerf of Random House, on the historical strength of *Shiloh*, offered Foote a contract for a short history of the Civil War aimed at the mass market. Foote agreed but quickly found that the scope of the projected work well outran the length proposed; he was able to outline three volumes and made Cerf the offer of a multivolume history, which was accepted. Here was the heir of Flaubert, Joyce, and Proust voluntarily abandoning his privileged position as artist to commit a significant portion of his career to a history, placing himself between the Sylla of the academic historians and the Charybdis of the fickle public. As novelist George Garrett points out in a review of the final volume, "The chances for loss, the risks involved, were staggering."[18] The other figures we have looked at over the course of this study all turned to history as an exercise in piety and polemic to various degrees; Foote would write, as he always did, for art and the truth that art alone can reveal.

Foote's title, *The Civil War: A Narrative*, reflects his decision to write from his strength—narrative—rather than from the foreign ground of professional history. Several of the professional historians reviewing the first volume noted Foote's failure to provide the scholarly apparatus of extensive attribution and footnotes, and Foote, anticipating such a reaction, takes pains in his "Bibliographic Note" at the end of the volume to justify his methods. He provides an overview of the primary sources used and the secondary sources he relied on most extensively, but he stands his ground: "I have left out footnotes, believing that they would detract from the book's narrative quality by intermittently shattering the illusion that the observer is not so much reading a book as sharing an experience."[19] Foote's methods in the narrative ran squarely athwart the dominant vein of American historiography; the academic historians had long since won the field and history shifted, as Oscar Handlin writes, from "loose discursive narrative to the heavily footnoted monograph."[20] By the forties and fifties, this tendency had been strengthened by the rise of quantitative methods and the view of history as a social science; the new keepers of the gate were the "cliometricians" and "psychohistorians" C. Vann Woodward identified in defending Foote's work against some early attacks on it by academic historians.[21] Foote's is a narrative rather than scholarly authority, sustained by the command of the narrative voice and the structural mastery of the form; as Rubin writes, the history is "given its authority by the assertion of the stylist-historian rather than by the meticulous citation of sources."[22] All the constituent elements—official records, memoirs, letters, diaries, historical accounts, photographs—are dissolved and merged into a flow controlled by a single narrative consciousness. Foote's object is not to provide an objective recounting with authorial judgment but to impart a quality of vision to the reader and create a massive simulacrum of the war that is experience rather than commentary. His effort anticipates a shift in the practice of history in the second half of the century as the linguistic turn forced historians to confront the epistemological foundations of their work and the extent to which the historian's authority is essentially narrative authority.[23]

Although Foote clearly has a southern perspective on the war, he works as an equal-opportunity critic. He addresses the question of sectional bias in the closing portion of the bibliographical note to the first volume: "Biased is the last thing I would be; I yield to no one in my admiration for heroism and ability, no matter which side of the line a man was born or fought on when the war broke out, fourscore and seventeen years ago. If pride in the resistance my forebears made against the odds has leaned me to any degree in their direction, I hope it will be seen to amount to no more, in the end, than the average American's normal sympathy for the underdog in a fight" (1:816). This statement seems fairly accurate. The pantheon of Foote's heroes is consistent with that of Tate and a great many other southern partisans: the triumvirate of Lee, Jackson, and Forrest evokes Foote's greatest admiration, having achieved the most against the longest odds. But, again as in Tate and even Page, the other great figure here is Lincoln, who overcame the longest (albeit political more than military) odds to prosecute the war at all and see it through to its conclusion. More striking, Foote accords a great deal of respect to Sherman on the score of vision and artistry (as we will see below), something that would have been anathema to an earlier generation. More significant is his use of varying perspectives on events. Throughout, he broadens the base of experience in the narrative by using alternate centers of consciousness to convey various limited perspectives without compromising the consistency of his narrative voice. In the prologue, for example, as Foote establishes the characters of Davis and Lincoln, we have no authorial analysis of the sources of the conflict but alternation between the northern and southern perspectives as individuals grapple with changing circumstances. We encounter a comparison of Davis and secession to Washington and the Revolution in what seems to be the authorial voice, but we find not thirty pages later a compelling case from Lincoln's perspective for the coming war as a second American Revolution. Clearly, from the opening pages, the imperatives in the narrative are artistic rather than polemical. Not that Foote withholds any larger cultural critique of the warring sides and their respective cultures; at various points in the narrative, he points to salient features of North and South in a mode sometimes verging on satire. Much as Foote is skeptical of the heroic claims of the ancestral plantation order, he refuses to let either side off easily on the score of limitations and excesses. The war was extraordinary and certain people were proven extraordinary by it, but the cultures (as all cultures) had faults that, to borrow from Warren, provided ironic counterpoint to their virtues.

Little is surprising in Foote's critique of the North. Much as he respects the men and certain of their leaders, he provides an assessment that is not much different from that of the Agrarians, Page, or Simms. From comments and sections here and there throughout the narrative, a cumulative picture emerges of a culture that is materialistic, morally overbearing, and somewhat lacking in social graces (though Foote certainly does not stress the last). But Foote writes as an American assessing faults in a broadly American culture; it simply happens that many of the dominant traits of our culture tend to be those associated with the North. As he says in a letter to Percy, shortly before going on to discuss American failings in the Cold War: "What a war! Everything we are or will be goes right back to that period. It decided for once and all which way we were going, and we've gone."[24] At times, Foote's critique is a matter of portrayal and tone, particularly when dealing with the crusading earnestness of the abolitionists; of course, his treatment is that afforded to the crusaders by Lincoln himself on several occasions. Writing of the abolitionist efforts after the Union fleet captures Port Royal and much of the surrounding plantation country, he comments that access provided the slaves "an opportunity not to be neglected by their abolitionist brethren, who presently arrived and began conducting uplift experiments among the Negro fieldhands" (1:120). More frequently, we find Foote's explicit critique mounted against that favorite southern target northern greed. He uses the rises and falls of the stock market as an index to the northern spirit as events unfold, referring to the "pocketbook barometer of Northern greed and fears,"[25] and elsewhere drives home his sense that the North felt pain acutely only when it struck the wallet: "a region where their threshold of pain was notoriously low" (3:462). In the most extended section of social commentary in the work, Foote treats the "Age of Shoddy" as manufacturing capacity expands and opportunists take advantage of the military's demand for supplies (and limited capital) to sell incredibly poor-quality products. He reads this phenomenon as "little more than the manifest awkwardness of national adolescence, a reaction to growing pains,"[26] and then turns to the deeper shift in the scale of government and the economy. Rather than simply taking potshots at the traditional targets of southern vitriol, Foote sees the profound changes as wrought by the war itself, not by the Yankees imposing their character, and the South, even during the war, as much altered as the North: "A change was coming upon the land, and upon the land's inhabitants; nor was the change merely a dollar and cents affair, as likely to pass as to last" (2:150).

Though Foote is unsparing in his critique of northern culture—and a later, broader American culture by implication—the South provides no viable alternative for him. It may well be, as he said to Percy, that "the worst cause won," but Foote is skeptical of the claims to southern virtue and details southern excesses as clearly as he does those of the North. As he points out in the note at the end of the second volume, the racial demagoguery rampant during the civil rights struggle provided ample evidence of the perversion of symbol and memory: "I am obligated also to the governors of my native state and the adjoining states of Arkansas and Alabama for helping to lessen my sectional bias by reproducing, in their actions during several of the years that went into the writing of this volume, much that was least admirable in the position my forebears occupied when they stood up to Lincoln" (2:971). The civil rights movement brought home a far different legacy of the war than lessons on sacrifice, heroism, and reconciliation, and Foote was writing his war when the battle over its meaning was at its most intense. He makes a stronger statement on his reaction to the southern political and social climate in a letter to Percy: "I feel death all in the air in Memphis, and I'm beginning to hate the one thing I ever really loved—the South. No, that's wrong: not hate—despise. Mostly I despise the leaders, the pussy-faced politicians, soft-talking instruments of real evil; killers of the dream, that woman called them, and she's right."[27] Foote attempted to escape by moving for a year to Gulf Shores, Alabama, only to find himself in conflict with the local KKK over the use of the Confederate battle flag: "I told them they were a disgrace to the flag, that everything they stood for was almost exactly the opposite the Confederacy had stood for, that the Confederacy believed in law and order above all things. . . . I created a good deal of resentment against myself down there until they decided I was crazy and then they were more sympathetic."[28] Such experiences reinforced Foote's artistic detachment while reinforcing his sense that the war and its memory mattered a great deal in the present.

It is clear throughout that Foote has no intention to "set up the grave in the house," to borrow a line from Tate, and participate in the cult of memory. On the most basic level, he does not paper over those crimes in the war that southern apologists traditionally have, such as the bayoneting of surrendered black soldiers at Fort Pillow and Petersburg, Quantrill's savagery in Kansas and Missouri, or the hanging of northern loyalists in eastern Tennessee. Further, like Tate, he faults the southern critics of Davis—the "impossibilists," as he calls them—for undermining the war effort in the name of rights that could be secured only by a successful war. Of these men, who "launched a conservative revolution," he says that "their anomalous devotion to an untimely creed amounted to an irresistible death-wish. But that was precisely their pride" (2:951). More important, Foote makes clear that the end of the Old South is not the product of a losing struggle, whoever might be to blame for it; the South, like the North, became something fundamentally different in the course of the war: "That was perhaps the greatest paradox of all: that the Confederacy, in launching a revolution against change, should experience under pressure of the war which then ensued an even greater transformation . . . than did the nation it accused of trying to foist upon it an unwanted metamorphosis, not only of its cherished institutions, but also of its very way of life" (2:158). Here we have the key to Foote's credibility as a narrator. He recognizes the war as a powerful shaping force on American culture, rather than a simply a reflection of it, and he sets out to recapture its totality—a massiveness obscured and reduced by polemic.

All that Foote learned as a novelist, serving his apprenticeship under such masters as Henry James, Proust, Joyce, and Faulkner, contributes to a narrative voice that is no less distinctive and compelling than Foote's spoken voice would be in the Ken Burns PBS miniseries on the Civil War years later. It is at once that of the teller of a several-nights' tale and a sensorium responsive to the innumerable voices speaking from the documents. Foote repeatedly cites Gibbon as one of his primary influences; his great lesson for Foote was the creation of an authoritative narrative voice that remains Foote's own (and the occasional rolling period). Phillips puts his finger on the primary quality of Foote's voice, saying that "he tells his story with a dignified informality" (184). Foote makes liberal use of colloquialisms, as when he asks about such a sacred document as the

Emancipation Proclamation, "What sort of document was this anyhow?" (1:708), or says that a bridge was built in "jig time." Foote uses a more Latinate diction sparingly—on the dead at Sharpsburg, "the effluvium of the bloodiest day of the war" (1:702)—as he builds outward from his core without tending toward abstract language. This demotic style, which Foote praised in an early review of Faulkner, provides the bedrock Anglo-Saxon base of Foote's writing, but the work as a whole encompasses a staggering register.

It is a voice that gains its authority by alternating between the modes argued for by Foote's characters in *Shiloh*. We see the war from the inside ("what each . . . of us saw in our own little corner") while maintaining a broader perspective that allows the reader a command of the whole ("looking out of that big Eye in the sky, playing God") (164). He consistently maintains a dual vision of each battle, contrasting the broader perspective of the commanders with the more immediate, close-up view of the men involved. We see the developments from a more abstract tactical standpoint—movements and countermovements, assaults that succeed or fail, enfilade and defilade, bombardments of various positions—but Foote frequently shifts our focus to the human experience of these actions on the ground. Fredericksburg provides the clearest example of this contrast of the abstract and the concrete. He writes of it as one of the "grandest as a spectacle" of the war's major battles: "Staged as it was, with a curtain of fog that lifted, under the influence of a genial sun, upon a sort of natural amphitheater . . . it quite fulfilled the volunteers' early-abandoned notion of combat as a picture-book affair" (2:20). In addition to the perfect view of the display from the respective heights, Burnside's observation balloons render a scene of "war reduced to miniature," which Foote sets in contrast to the reality encountered by the soldiers and the burial details. These last had a "nearer view of the carnage": "No one assigned to the burial details ever forgot the horror of what he saw; for here, close-up and life-size, was an effective antidote to the long-range, miniature pageantry of Saturday's battle as it had been viewed from the opposing heights. Up close, you heard the groans and smelled the blood. You saw the dead" (2:43). Foote strengthens the sense of concrete immediacy by shifting to the second person here before going on to give grisly details of the men's descriptions. During his treatment of Pickett's charge at Gettysburg, Foote writes of a strange phenomenon: the men step from deep shade to bright sunlight, and "the result was not only dazzling to the eyes but also added a feeling of elation and release. 'Before us lay bright field and fair landscape,' one among them would recall" (2:553). But this effect lasts only until their pupils contract and the enormity of their task dawns upon them. Dilation and contraction serves as an apt metaphor for Foote's method throughout the history; we see the broad sweep and large-scale movement of men and arms, but then the close-up gives us the concrete experience of which these consist. At Missionary Ridge (Chattanooga), Foote begins a paragraph on the Union assault with a Union colonel's perspective from Grant's command post as he watches the "gallant rivalry" of the colors progressing up the ridge and compares them to a "flock of migratory birds" but then shifts: "That was how it looked in small from Orchard Knob. Up close, there was the gritty sense of participation, the rasp of heavy breathing, the drum and clatter of boots on rocky ground, and always the sickening thwack of bullets entering flesh and striking bone" (2:855). In the long hours in the Bloody Angle at Spotsylvania, the larger perspective fades altogether, and there is only the struggle for survival and sanity, the savage "intimacy" of close-quarters fighting.[29]

The primary strength of the narrative form is that it allows events to unfold according to the logic of narrative flow rather than the demands of historical analysis. Foote's history is replete with a sense of historical contingencies that impinge on human actions and in large measure determine whether they are effective or praiseworthy; with a subject so completely known as the Civil War, it becomes easy to forget that the participants could not know the many things that seem obvious in retrospect. The narrative form rehumanizes history by recapturing the context of human action, as White and Sugg write: "Knowing what the human experience felt like involves imagining past events as developing process, replete with contingencies, and requires, therefore, the narrative form. The monograph is an account of past events as accomplished facts, winnowed from the contingencies, and requires the form of exposition" (95). In each section, Foote almost always limits himself to what was known to the participants themselves and uses alternate centers of consciousness for his narrative voice. For example, when describing Lee's plans for his first invasion of the North and then McClellan's subsequent counteroffensive after finding Special Orders 191, the same formula is repeated, "The war would be over—won"; both plans, of course, go awry, and hopes for a one-stroke end to the war fade by the end of the first volume. Most important, when dealing with the opening phases of the battles, Foote approaches each contest from the point of view of the commander who knows the least before turning to give the detailed background from another perspective. When dealing with Second Manassas, we have the early movements—Lee's division of his forces and Pope's futile attempt to destroy Jackson's detachment—but before the armies engage, Foote shifts our view away from the scene to follow McClellan as he tries to hurry reinforcements and follow developments at a distance: "Then Tuesday night the line went dead. All was silent beyond Manassas Junction, where there had been some sort of explosion" (1:614). Earlier, after dealing with the Confederate preparations for the Shiloh offensive, Foote moves to the complacency of the Union commanders and gives us the opening from Grant's perspective: "Next morning he heard a distant thunder from the south. The guns of Shiloh were jarring the earth" (1:332). We find the same use of a limited perspective in the experience of the soldiers as well as commanders, as when, at the opening of the Seven Days, Longstreet's men are sent forward to assault an unknown position from which A. P. Hill's troops had just stumbled back:

> Again that sudden clatter erupted, now with the boom of guns mixed in, and again the men came stumbling back, as wild-eyed as before.
>
> Penetrating deeper into the swampy woods, they had come face to face with the death-producing thing itself: three separate lines of Federal infantry, dug one above another into the face of a long, convex hill crowned with guns. (1:486)

Only then does Foote give us a description of the Federal position and set the stage for the battle of Gaines' Mill. Here as elsewhere we enter into the experience as the men themselves—blind—and only slowly grasp the true nature of the situation.

This same point about the role of contingency in shaping people and events over the course of the war applies to Foote's dynamic characterization. Early in the first volume, he writes, "It was [the participants'] good fortune, or else their misery, to belong to a generation in which every individual would be given a chance to discover or expose his worth, down to the final ounce of strength and nerve" (1:164). Foote allows the narrative itself to do this testing. He does not succumb to the historian's temptation to deal with character by inserting the set piece establishing the total character of the actor and then allowing him to play his role in the account; rather, drawing on his experience as a novelist, he sets certain fundamental aspects of the characters' temperament but reserves certain aspects of character to reveal only later, when those aspects are revealed by event in the course of the narrative. Foote comments repeatedly that various figures acted "according to their natures," but exactly what that deepest nature is remains opaque—certain relatively simple characters like Banks or Van Dorn excepted—until we have the entire span of the work. As Garrett writes, "The consistency, the core of character, is there by inference and implication. Which is to say characterization is dramatic and dynamic and becomes a source of narrative suspense, thus of forward motion in the whole narrative. . . . One way [to do this] is in finding the exact and appropriate moment in the action, and usually only once in the entire narrative, to present certain relevant details" (88). An example of this method comes when Grant undergoes his major transformation in the eyes of the North after his elevation to overall commander of Union forces. Foote reserves the most extensive description of Grant for the opening of the third volume, as the newest western hero and the man Lincoln recognizes as the "killer arithmetician" he has sought since early in the war comes unrecognized into the lobby of Washington's famous Willard's Hotel. We have the desk clerk's slightly contemptuous description of Grant's "seedy-looking" appearance followed by another paragraph on the absolute transformation following the "authentication that came with the fixing of the name": "It was as if the prayers of the curious had been answered after the flesh. Here before them, in the person of this undistinguished-looking officer—forty-one years of age, five feet eight inches tall, and weighing just under a hundred and forty pounds in his scuffed boots and shabby clothes—was the man who, in the course of the past twenty-five months of a war in which the news had been mostly unwelcome from the Federal point of view, had captured two rebel armies, entire, and chased a third clean out of sight beyond the roll of the southern horizon" (3:4).

Much the same evolution of character takes place with Lee. Only midway through the first volume, after the Seven Days, does Foote record his transformation into the familiar heroic figure in the eyes of his men. Using the second person, Foote presents the disparities in Lee's appearance—upper and lower body, mounted and afoot—before giving us the final effect of Lee's presence: "Quickly, though, you got over the shock (which after all was only the result of comparing flesh and perfection. However he *was* was how you preferred him) and when you saw him thus in the field your inclination was to remove your hat—not to wave it: just to hold it—and stand there looking at him: Mars Robert" (1:586). If some of the figures become larger than life, they do so because of the larger-than-life character of the war; the characters are transformed by it as the narrative proceeds, some for the better and some for the worse.

Creating a sense of "how it was" for Foote involves the conjunction of memory and sensation. In the most literal sense, here is where Foote combines the historian's purpose of communicating facts and the novelist's of communicating sensation. He says of the artist's aim: "With luck and talent, then, a man can *show* another man something; that is, he can make him see and hear and maybe even feel and smell it" ("Novelist's View" 225), and his history is charged with the full range of these sensations. He gives us the smell of burning bacon filling the air when Johnston burns a meat-packing plant during his withdrawal to the Rappahannock (1:239); we see a "blue-flame river of bourbon" and smell the "burnt liquor, roasting coffee beans, and frizzled bacon, wafting . . . through the reek of gunsmoke" during Forrest's raid on Johnsonville (3:620); and are tortured along with the Union sailors stranded in the Red River by a southern belle whose pet squirrel runs into her bodice (3:66). Cannon fire in rain had "a metallic ring in the saturated air" (1:411), small-arms fire the sound of tearing canvas, and a Union column moving past a Confederate position at Sharpsburg "struck sparks, like a file being raked across a grindstone" (1:685). These descriptions certainly help to bring the narrative alive, but they serve a deeper purpose for Foote: drawing on his lessons from Proust, he creates a link to the past through the connection of memory and sensation. In a letter to Percy on August 5, 1970, he encloses a long passage from Proust:

An hour is not merely an hour, it is a vase of scents and sounds and projects and climates, and what we call reality is a certain connection between these immediate sensations and the memories which envelop us simultaneously with them—a connection that is suppressed in a simple cinematographic vision . . . a unique connection which the writer has to rediscover in order to link forever in his phrase the two sets of phenomena which reality joins together. He can describe a scene by describing one after another the innumerable objects which at a given moment are present at a particular place, but the truth will be attained by him only when he takes two different objects, states the connection between them . . . encloses them in the necessary links of a well-wrought style; truth—and life too—can be attained by us only when, by comparing a quality common to two sensations, we succeed in extracting their common essence and in reuniting them to each other, liberated from the contingencies of time and place, within a metaphor.[30]

This "common essence" provides a concrete substrate that allows us to experience the war through Foote's narrative in a much more immediate way than a recounting of fact and event. It links the distant memory of the war with our personal pasts and so recaptures the complex tissue of event, the web of associations that link our present with past event or, as Warren showed in *All the King's Men*, self and past selves.

Foote's prose does not simply describe experience; it re-creates it through rhythm and syntax. Here, in addition to his skill at characterization, managing plot, and structuring the work, we find his greatest advantage as a novelist. In an interview, Foote described this attention to crafting the smallest portions of his work: "I'm working with a very large canvas, but at the same time I'm trying to do each paragraph the way you'd write a sonnet."[31] The comparison to poetry is apt, since Foote goes far beyond mere description to a use of language that makes the prose an experience in itself. When treating First Manassas, for example, he writes of the death of General Bee—"Bee fell, shot as he rallied his men, who leaderless gave back before the cheering ranks of the Federal attackers" (1:79)—and the phrase "who leaderless gave back" mirrors the regressive movement of the troops. In the same section, when treating the devolution of the struggle to the level of individuals, he writes, "There, while the battle raged on the forward slope—*disintegrated by now into a strung-out, seemingly disconnected series of hand-to-hand skirmishes by knots of men clustered about their shot-ripped flags, each man fighting as if the outcome of the battle depended on himself alone*—Beauregard used them to strengthen the line" (1:79; emphasis mine). In the inserted description of the battle here, Foote captures the fragmented scene of the battle through the use of monosyllabic words in clusters loosely joined by a string of prepositions. Rather than relying on extended description to make the narrative vivid, Foote compresses his description into lines that carry the force of his vision. At times, his style simply allows us to see a detail that otherwise would have been missed, as in the description of the Union charge on the Confederate entrenchments before Kennesaw Mountain: "A long, low cloud of smoke boiled up and out, billowing as it grew, lighted from within by the pinkish yellow blink and stab of muzzle flashes" (3:349–50). Foote's prose captures the things present to consciousness in the moment of action. At some points, the reader becomes the astonished witness; treating the doomed Union charges at Fredericksburg, Foote writes of the bluecoats falling as if they had struck a trip wire, but then, "Again they rose. Again, incredibly, they charged" (2:35). At others, Foote uses juxtaposition to carry the force of aspects of experience held in tension, such as when he deals with the abrupt shift from conception to confused violence during the Union charge at Spotsylvania, when General Warren "went forward, around 4 o'clock; into chaos" (3:207). The casual insertion of the time here serves as more than documentation; it carries the sense of moving from the battle plans, when time seems precise, to the world of the battle, in which the mundane bounds of time are stretched and distorted, and so prepares the way for the greatest distortion of time in the hours-long close-quarters fighting in the Mule Shoe. Through Foote's simulacrum of the war, the reader does not simply read description— he or she shares experience; "how it *was*" becomes "how it *is*" in the reader's present.

One of the most striking aspects of Foote's style is the way in which the many voices of political leaders, military commanders, civilians—slaves, women, journalists—and, most important, the common soldier are incorporated into the flow of the narrative. Foote marks the importance of these voices at the outset of his bibliographical note to the first volume when introducing the early works that form his most important sources: "There you hear the live men speak—there and in their diaries and letters, their newspapers and periodicals—although not always as they spoke in later life, when they got around to writing their memoirs, regimental histories, and a host of articles such as the ones collected in four large volumes and published in 1887 under the title *Battles and Leaders of the Civil War*. Early or later, taken in conjunction with the diplomatic correspondence and the congressional transcripts, these complete the first-hand testimony by soldiers and civilians, some of high rank, some of low rank, some of no rank at all" (1:813). "The live men speak" again in Foote's work, with the words placed in the larger flow of the narrative and in the context of the events that gave rise to them, not as duly cited words from documents; as James Cox notes, "By freeing himself from footnotes, the speeches and anecdotes are freed from their prior textuality to become voices in this text."[32] There are, of course, the great words from the great men, but Foote seems to take a special pleasure in giving us the words of more obscure men and women that speak to the larger human dimension of the war and provide ironic counterpoint to the words and records meant for posterity. Frequently, he draws on those words that convey the common soldier's "abiding sense of the ridiculous" that sustains him during the suffering in which all larger meaning is obscure at best. During the Seven Days, some of McClellan's soldiers feel that A. P. Hill has reserved a special portion of fury for them because of an earlier romantic rivalry between the commanders; waiting for the assaults, Foote tells us, they would wonder aloud, "God's sake, Nelly— why didn't you marry him?" (1:480). In another place, a Union soldier at Chickamauga marvels at seeing two birds mirroring the human conflict and exclaims, "Moses, what a country! The very birds are fighting!" This comic perspective shapes our perceptions of leaders as well as events. The voices of the common soldiers and lower officers rehumanize the primary figures by providing a slant of vision that works against the mythologizing tendencies of popular history. (It also, as Foote might have learned from Shakespeare, prevents tragedy from devolving into sentimentality or morbidity.) As Lee moves through Maryland on his way to Pennsylvania, for example, the natives are delighted by his perfect, gallant appearance—"Oh, I wish he was ours!"; one admiringly notes the large neck he has, only to be answered by one of Lee's men that "it takes a damn big neck to hold his head" (2:444). In another instance, a wounded, captured Federal asks to be raised up to catch a glimpse of the already legendary Stonewall but is so utterly disillusioned by the sight that he proclaims, "Oh my God! Lay me down"—a refrain taken up in good spirit by Stonewall's own men. As Phillips notes (194), Foote frequently uses anecdotes to convey the perspective and uncertainty of the men about the purposes of their commanders, as when he presents an exchange between two Union soldiers in the early stages of Fredericksburg; one espouses a psychological theory about Lee's motivation, but the other, a "veteran private," arrives at a direct, intuitive assessment: "Shit," he said. "They *want* us to get in. Getting out won't be quite so easy. You'll see" (2:30). Foote ends the section with his words, soon to be borne out in what follows.

This same measurement of the commanders and political leaders, as well as the war itself, brings the voices to serve as a gigantic chorus for the grand actions on the stage. Frequently Foote turns to the songs of the troops, usually improvised on the spot, that give them a voice to respond to the decisions of their leaders. Whenever the troops are badly mishandled, by Pope, Burnside, Bragg, Banks, or others, they express their cynicism in the songs that allow them to speak as one. But Foote makes clear that these songs are far from the easy cynicism of the New York or Richmond newspapermen: it is an earned perspective borne of suffering. As a corrective to the traditional focus on the obedience to duty and bravery of the common soldier—conceived as simple and absolute qualities—Foote uses the songs and anecdotes to place a deeper wisdom among the soldiers as agents capable of valor and heroism in the face of suffering (much of which could have been avoided) and undeniable shortcomings among their leaders. For example, when word gets out of a modified sea chantey going about among the troops after Fredericksburg, some of the northern press and leadership fear a loss of the will to fight:

> Abraham Lincoln, what yer 'bout?
> Stop this war. It's all played out.
> We'll all drink stone blind:
> Johnny, fill up the bowl! (2:117)

Foote writes of the troops, "Once they had pretended cynicism as a cover for their greenness and fears, but now they had earned it and they found the phrase descriptive of their outlook through this season of discontent" (2:117). He, as Lincoln and some other northern leaders and correspondents did, recognizes this kind of disillusionment as marking a stage of maturity: "Yet it was at this point, near the apparent nadir of its self-confidence and pride, with disaffection evident in all of its components, from the commander down to the youngest drummer boy, that the one truly imperishable quality of this army began to be discerned, like a gleam that only shone in the darkness. If men could survive the unprofitable slaughter of Fredericksburg—the patent bungling, the horror piled on pointless horror, and the disgust that came with the conclusion that their comrades had died less by way of proving their love for their country than by way of proving the ineptness of their leaders—it might well be that they could survive almost anything" (2:118). Endurance is a virtue for Foote in much the same way as it was for Faulkner. This kind of endurance with knowledge of cost and senselessness expands the human range of the narrative to encompass the soldiers as actors, rather than mere counters or ciphers moved about by larger forces. Their action many times is that of a witness, a role that seems passive but which Foote uses to mark internal change. After Hood takes over the Army of the Tennessee, for example, the army's progress toward destruction is marked by the responses of individual men. Outside Atlanta, after a grueling and ill-advised effort to forestall one of Sherman's sidles, we have this exchange: "'Say, Johnny,' one of Logan's soldiers called across the breastworks into the outer darkness,

'How many of you are there left?' 'Oh, about enough for another killing,' some butternut replied" (3:490). Hood wrecks his army on his advance into Tennessee by charging works at Franklin and allows it to be destroyed by greatly superior forces in front of Nashville, and the final passage of the remnants southward is closed with the voices of the men: "'Ain't we in a hell of a fix?' one ragged Tennessean groaned as he picked himself up, slathered with mud from a fall on the slippery pike. 'Ain't we in a hell of a fix: a one-eyed President, a one-legged general, and a one-horse Confederacy!'" (3:709).

The choral speakers on Foote's tragic stage extend far beyond the soldiers to encompass journalists, politicians, slaves and free blacks, and women, North and South. The women's words, in particular, help to measure the cost of the war and to foreshadow the end. We hear from them frequently, usually in the form of diary entries or letters, and the intimacy of their private voices provides the greatest counterpoint to the public statements of the men. The diary of Mary Chesnut, of course, provides the greatest wealth of these words, but Foote uses those of more obscure women to powerful effect, as when an unnamed "matron diarist" observes the trains taking Longstreet's troops to join Bragg before Chickamauga: "It was a strange sight. What seemed miles of platform cars, and soldiers rolled in their blankets lying in rows with their heads all covered, fast asleep. In their gray blankets packed in regular order, they looked liked swathed mummies. . . . A feeling of awful depression laid hold of me. All those fine fellows going to kill or be killed, but why?" (2:710). All these voices serve the same function in Foote's narrative as the chorus served in the tragedies of ancient Greece: they mark the participation of the entire polis in the drama unfolding on stage and so serve to extend the significance of the action to the whole. Further, the chorus in the ancient tragedies, however much it might err in the early stages, moves ahead of the protagonist to an aggrieved acceptance of the work of fate.

Foote's narrative is fundamentally a war of words. Language, for Foote, is not simply a reflection of reality but a medium in which human reality can be shaped and given meaning and direction. As an artist he claims for the great forms of literature only a higher order of a claim for all human language, and he pays particular attention to the use of language by the participants in the struggle he records and measures them accordingly. Much as Tate saw the demise of the Old South as a failure of mind, Foote sees the failures in the war as failures of imagination; those individuals who succeed, as the war unfolds, are those—like Foote's artist—who are able to bring genius to fruition through labor and whose imagination is sufficiently powerful that they see into events deeply enough to divine the suitable form for action.

Foote casts the primary struggle between Lincoln and Davis as that between a great artist and a lesser. Davis is largely limited to received forms of language and thought, and, while he does respond to contingencies, he does so belatedly and insufficiently; Lincoln, in contrast, uses a more flexible, organic language and freely responds pragmatically to events as they develop. He sees into the essential nature of events and is able to use language to shape their course. Foote repeatedly contrasts the presidential addresses of Davis and Lincoln as both seek to define the conflict to their own advantage, and Lincoln gets the better of the rhetorical struggle. In their crucial presidential addresses to the legislatures late in 1862, Lincoln successfully marks a new phase of the war and shifts the focus to slavery and Union, making Davis's rhetoric of states' rights seem "destructive of world democracy" ("the last best hope of earth"). Foote draws the moral: "Davis in time, like other men before or since, found what it meant to become involved with an adversary whose various talents included those of a craftsman in the use of words" (1:806).

Foote sketches Lincoln as the true artist, toiling in his workshop and gaining his effects by hard labor; his style—the "Lincoln music" that Foote marks again and again—is an American voice, something his numerous critics fail to understand: "That there was such a thing as the American language, available for literary purposes, had scarcely begun to be suspected by the more genteel" (1:804). We see Lincoln choosing his words almost as often as we see him acting, and in fact his actions often take the form of words. He writes letters never intended to be mailed to clarify his thoughts, others in sealed envelopes to enforce the allegiance of his cabinet; makes calculated use of the Emancipation Proclamation; and creates the great epitome of the war in his address at Gettysburg. He shapes his words and so shapes the war; his adversary, in contrast, speaks in the high mode of southern oratory in language that is polished but divorced from life. Perhaps no more damning anecdote concerning Davis appears in the work than that in which we see him weeping over passages in a sentimental novel he has asked his wife to read to him; in fact, Foote places this section within a few pages of the most extensive treatment of Lincoln as artist. Although Davis does have moments such as his well-known letter refusing Lee's resignation after Gettysburg, he normally speaks according to the world he knew—or rather according to an abstract conception of it—instead of the world as it comes into being over the course of the war. Little changes in Davis's rhetoric over the course of the war, so that by the late stages it seems something akin to dementia, as when he speaks in an 1864 address of the "smiling face of our land and the teeming evidences of plenty which everywhere greet the eye" (3:609). Or, more telling, while on his flight from Richmond, with a rapidly diminishing cabinet and Lee's army defeated, he speaks to his remaining generals of strategic options "like a dreamy madman" (3:967). So important to Foote is the difference between the antagonists on this score that he devotes the final page—after Davis has spent his declining years playing the living martyr to Lincoln's dead one and attempting his apologia in prose and speech—to a comparison not of their politics or principles but of their style, from which all the rest might be inferred.

The various commanders are judged as artists as well, sometimes on their actual language and sometimes on a broader faculty of imagination. They fall roughly into groups of artists and unsuccessful imitators. The greatest of the former are men like Sherman and Lee whose vision, like Lincoln's, is powerful enough that they envision a reality greater than the everyday world—"a world," as Foote said of his early reading, "more real than the real world"; through their innovation, they shape the course of battle rather than merely responding according to developments. We see them at moments of inspiration borne of labor, such as when Sherman realizes how he can securely flank Johnston out of a strong position and "experienced a surge of joy not unlike that of a poet revising the rejected draft of a poem he now perceives will become the jewel of his collection" (3:322), or when Lee, standing atop Clark's Mountain with his lieutenants, prophetically extends a "gauntleted hand" to predict the routes of Grant's invasion to begin the Forty Days. His prophecy is fulfilled, as is his greater one concerning the three components of Grant's overall strategy, and Foote remarks on this seeming "mind reading" or how he could *become* that man [his adversary]": "Like artists in other kinds of endeavor, Lee produced by hard labor, midnight oil, and infinite pains what seemed possible only by uncluttered inspiration" (3:144). These are men whose style is of a piece with their vision of the world and whose respective genius produces different kinds of innovation. We hear Lee's grand but understated assurance of manner that belies a supreme command of men and events and witness an audacity that never becomes rashness (except perhaps at Gettysburg). Apart from his success on the field, Lee achieves a greater triumph of style in defeat as the joint work authored by him and Grant at Appomattox becomes the great image of the war's closure, and Foote focuses our attention on the craftsmanship behind this event by spending a fair amount of time dealing with Lee's editing of his secretary's drafts of the acceptance of terms and the address to his troops. With Sherman, his more abrupt, jagged style—"War is cruelty. You cannot refine it"—bespeaks his grasp of a new kind of total war, and his great work, the march to the sea, is more a work of imagination than tactics; the tactical victory achieved over Johnston and Hood in turn, Sherman reaches for the grand gesture capable of altering the people's perception of the war, North and South. Sherman envisions a role for himself and his army, that of avenging angel, and proceeds to fashion word and act suited to the role: pines burning by the roadsides along the route of march, his troops singing "John Brown's Body," and Sherman writing, "Read to them this letter . . . and let them use it so as to prepare for my coming" (2:940). These artists are joined by those commanders such as Jackson, Nathan Bedford Forrest—who fights all his battles "by ear" without ever reading a tactics manual—and U. S. Grant, who is "tone deaf" in many respects but who envisions the Grand Strategy that ends the war.[33]

The failed commanders are the unsuccessful artists, the imitators who lack the vision of their greater counterparts. Unlike the artists, they prove to be incapable of penetrating the surface of events and discovering new forms. Frequently we see this failure accompanied by a high rhetoric, as well as the imaginative categories such rhetoric implies, which separates them from the flow of events and so blinds them to contingency. Early on, Foote recounts the ill-advised and badly executed Union assault on Ball's Bluff and the conflict between romantic preconceptions of the war and the brutal reality. Colonel Edward Baker, a warhawking former U. S. senator and friend of Lincoln's, takes command of the field quoting Scott and oblivious to strategic concerns: "Then, by way of climax, he who had called for sudden, bold, forward, determined war received it in the form of a bullet through the brain, which left him not even time for a dying quotation" (1:106). This split between rhetoric and reality is reinforced repeatedly on both sides via the examples of Pope, Morgan, Bragg, and a great many others, and at certain points Foote makes clear that this is an artistic failure, a failure of imagination. Most pointedly, we see this failure in the efforts of first Bragg and then Hood to emulate Jackson's exploits, with effects ranging from insufficiency to disaster. After Bragg's failed invasion of Kentucky, when he has abandoned the aggressive Jacksonian rhetoric in favor of a defensive account of his gains, Foote claims a trouble "deep inside Bragg himself" and remarks: "For all his audacity of conception, for all his boldness through the preliminaries, once the crucial instant was at hand he simply could not screw his nerves up to the sticking point. It was strange, this sudden abandonment of Jackson as his model. It was as if a lesser poet should set out to imitate Shakespeare or Milton. With luck and skill, he might ape the manner, the superficial arrangement of words and even sentences; but the Shakespearean or Miltonic essence would be missing. He lacked the essence" (1:660). Hood's failing in the third volume corresponds to Bragg's in the first (even to the precise location in the volumes), but with far bloodier consequences. His lack is not one of nerve but of perception. From Atlanta to Nashville, he blindly carries out his imitation of Jackson and Lee with no regard to the change in conditions or the raggedness of his troops, without stopping "to consider what he asked of them in designing still another of those swift Jacksonian movements that had worked so well two years ago in Virginia; whereas the fact was, not even Lee's army was 'Lee's army' any longer; let alone Hood's" (3:661–62). Phillips gives extensive treatment to the measure of artistry in Foote's work, and he comments on the sources of various generals' ineptitude: "Among the sources that seem particularly important to Foote's history are the rhetorical posturing, ambition, and inflexibility, all of which inhibit contact with the more basic rhythms of history and a spontaneous response to them" (203). Though the second of these might need qualification (witness the examples of Sherman or Jackson, hardly men free of ambition), Phillips's larger point about the connection between imagination and success through the trial of war is certainly a valid one. Art for Foote is not mere window dressing for the "real" events of history but the stuff of history itself—the vision necessary to penetrate the surface of event and act meaningfully in the world.

The presence of artists in the narrative extends far beyond the participants and the narrator himself; in the background, evoked through pervasive allusion, are those great masters who have shaped our understanding of humanity and human action. At times, the allusions are simply a matter of subtle word choice and diction, as when Foote writes of an attack that "exploded out of the darkling woods" at Chickamauga, recalling Keats and Hardy, or describes Forrest's angry parting with the commanders at Fort Donelson with "Bedford Forrest stood up in his wrath," evoking the image of Achilles. Elsewhere, the allusions are more explicit, describing a situation in a sort of literary shorthand. He compares Grant to Byron's Childe Roland as he moves toward Chattanooga and describes Pope's exile in the West using a line from *Othello*. In the most extended instance, Foote captures Hooker's failure of moral courage at Chancellorsville using Hemingway's bullfight terms. Hooker becomes the "morally frightened" bullfighter Gallo, surrendering authority (and responsibility) to his subordinates when facing Lee and saying, in effect, "You take him, Paco. . . . I don't like the way he looks at me" (2:280). The allusions are not simply a matter of Foote providing a literary gloss on his material; the participants themselves draw on literary sources to understand their own experiences. One soldier at Fredericksburg recalls a passage from Goethe about the landscape turning red when he is under the stress of battle. Lincoln draws metaphors from humorists such as Bill Arp to reduce a situation to its essentials and shortly before his assassination senses a dark prophecy of his own fate in that of Duncan in Shakespeare's *Macbeth*. Underlying the dense fabric of allusions in Foote's work is the implicit claim that art is not a decorative epiphenomenon standing apart from the events of history but a vital force that enters into the making of history and our understanding of it.

Part of the effect of Foote's making his Civil War a war of words is to elevate the status of the artist in relation to the accepted arbiters of history. As a self-conscious modernist devoted to art as the highest calling, Foote, like Joyce, Proust, and Eliot, sees the corruption of language as the corruption of civilizational order itself and the role of the artist as the restoration (in fact the remaking) of order through words. As Simpson writes of the Fugitive-Agrarians: "[Their inspiration] came from their struggle to imagine the authoritative role of the modern Southern writer in the attempted restoration of a politics of the Word or polity of letters" (*Man of Letters* 230). He continues, "In the years following the First World War they reaffirmed the notion of representing the literary existence as one of the orders of Western society—to support, that is to say, the faith that the 'spirit of letters' represents a separate realm of being and the belief that this realm offers the possibility of walling us against the abyss and of bringing order out of chaos" (231). Although the Agrarians asserted the authority of the literary through an expansion of their activity to encompass a broader cultural critique (much of it accomplished through polemic), Foote's implicit claim to cultural authority in his narrative is at once subtler and more radical: he renders the war in words and treats art and imagination as fundamental issues in the work, placing himself—the master narrator and artist—in the authoritative position superior to that of the professional historian. In "A Novelist's View of History" and in various interviews, as we have seen, Foote makes a claim for the common aim of historians and novelists, but the narrative itself establishes a more profound commonality between the participants in the war and the narrative that re-creates it. Seen in this light, a curious parallel between Foote and one of his subjects, Jefferson Davis, which might otherwise be taken as merely an inside joke, takes on a deeper significance. After being released from Fortress Monroe, Davis sets out in Memphis to write a three-volume history of the war, and Foote, who of course is completing his own three-volume history in the same city, remarks: "Bustling Memphis, hot in summer, cold in winter . . . seemed unconducive to the peace he believed he needed for such work. Who could write anything there, let alone a full-fledged three-volume history of the war?" (3:1052). A relatively insignificant instance, to be sure, but when combined with the pervasive concern with art and imagination throughout the work—the recurrent metaphors of poets revising or writers in their workshops, the attention to style and craftsmanship (or lack of it) in the participants' prose—we see a deeper claim emerge: Foote's *Civil War* is of a piece with its great subject.

With Foote as the master narrator in this war of words, meaning resides not in event but in the form given the event by the hand of art. Unlike meaning in the work of the professional historian, based on objective judgment of facts and sound generalizations from them, meaning here is rendered through artistic vision and sensed by the reader through the dynamic experience of the work's structure. Foote renders experience, rather than judgment, but it is experience distilled and shaped by art—drama. On this question, as on others, he yields no ground to the historian: "Drama *is* meaning, just as character is action, provided it is clear."[34] Art for Foote is the process of discerning the hidden form beneath the surface of event and rendering it visible, and he uses a striking metaphor to distinguish this idea from art conceived as idea or history conceived as statement: "[The artist] can be fascinated by the shape of his own hand, watching it by lamplight hold the pen; for him 'understanding' is merely description—that is enough. Your wise-man says 'There is my hand; all right; [let's] get on to important things. How about the relation of God to man?' But the artist, I believe, concentrating on the hand itself, without even a thought of God, comes closer to finding the meaning simply by observing how the hand, held between his eye and the lamp, becomes semi-transparent, showing the skeleton hand beneath."[35] Whereas this metaphor makes it sound as though the structure is inherent, Foote combines a romantic notion of form with a classical one that holds form as a matter of models of order inherited from tradition; adapting Wordsworth, form is what we half perceive and half create. Foote seems to hold a conception of form inhering in experience, but his high-modernist sensibility recognizes the formulations of order the artist—along with the culture at large—inherits; as Phillips notes, "While form in art, just as the form of the bones in the artist's hand, may have its origins in what lies beyond time, it is equally important that form has its evolution in history and time" (165). Writing of the novel, Foote tells Percy in a letter, "What the novel needs is a sense of proceeding from generations of knowledge."[36] When Foote assesses his debts to his artistic forebears, we see that the phrase "generations of knowledge" has a very real meaning; he learned his lessons on form not in classes on historical methodology but from Proust, Gibbon, Thucydides, Aeschylus, and Homer.

The structure of Foote's history reflects his insistence on an artistic prerogative. One of his lessons from Gibbon, as White and Sugg point out, was the use of a "candidly provisional coherence" for his history (91); as with the narrative voice, the effect here is to lessen the claim to the historical authority of the specialist but heighten the narrative authority of the author. Even a cursory glance at Foote's table of contents for the entire narrative reveals a structure too perfectly balanced to even pretend to represent the war "as it was" in some positivistic sense.[37] We see the same love of tripartite divisions that guided much of Foote's other work, particularly *Jordan County* and *Follow Me Down*; the three volumes are divided into three parts each, and each of these parts is divided into three chapters, with the exception of part 2 in volumes 1 and 3 (which have two chapters each). The exception proves the rule, here, just as a metrical variation in Milton or Browning achieves a desired effect on the reader because of the regularity of the other lines. The missing chapters in those second parts highlight the three-chapter second part of volume 2; they create a center of the work to be occupied by Gettysburg, the "keystone of the arch," in Phillips's phrase (209). On the most basic level, this structure creates the classic dramatic trajectory of rising action, climax, and falling action, but Foote goes beyond this basic cultural inclination to strive for a greater symmetry both in the number of chapters (as we saw above) and in the heightening of parallels between the first half of the narrative and last.

These parallels reflect the changing reality of the war as it progresses and reinforce the sense of the war as an entity in itself much greater than the forces that try to direct it. The cases of Bragg and Hood as unsuccessful imitators of Jackson in the West, cited above, both highlight failure to adapt to very different contexts of action, early and late, and Foote reinforces the parallel by setting them in precisely the same position in their respective volumes. But where Bragg's failure of nerve allows the offensive potential of the early campaigns to go unfulfilled, Hood's rashness leads to catastrophe because that offensive potential is no longer there. The war changes; early impetus no longer provides sufficient cause, and the means of warfare changes radically. The contrast between two of what Foote calls the "great marches of all time"—Henry Sibley's doomed expedition to the Far West in volume 1 and Sherman's march to the sea in volume 3—set a profound contrast between competing visions. Sibley's march represents the once powerful dream, familiar from the heady days of southern nationalism in the 1850s, of a grand Confederate empire stretching down into Latin America—an alternate vision of the great modern nation. As the survivors struggle simply to live long enough to return to Texas, we have the first ending in the work, that of the war in the Far West. Already the Confederacy is drawn inward. Sherman's is a march to the sea as well, but the Atlantic rather than the Pacific, and it represents a victory of the northern vision of empire over the southern, a vision that would lead to the so-called Second American Republic. Sherman is the great visionary of modern warfare, and Foote emphasizes the link between the transition to modern warfare and the transition to modernity. The two "short" parts in volumes 1 and 3 have corresponding titles; the two chapters of each part draw their titles from an epigram produced by two of the great artists of warfare, Forrest and Sherman. In the first volume, Foote uses one of Forrest's dicta—"War Means Fighting" (chapter 4) and "Fighting Means Killing" (chapter 5)—to head chapters in which, with Shiloh and Seven Pines, the chaotic nature and price of the continental war become clear; Forrest, having no received notions of the conduct of war, freely improvises and adapts successfully, but in his savagery and common origins, he is far removed from Chevalier Bayard or Jeb Stuart. The implication: success in this war could come only at the cost of the South's idea of itself. Whereas Forrest, fighting by instinct and "ear," was far from concerned with any larger implications, Sherman always kept one eye on the larger view, the grand implications of his acts. He is the one Foote presents as first grasping what victory over the South would entail, and his grand gesture of total war, the march to the sea, takes place in chapters in volume 3 headed with one of his dicta: "War Is Cruelty . . . " (chapter 4) and "You Cannot Refine It" (chapter 5). Sherman grasps better than anyone, even Grant and Lincoln, the changing demands of the war, and he willingly authors the work of "total war" that would be one of the Civil War's great legacies to the coming century. Through these kinds of structural parallels, Foote brings us to feel the force of changes in the war—to experience them through the form— in a far more immediate (if not always conscious) way than that allowed by commentary.

We feel the tragedy of the war through the structure of the narrative. On one level, the war is an epic story, and Foote indicates as much both in the sweep of the work and, as White and Sugg note, by modeling the work on the *Iliad*, with twenty-four chapters and an epic prologue (111). As epic, it is an *Iliad* rather than an *Aeneid*, concerned with character, event, and fate rather than the founding of the new empire. But the tragic vision predominates and pervades the structure, and, following C. Vann Woodward's assessment of the tragic vision of southerners, we see this tragic sense as most clearly marking Foote's vision as southern (*Burden* 19–21). Not tragic in the superficial sense of ruefully tallying the better than half a million men who died on both sides, the cost in blood and treasure, or speculating on how the war might have been avoided, but tragic in the more profound sense of seeing limitations on human knowledge, of the mixture of motives in any act and the unintended consequences following from it—in a phrase, of having always to act in the realm of innumerable contingencies. As Woodward wrote in his review of Foote, however much Foote's artistic brilliance might seem irrelevant to the concerns of professional historians, it "might serve to expose them to the terrifying chaos and mystery of their intractable subject and disabuse them of some of their illusions of mastery" ("Great American Butchery" 12).

Fate plays a large role on Foote's stage; if God is dead in the bleak wasteland of the modernist vision, Foote makes clear that Fate is not. The individual's confrontation with fate pervades the narrative, as in the repeated motif of stars in the work marking the ineffable forces operative beyond human control or even knowledge. We see the stars of individuals rising and falling, stars impassive above the troubled landscape, and stars as emblems of fate governing events, most notably when Foote uses the biblical words to describe Lee's failure in Pennsylvania: as if "the stars in their courses had fought against him." Careers are made and unmade at the crossing of ways, as with Longstreet refusing to yield the right-of-way to Huger at Seven Pines—"the making of one career and the wrecking of another" (1:446)—or Garfield and Rosecrans taking different roads in different directions after Chickamauga, one to the White House and the other to obscurity. Fate bespeaks the significance of action hidden from the actors in the present, and the deeper currents running beneath the surface of event, as Foote speaks of the "trembling instant when the battle scales of Fortune signal change" when Longstreet strikes at Second Manassas and Pope's flank crumbles (1:638). At times, certain characters—Banks, Early, Pope among them—display a hubris that invites their downfall, but Foote is more concerned, as Aeschylus was, with the human response to the web of contingency than with drawing moral lessons. Many of the great images in his narrative are images of pathos, such as Lee bedridden in his tent, unable to spring his trap for Grant on the North Anna: "'We must strike them a blow!' Betrayed from within, he raged against fate" (3:273); Hood, having returned east after the destruction of his army, staring into the firelight and, in the words of an observer, "going through in his own mind the torture of the damned" (3:760); and, greatest of all, Lincoln with his recurrent dreams of his own death. Fate begins to play the largest role in the third volume as the participants start to sense events working themselves toward a conclusion. After heightening the uncertainty of the first two volumes, Foote begins to foreshadow the end as the events play out like actions in a preordained drama.

The tragic element in the narrative is significant because Foote does not comment on tragedy, he enacts it, and so brings the reader to the catharsis of pity and fear as part of the audience. Through its immediacy, the sense of a progressive unfolding, and the artistic shaping of form, the reader becomes witness to the massive event. What Warren, in the mature vision we saw in the last chapter, merely prescribes, Foote accomplishes in prose. In "The Use of the Past," Warren cites Melville's hope that the war might teach us pity and fear and offers his own hope that, in its scope and nature, the Civil War might restore to us something of the tragic sense beyond the Great Alibi or the Treasury of Virtue. But such a response cannot come about for the mass of Americans through documents, reflection, or history as it is normally written; it can come through experience, through Foote's simulacrum of the war in words. Rubin writes that "Shelby Foote was not himself involved in fighting the war over," but in a crucial sense that is precisely what he *was* doing ("Shelby Foote's Civil War" 191). It is why he gave himself, and his art, over to the writing of a three-thousand-page narrative that would consume twenty years of his career. Foote gives the reader a means to relive the war and so achieve the perspective that Warren hoped for, beyond pride and self-pity. Only then can Foote say, as he does in the final words of the closing note to the final volume, "The conflict is behind me now, as it is for you and it was a hundred-odd years ago for them" (3:1065).

Such is the triumph of Foote's narrative: by reliving "what was" through "what *is*" in the text, he effectively forecloses the "might have been" that haunted southern letters through midcentury. Foote's form is a closed form, a grand completed action of such massiveness that the experience of it, by its very extent and duration, forces us beyond the settled ways of understanding the war we bring to the text. Simms, as we saw at the outset, turned to the Revolution as the great originary moment with confidence that it provided the ground for a unified national narrative; he was forced to yield that ground when competing narratives came into play, and finally into bloody conflict. Foote turned to the Civil War as the ground of our nationhood, but not one providing a unified idea; instead, it is the ground of tragedy, one that forces the recognition of human flaws and limitations on knowledge, of acts determined by innumerable contingencies. Such a perspective—such an experience—breeds humility in the face of history and a recognition that an event such as the Civil War takes us beyond the narrow view of the partisan and the use of history for ideological ends. Foote's view is a long one, as we see in the opening words of his epilogue:

> All things end, and by ending not only find continuance in the whole, but also assure continuance by contributing their droplets, clear or murky, to the stream of history. Anaximander said it best, some 2500 years ago: "It is necessary that things should pass away into that from which they were born. For things must pay one another the penalty and compensation for their injustice according to the ordinance of time." So it was with the Confederacy, and so one day will it be for the other nations of the earth, if not for earth itself. (3:1040)

Foote makes clear that our sense of nationhood emerged from the war, from a common ordeal, but the meaning and ultimate fate of that nation are hidden from us; we, as the war's participants, cannot know the "ordinance of time," and Foote drives this point home in the narrative's final line. He chooses the words of Davis toward the end of his life, given to a journalist who had asked what words he had for future generations: "Tell them. . . . Tell the world that I only loved America" (3:1060). Percy objected to the ambiguity of Foote's focus on Davis and the "sense of nationhood" he describes in his epilogue: "It is not clear whether the 'sense of nationhood' you mention means in USA with a Solid South, or the USA for northern vets or SS [Southern States] for Southerners, or both. Finally, it appears you mean both." Foote replied that "it was intended to be [ambiguous] in just the way it struck you. . . . Just so—a gradual dawning, a gradual realization that it is both I mean," and added in a note that the realization is "for the reader, as it was for them [the participants]."[38] He insists on holding competing visions in tension and resists the temptation to overwrite them with a single narrative to make the war's meaning "clear." In so doing, he moves us beyond ideology and forces us into a deeper confrontation with the war, our nationhood, and ourselves.

CONCLUSION

William Gilmore Simms in the 1820s to 1840s found in the memory of another war an image of unity and national purpose. The narrative he lovingly embellished in his Revolutionary War novels and historical work was in his mind simply a southern variant of a national story: one of hope, progress, and the gradual emancipation of the human spirit. But the image of the landed aristocrat as partisan warrior and champion of freedom contained within it the fatal contradiction that would lead to the historiographic struggle of the 1850s and finally the Civil War itself; narratives of the national past, and finally armies in the field, would compete for supremacy. Only one army could emerge victorious, but the struggle of narratives was not so easily settled. William Wells Brown would find his hopes for a victory of the northern narrative, modified to include the expansion of freedom and the contributions of African Americans, dashed with the failure of Reconstruction. Thomas Nelson Page was more concerned with the second American revolution than the first, and he found its use in a sort of victory in defeat: the "heritage of an untarnished sword," he called it. What the Old South had failed to achieve as a physical nation it might yet achieve as a spiritual one. His figuration of the South as Christ risen from the tomb at the beginning of the "The Old South" is not simply a rhetorical flourish; the historical Jesus as revolutionary was a failure, but the risen Christ could determine the course of an empire and ultimately a civilization. Freed from the destructive aberration of slavery, Page's South could regain its rightful place as standard-bearer for Anglo-Saxon civilization on the continent. The Fugitive-Agrarians were wary of the inheritance of Page and the cult of memory—"the old atavism and sentimentality," in Allen Tate's phrase (qtd. in Simpson, *Man of Letters*, 245)—but still sought in an agrarian South the image of a traditional order to set against the ills of modernity. In seeking a use for the past, Tate and Robert Penn Warren wrestled with the meaning of the Civil War as the great crisis of our culture, but both were driven beyond a simple opposition of North and South to a recognition that the roots of the modern crisis were to be found in both of the competing orders. Warren made a great contribution toward redefining the public role of the artist in relation to history, but Foote did something more: he became the artist as historian. Using the means of art to craft a history that carries the force of lived experience, Foote restored the massiveness and density of the war beyond the imperatives of justification.

Although Foote did not attempt to construct a redemptive history, as earlier southern writers of a conservative bent were tempted to do, he did share their tendency to turn to the southern past for meaning and their sense of responsibility for giving it shape and coherence. Southern writers after those like Warren, Foote, and William Styron would not be obsessed with history in the same way; nor would they feel the compulsion of the writers we have examined to turn from fiction to historiography. Foote's grand achievement was made possible by the fact that he shared something of an older southern sensibility, but the future lay much more with his childhood counterpart Walker Percy, a writer more suited to grappling with life in the postmodern age. The time of Foote's work on the Civil War trilogy—from his start in 1952 to the publication of the third volume in 1974—roughly corresponds to the period of an economic and cultural revolution in the South. One enormous change was the civil rights movement, and by the mid-seventies there was a sense that the South, as Fred Hobson notes, had "come through" and was, while far from perfect, at least on a par with the other regions; with this shift, the "rage to explain," to attack or defend the South as a special entity, was ameliorated in large measure, and history no longer lay so heavy a burden.[1] At the same time, the ever increasing prosperity of the South after World War II wrought permanent changes in the cultural landscape. Beyond the obvious transformation from Bible Belt to Sun Belt, there was a movement into the mass culture transforming not just the South but the world. In a new age of media images, consumer culture, and physical and social mobility, the prototypical young intellectual southerner is apt to be closer to Percy's Williston Bibb Barrett of *The Last Gentleman* than Faulkner's doomed Quentin Compson: bemused and aimless, vaguely discontented in a world promising contentment, a world in which things and the self seem to have strangely lapsed. Far from the oppressive matrix of place, culture, and history that provides the reference points for much southern fiction, the situation now is precisely the absence of such a matrix and how to locate the self in an age when the defining experience is fluidity of self—identity by means of a succession of identifications with images from popular culture.

What distinguishes the situation of the contemporary southern writer from that of the writers I have examined in this study is the lack of any sense of a responsibility for a larger corporate entity known as the South. The traditional lines of community (and the self in relation to it) have simply shifted too radically for the older unifying narratives to carry much force. Southern writers continue to be concerned with community and threats to it, but this community takes on far different forms and does not have the lingering overtones of southern nationalism. Wendell Berry, for example, might have inherited the mantle of agrarianism, but his is an agrarianism of the Sierra Club rather than the Southern League. His concern with the proper relationship of life to land as the true basis of community has much in common with the Agrarians, as he has acknowledged, but his critique has no sectional component.[2] The memory Berry seeks to preserve is that of the small community and the families composing it, and many southern writers have taken a similar path. If there is a concern with writing history, it is not in the broad sweeping narratives demanded of the southern keeper of memory but the narrative of the personal and the local. The memoir in particular has maintained its vitality, but we can measure the distance of the southern writer from redemptive history by setting William Alexander Percy's requiem for the plantation order in *Lanterns on the Levee* alongside a work such as novelist Harry Crews's *Childhood: The Biography of a Place*.[3] Crews's treatment of the harsh realities in the life of poor whites in south Georgia heightens the internal lines of difference—even among whites—that challenge the coherence of "the South" and its historical identity. These are some of the southerners left unredeemed by history.

This heightened reliance on private memory has expanded our notion of the South and its history, but there may yet be a return among creative writers to a more public role. Against the trend of mass culture and cultural homogenization, we have already begun to see a resurgence of regionalism in some quarters, and a region is defined largely by its past. The view of history as a tissue of competing fictions offers a kind of liberation, but taken too far, that liberation can simply be an imprisonment of a different kind—history as a hall of mirrors. As Warren has a chastened Thomas Jefferson say in *Brother to Dragons*, "without the fact of the past we cannot dream the future."[4] The examples of Warren and Foote, as we have seen in this study, demonstrate the latent power of the tradition of the southern artist as keeper of memory, beyond the old work of cultural justification and redemptive history. By limiting the prerogatives of subjective vision and taking on a responsibility for the facts of the past, the artist can extend the province of the literary and perhaps reclaim some of the ground too easily yielded to the historical specialist. In doing so, he or she might restore to readers something of their own responsibility for the making of history. "Historical sense and poetic sense," Warren tells us in *Brother to Dragons*, "should not, in the end, be contradictory, for if poetry is the little myth we make, history is the big myth we live, and in our living, constantly remake" (xii).

NOTES

INTRODUCTION

1. Three seminal books in southern literary studies mix genres in this fashion: Fred Hobson, *Tell about the South: The Southern Rage to Explain* (Baton Rouge: Louisiana State University Press, 1983); Michael O'Brien, *The Idea of the American South* (Baltimore: Johns Hopkins University Press, 1979); and Daniel Singal, *The War Within: From Victorian to Modernist Thought in the South, 1919–1945* (Chapel Hill: University of North Carolina Press, 1982). One encounters figures such as the sociologist Howard Odum and the historian Ulrich B. Phillips alongside canonical literary figures.

2. See Richard Weaver, "Aspects of the Southern Philosophy," in *The Southern Essays of Richard M. Weaver*, ed. George M. Curtis III and James J. Thompson Jr. (Indianapolis: Liberty Fund, 1987), 189–208, and C. Vann Woodward, "The Search for Southern Identity," in *The Burden of Southern History*, rev. ed. (Baton Rouge: Louisiana State University Press, 1968).

3. Simpson, *The Man of Letters in New England and the South: Essays on the History of the Literary Vocation in America* (Baton Rouge: Louisiana State University Press, 1973), 209; Robert Penn Warren, *The Legacy of the Civil War: Meditations on the Centennial* (New York: Random House, 1961), 274.

4. W. J. Cash, *The Mind of the South* (New York: Knopf, 1941); Lillian Smith, *Killers of the Dream* (New York: Norton, 1949).

5. On this shift in the social sciences to a positivistic model, see Eric Voegelin, *The New Science of Politics: An Introduction* (Chicago: University of Chicago Press, 1952), 1–26.

6. See Michael O'Brien's comments on the conservative character of historians, *Rethinking the South: Essays in Intellectual History* (Baltimore: Johns Hopkins University Press, 1988), 7–14. More radically, Hayden White has challenged historians to recognize the way in which modes of discourse shape ostensibly "objective" analysis. Historians use the conventions of figurative, not technical (i.e., scientific), language and fail to recognize the way in which their narratives are necessarily shaped by conventions received from literary tradition. See *Metahistory: The Historical Imagination in Nineteenth-Century Europe* (Baltimore: Johns Hopkins University Press, 1973), and *Tropics of Discourse: Essays in Cultural Criticism* (Baltimore: Johns Hopkins University Press, 1978).

7. Richard J. Gray, *Writing the South: Ideas of an American Region* (Cambridge: Cambridge University Press, 1986).

8. Benedict Anderson, *Imagined Communities: Reflections on the Origin and Spread of Nationalism* (London: Verso, 1991).

9. See "The Southern Writer and the Great Literary Secession," in Simpson, *Man of Letters*, 229–55. For Simpson's treatment of the problematic nature of southern pastoral, see *The Dispossessed Garden: Pastoral and History in Southern Literature* (Athens: University of Georgia Press, 1975) and his extensive analysis of the South in relation to modernity in *The Brazen Face of History: Studies in the Literary Consciousness of America* (Baton Rouge: Louisiana State University Press, 1980).

10. Allen Tate, "Ode to the Confederate Dead," in *Poems* (New York: Charles Scribner's Sons, 1960), 19–26.

11. Tate to Davidson, August 10, 1929, in *The Literary Correspondence of Donald Davidson and Allen Tate*, ed. John Tyree Fain and Thomas Daniel Young (Athens: University of Georgia Press, 1974), 229.

12. Shelby Foote, *The Civil War: A Narrative*, vol. 3, *Red River to Appomattox* (New York: Random House, 1974), 1065.

1

"MEMORY ENOUGH FOR THE BEST AND BRAVEST OF US ALL"

1. There is still some debate over whether to include the biography of Gen. Nathanael Greene, which Simms edited for publication in 1849, among his works. It certainly bears signs of his handiwork, but the question of authorship has been answered to my satisfaction by Frederick Wagner in "Simms's Editing of *The Life of Nathanael Greene*," *Southern Literary Journal* 11 (Fall 1978). He establishes that Simms was indeed the editor, not the author, of the work, and I will therefore leave it aside.

2. This transference and its implications lie at the core of most of Simpson's work. See also *Mind and the American Civil War: A Meditation on Lost Causes* (Baton Rouge: Louisiana State University Press, 1989), 1–32, and Simpson, *Man of Letters*, 1–31, 201–28.

3. St. Jean de Crèvecoeur, *Letters from an American Farmer*, in *The American Tradition in Literature*, ed. George Perkins and Barbara Perkins, 11th ed. (New York: McGraw-Hill, 2007), 251; Ralph Waldo Emerson, *Nature*, in Perkins and Perkins, *American Tradition in Literature*, 882; George H. Callcott, *History in the United States, 1800–1860: Its Practice and Purpose* (Baltimore: Johns Hopkins University Press, 1970), 25.

4. For example, Irving made his name as a historian with his biography of Columbus (1828) and *A Chronicle of the Conquest of Grenada* (1829); he later followed with his highly regarded life of Washington (1856–59). Cooper turned his hand to a history of the U.S. Navy (1839).

5. On the status of the novel in the early Republic, see Cathy Davidson's *Revolution and the Word* (New York: Oxford University Press, 1986).

6. William Gilmore Simms, *Views and Reviews in American Literature, History and Fiction: First Series*, ed. C. Hugh Holman (Cambridge, MA: Belknap Press, 1962), 33–34.

7. For an assessment of the value of Simms's work to the historians, see Stephen Meats, "Artist or Historian: William Gilmore Simms and the Revolutionary South," in *Eighteenth-Century Florida and the Revolutionary South*, ed. Samuel Proctor (Gainesville, FL: University Press of Florida, 1975), 95–108.

8. Quoted in Jon L. Wakelyn, *The Politics of a Literary Man: William Gilmore Simms* (Westport, CT: Greenwood Press, 1973), 88–89.

9. [Nathaniel Beverly Tucker], "Literary Notices," *Southern Literary Messenger* 1 (June 1835).

10. C. Hugh Holman, ed., introduction to *Views and Reviews in American Literature, History and Fiction, First Series*, by William Gilmore Simms, ed. Hugh C. Holman (Cambridge, MA: Belknap Press, 1962), xxii.

11. William Gilmore Simms, dedication to *The Wigwam and the Cabin* (1856), in John Caldwell

Guilds, ed., *The Simms Reader: Selections from the Writings of William Gilmore Simms* (Charlottesville: University of Virginia Press, 2001), 9.

12. Louis D. Rubin Jr. *The Edge of the Swamp: A Study in the Literature and Society of the Old South* (Baton Rouge: Louisiana State University Press, 1989), 63.

13. This question of Simms's relationship to Charleston pervades much of the criticism. For two different perspectives on the issue, see Louis D. Rubin Jr., "Simms, Charleston, and the Profession of Letters," in *"Long Years of Neglect": The Work and Reputation of William Gilmore Simms,* ed. John Caldwell Guilds (Fayetteville: University of Arkansas Press, 1988), 242–64, and John Caldwell Guilds, *Simms: A Literary Life* (Fayetteville: University of Arkansas Press, 1992), particularly 3–14.

14. Quoted in Mary Ann Wimsatt, *The Major Fiction of William Gilmore Simms: Cultural Traditions and Literary Form* (Baton Rouge: Louisiana State University Press, 1989), 17.

15. William Gilmore Simms, *The Social Principle: The True Source of National Permanence* (Tuscaloosa: Eurosophic Society of the University of Alabama, 1843), 7.

16. William Gilmore Simms, *The Partisan: A Romance of the Revolution* (1835; New York: Redfield, 1856), 355–56.

17. William Gilmore Simms, *The Life of Francis Marion* (New York: Langley, 1844), 9.

18. John McCardell, "Poetry and the Practical: William Gilmore Simms," in *Intellectual Life in Antebellum Charleston,* ed. Michael O'Brien and David Moltke-Hansen (Knoxville: University of Tennessee Press, 1986), 202.

19. William Gilmore Simms, *The Letters of William Gilmore Simms,* ed. Mary C. Simms Oliphant, Alfred Taylor Odell, and T. C. Duncan Eaves (Columbia: University of South Carolina Press, 1952–82), 2:297.

20. Simms's admiration of dueling is certainly qualified, as we see here and in his biography of Bayard. Critics such as Charles S. Watson, *From Nationalism to Secessionism: The Changing Fiction of William Gilmore Simms* (Westport, CT: Greenwood Press, 1993), imply that Simms gave wholehearted approval to the chivalric code of honor; see 36–40.

21. For another treatment of this balance between stability and change, see David Moltke-Hansen, "Ordered Progress: The Historical Philosophy of William Gilmore Simms," in Guilds, *"Long Years of Neglect,"* 126–47.

22. William Gilmore Simms, *The Life of Captain John Smith* (New York: Geo. F. Cooledge, 1846), 61.

23. William Gilmore Simms, *The Life of Chevalier Bayard* (New York: Harper, 1847), 2.

24. David D. Van Tassel, *Recording America's Past: An Interpretation of the Development of Historical Studies in America, 1607–1884* (Chicago: University of Chicago Press, 1960), 135.

25. See ibid., 134–41, and Callcott, *History in the United States,* 215–26.

26. William Gilmore Simms, "South Carolina in the Revolution," *Southern Quarterly Review* 14 (July 1848): 37–77; (October 1848): 261–337, later published as part of *South Carolina in the Revolutionary War: Being a Reply to Certain Misrepresentations and Mistakes of Recent Writers, in Relation to the Course and Conduct of this State* (Charleston, SC: Walker and James, 1853). All citations refer to the pamphlet.

27. William Gilmore Simms, "*Domestic Manners of the Americans,* by Mrs. Trollope," *American Quarterly Review* 12 (September 1832): 110; William Gilmore Simms, "Miss Martineau on Slavery," *Southern Literary Messenger* 3 (1837).

28. Simms to Nathaniel Beverly Tucker, May 6, 1849, in Simms, *Letters*.

29. William R. Taylor, *Cavalier and Yankee: The Old South and the American National Character* (New York: George Braziller, 1961), 280.

30. William Gilmore Simms, *The History of South Carolina*, rev. ed. (Charleston: Russell and Jones, 1860), 6.

31. William Gilmore Simms, *Sack and Destruction of the City of Columbia, S.C.* (Columbia, SC: Daily Phoenix, 1865), 84.

2
"IT WILL BE AS I NOW REMEMBER IT"

1. Harriet R. Holman, "The Literary Career of Thomas Nelson Page, 1884–1910" (PhD diss., Duke University, 1947), 183.

2. Henry Adams, *The Education of Henry Adams*, in *Novels, Mont Saint Michel, The Education*, Library of America (New York: Literary Classics of the United States, 1983), 723.

3. Thomas Nelson Page, "Recollections and Reminiscences," manuscript, box 37, Thomas Nelson Page Papers, Duke University, 4.

4. Lucinda Hardwick MacKethan, *The Dream of Arcady: Place and Time in Southern Literature* (Baton Rouge: Louisiana State University Press, 1980), 40.

5. C. Vann Woodward, *The Origins of the New South, 1877–1913*, vol. 9, *The History of the South*, ed. Wendell Holmes Stephenson and E. Merton Coulter (Baton Rouge: Louisiana State University Press, 1951), 155.

6. See Woodward, *Origins of the New South*, particularly 107–74.

7. Wayne Mixon, *Southern Writers and the New South Movement, 1865–1913* (Chapel Hill: University of North Carolina Press, 1980), 8.

8. Page to Mrs. Sarah Seddon Bruce, London, October 9, 1890, Thomas Nelson Page Papers, Duke University.

9. Thomas Nelson Page, *The Old South: Essays Social and Political* (1892; New York: Scribner's, 1906), 171.

10. Homi K. Bhabha, "DissemiNation: Time, Narrative, and the Margins of the Modern Nation," in *Nation and Narration*, ed. Homi Bhabha (London: Routledge, 1990), 299.

11. Lloyd Kramer, "Historical Narratives and the Meaning of Nationalism," *Journal of the History of Ideas* 58 (1997): 537.

12. Page here is responding directly to an address by George Washington Cable to the Massachusetts Club of Boston on February 22, 1890. For Cable's views, see Arlin Turner, ed., *The Negro Question: A Selection of Writings on Civil Rights in the South by George W. Cable* (New York: Norton, 1958).

13. Woodward paints a portrait of Hayne's life in his cropper shack that provides a stark contrast to Page. See *Origins of the New South*, 162.

14. Thomas Nelson Page, *The Old Dominion: Her Making and Her Manners* (New York: Scribner's, 1908), viii.

15. William E. Dodd, "The Old Dominion: Her Making and Her Manners," *American Historical Review* 14 (October 1908).

16. Page revised and expanded the biography largely because of criticisms of inaccuracies in the first version (many made by Confederate veterans). See Holman, "Literary Career of Thomas Nelson Page," 117. For my purposes, the first version contains all of Page's essential claims about Lee and his relationship to Virginia and the broader South; the later work simply expands the accounts of the various campaigns.

17. Thomas Nelson Page, *Robert E. Lee: The Southerner* (New York: Scribner's, 1898), 278.

18. In Bonhoeffer's account, "cheap grace" resulted when "the justification of the sinner in the world degenerated into the justification of sin and the world" (53). See Dietrich Bonhoeffer, *The Cost of Discipleship*, 2nd ed. (New York: Macmillan, 1959), 45–60.

3
"THE EXASPERATED GENIUS OF AFRICA"

1. Dickson D. Bruce Jr., *The Origins of African American Literature, 1680–1865* (Charlottesville: University of Virginia Press, 2001), 100.

2. Wilson Jeremiah Moses, *Afrotopia: The Roots of African American Popular History* (Cambridge: Cambridge University Press, 1998), 39.

3. Eric Sundquist, "The Literature of Slavery and African American Culture," in *The Cambridge History of American Literature*, vol. 2, *American Prose Writing, 1820–1862* (Cambridge: Cambridge University Press, 1995), 241.

4. William Edward Farrison, *William Wells Brown: Author and Reformer* (Chicago: Chicago University Press, 1969), 172.

5. William Wells Brown, *St. Domingo: Its Revolutions and Its Patriots. A Lecture. Delivered before the Metropolitan Athenaeum, London, May 16, and at St. Thomas' Church, Philadelphia, December 20, 1854* (Boston: Bela Marsh, 1855; repr., Philadelphia: Rhistoric Publications, 1969), 9.

6. William Wells Brown, *The Black Man: His Antecedents, His Genius, and His Achievements*, 2nd ed. (New York: Thomas Hamilton, 1863; repr., New York: Johnson Reprint Co., 1968), 6.

7. See Elizabeth Elkin Grammar, "Collective Biography," in *The Oxford Companion to African American Literature*, ed. William L. Andrews et al. (New York: Oxford University Press, 1997), 161–62.

8. William Wells Brown, *Anglo-African*, August 13, 1864, 2–3.

9. William Wells Brown, *The Negro in the American Rebellion: His Heroism and His Fidelity* (Boston: Lee and Shepard, 1867; repr., New York: Johnson Reprint Co., 1968), v.

10. Alonzo Moore, foreword to *The Rising Son: or, The Antecedents and Advancement of the Colored Race*, by William Wells Brown (Boston: A. G. Brown, 1874; repr., Miami, FL: Mnemosyne Publishing, 1969), 9.

11. William Wells Brown, *The Rising Son: or, The Antecedents and Advancement of the Colored Race* (Boston: A. G. Brown, 1874; repr., Miami, FL: Mnemosyne Publishing, 1969), 50.

4
"A DISTURBING AND ALIEN MEMORY"

1. In addition to the works dealt with here, other historical works emerging from the Fugitive-Agrarian circle include Andrew Nelson Lytle, *Bedford Forrest and His Critter Company* (New York:

Milton, Balch, 1931); John Gould Fletcher, *The Two Frontiers: A Study in Historical Psychology* (New York: Coward-McCann, 1930); *Arkansas* (Chapel Hill: University of North Carolina Press, 1947); Donald Davidson's Pulitzer Prize–winning *The Tennessee*, vol. 1, *The Old River: Frontier to Secession* (New York: Rinehart, 1946); and *The Tennessee*, vol. 2, *The New River: Civil War to TVA* (New York: Rinehart, 1948).

2. See Louis D. Rubin Jr., *The Wary Fugitives: Four Poets and the South* (Baton Rouge: Louisiana State University Press, 1978) and his introduction to Twelve Southerners, *I'll Take My Stand: The South and the Agrarian Tradition* (New York: Harper, 1930); for more recent reassessments of the Fugitive-Agrarians, see Singal, *War Within*, 198–231; O'Brien, *Idea of the American South*, 117–212; and Michael Kreyling, *Inventing Southern Literature* (Jackson: University Press of Mississippi, 1998), 3–18.

3. Radcliffe Squires, *Allen Tate: A Literary Biography* (New York: Pegasus, 1971), 38.

4. Tate, "Ode to the Confederate Dead," 19–26.

5. The genesis of the Agrarian movement has been placed in 1926, but Singal makes a convincing case that the relevant letters of Tate, Ransom, and Davidson were written in 1927; *War Within*, 398 n. 5.

6. Donald Davidson, "Stonewall Jackson's Way," in *The Spyglass: Views and Reviews, 1924–1930*, ed. John Tyree Fain (Nashville: Vanderbilt University Press, 1963), 201.

7. Tate to Davidson, April 28, 1927, in Fain and Young, *Literary Correspondence*, 198.

8. Thomas Landess, preface to *Stonewall Jackson: The Good Soldier*, by Allen Tate (Nashville: J. S. Sanders, 1991), viii.

9. Allen Tate, *Stonewall Jackson: The Good Soldier* (New York: Minton, Balch, 1928; Nashville: J. S. Sanders, 1991), 5.

10. See Wade, "The Life and Death of Cousin Lucius," in Twelve Southerners, *I'll Take My Stand*, 265–301, and Donald Davidson, *The Tall Men* (Boston: Houghton Mifflin, 1927).

11. Tate to Davidson, August 10, 1929, in Fain and Young, *Literary Correspondence*, 231.

12. Allen Tate, "Mother and Son," in *Poems*, 34.

13. Allen Tate, "Message from Abroad," *Poems* 10–13, 46–47.

14. M. E. Bradford, "Rumors of Mortality: An Introduction to Allen Tate," in *Generations of the Faithful Heart: On the Literature of the South* (La Salle, IL: Sherwood Sugden, 1983), 27.

15. Allen Tate, *Jefferson Davis: His Rise and Fall* (New York: Minton, Balch, 1929), 5.

16. Compare Tate's comment to Davidson in a letter from August 10, 1929: "We must be the last Europeans—there being no Europeans in Europe at present"; Fain and Young, *Literary Correspondence*, 230.

17. Tate to John Peale Bishop, June 1931, in *The Republic of Letters in America: The Correspondence of John Peale Bishop and Allen Tate*, ed. Thomas Daniel Young and John J. Hindle (Lexington: University Press of Kentucky, 1981), 34.

18. Lewis P. Simpson, *The Fable of the Southern Writer* (Baton Rouge: Louisiana State University Press, 1994), 33.

19. Bishop to Tate, October 19–26, 1932, Young and Hindle, *Republic of Letters in America*, 65.

20. Thomas A. Underwood, *Allen Tate: Orphan of the South* (Princeton, NJ: Princeton University Press, 2000), 196.

21. Tate to Bishop, February 11, 1932, Young and Hindle, *Republic of Letters in America*, 52.

22. Allen Tate to Ellen Glasgow, May 31, 1933, quoted in Squires, *Allen Tate,* 128–29.

23. Mark Malavasi, *The Unregenerate South: The Agrarian Thought of John Crowe Ransom, Allen Tate, and Donald Davidson* (Baton Rouge: Louisiana State University Press, 1997), 143.

24. Tate to Davidson, January 14, 1953, in Fain and Young, *Literary Correspondence,* 370.

25. Allen Tate, *Essays of Four Decades* (New York: William Morrow, 1968), 4–5.

5
"HISTORY IS BLIND, BUT MAN IS NOT"

1. On Warren's religious ambivalence, see Robert Koppelman, *Robert Penn Warren's Modernist Spirituality* (Columbia: University of Missouri Press, 1990), and James H. Justus, *The Achievement of Robert Penn Warren* (Baton Rouge: Louisiana State University Press, 1981), particularly 41–45.

2. Warren's final book, *Portrait of a Father* (Lexington: University Press of Kentucky, 1988), is an extended meditation on mystery of his father. For one example of his father's reticence, see 16–17.

3. Joseph Blotner, *Robert Penn Warren: A Biography* (New York: Random House, 1997), 12.

4. Rob Roy Purdy, ed., *The Fugitives' Reunion: Conversations at Vanderbilt* (Nashville: Vanderbilt University Press, 1959), 208–9.

5. Through Tate's contact with literary agent Mavis McIntosh, Warren was offered the commission for a John Brown biography by Payson and Clarke in 1929. Jonathan S. Cullick, *Making History: The Biographical Narratives of Robert Penn Warren* (Baton Rouge: Louisiana State University Press, 2000), 35.

6. See John Burt, *Robert Penn Warren and American Idealism* (New Haven, CT: Yale University Press, 1988).

7. Robert Penn Warren, *John Brown: The Making of a Martyr* (New York: Payson and Clarke, 1929; Nashville: J. S. Sanders, 1993), 19.

8. William Bedford Clark, *The American Vision of Robert Penn Warren* (Lexington: University Press of Kentucky, 1991), 5.

9. Robert Penn Warren, *Who Speaks for the Negro?* (New York: Random House, 1965), 320.

10. Victor Strandberg, *The Poetic Vision of Robert Penn Warren* (Lexington: University Press of Kentucky, 1977), 130–49.

11. Robert Penn Warren, *All the King's Men,* HBJ Modern Classics ed. (New York: Harcourt Brace Jovanovich, 1974), 200.

12. L. Hugh Moore Jr., *Robert Penn Warren and History: "The Big Myth We Live"* (The Hague: Mouton, 1970), 81.

13. "A Conversation" (interview with Bill Moyers, 1976), 218, quoted in Cullick, *Making History,* 74.

14. Robert Penn Warren, *Brother to Dragons: A Tale in Verse and Voices* (New York: Random House, 1953), 24.

15. Robert Penn Warren, "The Use of the Past," in *New and Selected Essays* (New York: Random House, 1989), 29, 31.

16. Robert Penn Warren, *Democracy and Poetry* (Cambridge, MA: Harvard University Press, 1975), 56.

17. Reinhold Niebuhr, *The Irony of American History* (New York: Charles Scribner's Sons, 1952).

18. T. Harry Williams, *Lincoln and the Radicals* (Madison: University of Wisconsin Press, 1941).

6
THE CONFLICT IS BEHIND ME NOW

1. Shelby Foote, "Faulkner's Depiction of the Planter Aristocracy," in *The South and Faulkner's Yoknapatawpha: The Actual and the Apocryphal,* ed. Evans Harrington and Ann Abadie (Jackson: University Press of Mississippi, 1977), 49.

2. Quoted in Helen White and Redding Sugg, *Shelby Foote* (Boston: Twayne, 1982), 11.

3. Walker Percy, "Uncle Will," in *Signposts in a Strange Land,* ed. Patrick Samway (New York: Farrar, Straus and Giroux, 1991), 55–56.

4. William Alexander Percy, *Lanterns on the Levee: Recollections of a Planter's Son* (New York: Knopf, 1941).

5. Interview with Helen White and Redding Sugg in *Conversations with Shelby Foote,* ed. William C. Carter (Jackson: University Press of Mississippi, 1989), 206–7.

6. Foote to Percy, December 11, 1973, in *The Correspondence of Shelby Foote and Walker Percy,* ed. Jay Tolson (Durham, NC: DoubleTake, 1997), 181.

7. Foote's war record is one of frustration. He served with a national guard artillery unit that was mobilized and sent to Ireland, only to be discharged for the minor offense of barely exceeding a fifty-mile limit to visit his girlfriend and soon-to-be wife in Belfast. After returning to the States, he made another attempt to find his way to the battlefield by enlisting in the Marine Corps, but the war ended before his deployment in the Pacific.

8. Foote to Percy, November 19, 1949, in Tolson, *Correspondence,* 21.

9. Foote to Percy, December 31, 1950, in Tolson, *Correspondence,* 39.

10. Quoted in Foote to Percy, February 12, 1952, in Tolson, *Correspondence,* 81.

11. Shelby Foote, *Tournament* (New York: Dial Press, 1949).

12. Robert L. Phillips, *Shelby Foote: Novelist and Historian* (Jackson: University Press of Mississippi, 1992), 158.

13. Shelby Foote, *Shiloh* (New York: Dial Press, 1952; repr., New York: Barnes and Noble, 1992), 164.

14. Shelby Foote, "The Novelist's View of History," *Mississippi Quarterly* 17 (Fall 1964): 220.

15. *Child by Fever* became the 150-page centerpiece of *Jordan County: A Landscape with Figures* (New York: Dial Press, 1954).

16. Foote to Percy, November 19, 1951, February 16, 1952, in Tolson, *Correspondence,* 65, 82.

17. Foote to Percy, March 23, 1952, in Tolson, *Correspondence,* 87.

18. George Garrett, "Foote's *The Civil War:* The Version for Posterity?" *Mississippi Quarterly* 28 (Winter 1974–75): 86.

19. Shelby Foote, *The Civil War: A Narrative,* vol. 1, *Fort Sumter to Perryville* (New York: Random House, 1958), 815.

20. Oscar Handlin, *Truth in History* (Cambridge, MA: Belknap Press, 1979), 61.

21. C. Vann Woodward, "The Great American Butchery." Review of *The Civil War: A Narra-*

tive, vol. 3, *New York Review of Books*, March 6, 1975. For one of the earlier negative assessments, see James I. Robertson Jr., Review of *The Civil War: A Narrative*, vol. 2, *American Historical Review* 69 (April 1964). For the positive shift in historians' view of the work, see Robertson's later review of the entire work in *Civil War History* 21 (June 1975), and Robert Hartje, review of vol. 3, *American Historical Review* 81 (October 1976).

22. Louis D. Rubin Jr., "Shelby Foote's Civil War," in *A Gallery of Southerners* (Baton Rouge: Louisiana State University Press, 1982), 181.

23. See Joyce Appleby, Lynn Hunt, and Margaret Jacob, *Telling the Truth about History* (New York: Norton, 1994), and Peter Burke, "History of Events and the Revival of Narrative," in *New Perspectives on Historical Writing*, ed. Peter Burke (Cambridge, England: Polity Press, 1991), 233–46.

24. Foote to Percy, November 29, 1956, in Tolson, *Correspondence*, 111.

25. Foote, *The Civil War: A Narrative*, vol. 3, *Red River to Appomatox*, 341.

26. Shelby Foote, *The Civil War: A Narrative*, vol. 2, *Fredericksburg to Meridian* (New York: Random House, 1963), 149.

27. Foote to Percy, August 13, 1963, in Tolson, *Correspondence*, 125. Foote refers here to Lillian Smith's *Killers of the Dream*, first published in 1949.

28. Interview with John Griffin Jones (1979) in Carter, *Conversations*, 181–82.

29. James Panabaker links the strange "intimacy" of the combat with the existential undercurrent in Foote's history; *Shelby Foote and the Art of History: Two Gates to the City* (Knoxville: University of Tennessee Press, 2004), 139–40.

30. Tolson, *Correspondence*, 150.

31. Interview in *Memphis Commercial Appeal*, July 15, 1973, in Carter, *Conversations*, 104.

32. James M. Cox, "Shelby Foote's Civil War," in *Recovering Literature's Lost Ground: Essays in American Autobiography* (Baton Rouge, Louisiana State University Press, 1989), 211.

33. Foote claims in an interview that the two geniuses developed over the course of the war were Forrest and Lincoln; interview with Jones in Carter, *Conversations*, 173.

34. Foote to Percy, November 29, 1956, in Tolson, *Correspondence*, 111.

35. Foote to Percy, November 8, 1951, in Tolson, *Correspondence*, 61.

36. Foote to Percy, December 11, 1951, in Tolson, *Correspondence*, 71.

37. In each volume of the Vintage paperback edition of the work, Foote includes a "Comprehensive Table of Contents." This table is not merely a finding aid for the reader (there was already a comprehensive index) but a testament to Foote's emphasis on structure. Essentially, he is giving the reader a glimpse of the structure he mapped out before writing the history.

38. Percy to Foote, July 7, 1974; Foote to Percy, July 11, 1974, in Tolson, *Correspondence*, 188–189.

CONCLUSION

1. See Hobson, *Tell about the South*, 297–300, 352–54.

2. For Wendell Berry's assessment of the Agrarians, see "Still Standing: Why the Prophecies of the Agrarians Should Not Have Been Ignored," *Oxford American* 25 (January/February 1999).

3. Harry Crews, *A Childhood: The Biography of a Place* (New York: Harper and Row, 1978).

4. Warren, *Brother to Dragons*, 193.

WORKS CITED

Adams, Henry. *The Education of Henry Adams.* In *Novels, Mont Saint Michel, The Education.* Library of America. New York: Literary Classics of the United States, 1983.

Anderson, Benedict. *Imagined Communities: Reflections on the Origin and Spread of Nationalism.* London: Verso, 1991.

Appleby, Joyce, Lynn Hunt, and Margaret Jacob. *Telling the Truth about History.* New York: Norton, 1994.

Berry, Wendell. "Still Standing: Why the Prophecies of the Agrarians Should Not Have Been Ignored." *Oxford American* 25 (January/February 1999): 64–69.

Bhabha, Homi K. "DissemiNation: Time, Narrative, and the Margins of the Modern Nation." In *Nation and Narration,* edited by Homi Bhabha. London: Routledge, 1990.

Blotner, Joseph. *Robert Penn Warren: A Biography.* New York: Random House, 1997.

Bonhoeffer, Dietrich. *The Cost of Discipleship.* 2nd ed. New York: Macmillan, 1959.

Bradford, M. E. "Rumors of Mortality: An Introduction to Allen Tate." In *Generations of the Faithful Heart: On the Literature of the South.* La Salle, IL: Sherwood Sugden, 1983.

Brown, William Wells. *The Black Man: His Antecedents, His Genius, and His Achievements.* New York: Thomas Hamilton, 1863. Reprint, New York: Johnson Reprint Co., 1968.

———. *The Negro in the American Rebellion: His Heroism and His Fidelity.* Boston: Lee and Shepard, 1867. Reprint, New York: Johnson Reprint Co., 1968.

———. *The Rising Son; or, The Antecedents and Advancement of the Colored Race.* Boston: A. G. Brown, 1874. Reprint, Miami, FL: Mnemosyne Publishing, 1969.

———. *St. Domingo: Its Revolutions and Its Patriots. A Lecture. Delivered before the Metropolitan Athenaeum, London, May 16, and at St. Thomas' Church, Philadelphia, December 20, 1854.* Boston: Bela Marsh, 1855. Reprint, Philadelphia: Rhistoric Publications, 1969.

Bruce, Dickson D., Jr. *The Origins of African American Literature, 1680–1865.* Charlottesville: University of Virginia Press, 2001.

Burke, Peter, ed. *New Perspectives on Historical Writing.* Cambridge, England: Polity Press, 1991.

Burt, John. *Robert Penn Warren and American Idealism.* New Haven, CT: Yale University Press, 1988.

Callcott, George H. *History in the United States, 1800–1860: Its Practice and Purpose.* Baltimore: Johns Hopkins University Press, 1970.

Carter, William C., ed. *Conversations with Shelby Foote.* Jackson: University Press of Mississippi, 1989.

Cash, W. J. *The Mind of the South*. New York: Knopf, 1941.

Clark, William Bedford. *The American Vision of Robert Penn Warren*. Lexington: University Press of Kentucky, 1991.

Connelly, Thomas. "Robert Penn Warren as Historian." In *A Southern Renascence Man: Views of Robert Penn Warren by Thomas L. Connelly, Louis D. Rubin, Madison Jones, Harold Bloom, and James Dickey*, edited by Walter B. Edgar. Baton Rouge: Louisiana State University Press, 1984.

Cox, James M. "Shelby Foote's Civil War." In *Recovering Literature's Lost Ground: Essays in American Autobiography*. Baton Rouge: Louisiana State University Press, 1989.

Crews, Harry. *A Childhood: The Biography of a Place*. New York: Harper and Row, 1978.

Cullick, Jonathan S. *Making History: The Biographical Narratives of Robert Penn Warren*. Baton Rouge: Louisiana State University Press, 2000.

Davidson, Cathy. *Revolution and the Word*. New York: Oxford University Press, 1986.

Davidson, Donald. *The Spyglass: Views and Reviews, 1924–1930*. Edited by John Tyree Fain. Nashville: Vanderbilt University Press, 1963.

Dodd, William E. "The Old Dominion: Her Making and Her Manners." *American Historical Review* 14 (October 1908): 182.

Fain, John Tyree, and Thomas Daniel Young, eds. *The Literary Correspondence of Donald Davidson and Allen Tate*. Athens: University of Georgia Press, 1974.

Farrison, William Edward. *William Wells Brown: Author and Reformer*. Chicago: University of Chicago Press, 1969.

Foote, Shelby. *The Civil War: A Narrative*. Vol. 1, *Fort Sumter to Perryville*. New York: Random House, 1958.

———. *The Civil War: A Narrative*. Vol. 2, *Fredericksburg to Meridian*. New York: Random House, 1963.

———. *The Civil War: A Narrative*. Vol. 3, *Red River to Appomattox*. New York: Random House, 1974.

———. "Faulkner's Depiction of the Planter Aristocracy." In *The South and Faulkner's Yoknapatawpha: The Actual and the Apocryphal*, edited by Evans Harrington and Ann Abadie. Jackson: University Press of Mississippi, 1977.

———. *Jordan County: A Landscape with Figures*. New York: Dial Press, 1954.

———. "The Novelist's View of History." *Mississippi Quarterly* 17 (Fall 1964): 219–25.

———. *Shiloh*. New York: Dial Press, 1952. Reprint, New York: Barnes and Noble, 1992.

———. *Tournament*. New York: Dial Press, 1949.

Garrett, George. "Foote's *The Civil War*: The Version for Posterity?" *Mississippi Quarterly* 28 (Winter 1974–75): 83–92.

Grammar, Elizabeth Elkin. "Collective Biography." In *The Oxford Companion to African American Literature*, edited by William L. Andrews et al. New York: Oxford University Press, 1997.

Gray, Richard J. *Writing the South: Ideas of an American Region*. Cambridge: Cambridge University Press, 1986.

Guilds, John Caldwell, ed. *"Long Years of Neglect": The Work and Reputation of William Gilmore Simms*. Fayetteville: University of Arkansas Press, 1988.

———. *Simms: A Literary Life*. Fayetteville: University of Arkansas Press, 1992.

———, ed. *The Simms Reader: Selections from the Writings of William Gilmore Simms*. Charlottesville: University of Virginia Press, 2001.

Handlin, Oscar. *Truth in History*. Cambridge, MA: Belknap Press, 1979.

Hartje, Robert. Review of *The Civil War: A Narrative*, vol. 3. *American Historical Review* 81 (October 1976): 975–76.

Havard, William C., and Walter Sullivan, eds. *A Band of Prophets: The Vanderbilt Agrarians after Fifty Years*. Baton Rouge: Louisiana State University Press, 1982.

Hobson, Fred. *Tell about the South: The Southern Rage to Explain*. Baton Rouge: Louisiana State University Press, 1983.

Holman, C. Hugh. Introduction to *Views and Reviews in American Literature, History and Fiction: First Series*, by William Gilmore Simms, edited by C. Hugh Holman. Cambridge, MA: Belknap Press, 1962.

———. *The Roots of Southern Writing: Essays on the Literature of the American South*. Athens: University of Georgia Press, 1972.

Holman, Harriet R. "The Literary Career of Thomas Nelson Page, 1884–1910." PhD diss., Duke University, 1947.

Justus, James H. *The Achievement of Robert Penn Warren*. Baton Rouge: Louisiana State University Press, 1981.

Koppelman, Robert. *Robert Penn Warren's Modernist Spirituality*. Columbia: University of Missouri Press, 1990.

Kramer, Lloyd. "Historical Narratives and the Meaning of Nationalism." *Journal of the History of Ideas* 58 (1997): 525–45.

Kreyling, Michael. *Inventing Southern Literature*. Jackson: University Press of Mississippi, 1998.

Landess, Thomas. Preface to *Stonewall Jackson: The Good Soldier*, by Allen Tate. Nashville: J. S. Sanders, 1991.

MacKethan, Lucinda Hardwick. *The Dream of Arcady: Place and Time in Southern Literature*. Baton Rouge: Louisiana State University Press, 1980.

Malavasi, Mark. *The Unregenerate South: The Agrarian Thought of John Crowe Ransom, Allen Tate, and Donald Davidson*. Baton Rouge: Louisiana State University Press, 1997.

McCardell, John. "Poetry and the Practical: William Gilmore Simms." In *Intellectual Life in Antebellum Charleston*, edited by Michael O'Brien and David Moltke-Hansen. Knoxville: University of Tennessee Press, 1986.

Meats, Stephen. "Artist or Historian: William Gilmore Simms and the Revolutionary

South." In *Eighteenth-Century Florida and the Revolutionary South*, edited by Samuel Proctor. Gainesville, FL: University Press of Florida, 1975.

Mixon, Wayne. *Southern Writers and the New South Movement, 1865–1913*. Chapel Hill: University of North Carolina Press, 1980.

Moore, L. Hugh, Jr. *Robert Penn Warren and History: "The Big Myth We Live."* The Hague: Mouton, 1970.

Moses, Wilson Jeremiah. *Afrotopia: The Roots of African American Popular History*. Cambridge: Cambridge University Press, 1998.

Niebuhr, Reinhold. *The Irony of American History*. New York: Charles Scribner's Sons, 1952.

O'Brien, Michael. *The Idea of the American South*. Baltimore: Johns Hopkins University Press, 1979.

———. *Rethinking the South: Essays in Intellectual History*. Baltimore: Johns Hopkins University Press, 1988.

O'Brien, Michael, and David Moltke-Hansen, eds. *Intellectual Life in Antebellum Charleston*. Knoxville: University of Tennessee Press, 1986.

Page, Thomas Nelson. *The Old Dominion: Her Making and Her Manners*. New York: Scribner's, 1908.

———. *The Old South: Essays Social and Political*. 1892. New York: Scribner's, 1906.

———. "Recollections and Reminiscences." Manuscript. Box 37, Thomas Nelson Page Papers, Duke University.

———. *Robert E. Lee: The Southerner*. New York: Scribner's, 1898.

———. *Social Life in Old Virginia before the War*. New York: Scribner's, 1897.

Panabaker, James. *Shelby Foote and the Art of History: Two Gates to the City*. Knoxville: University of Tennessee Press, 2004.

Percy, Walker. *Signposts in a Strange Land*. Edited by Patrick Samway. New York: Farrar, Straus and Giroux, 1991.

Percy, William Alexander. *Lanterns on the Levee: Recollections of a Planter's Son*. New York: Knopf, 1941.

Phillips, Robert L. *Shelby Foote: Novelist and Historian*. Jackson: University Press of Mississippi, 1992.

Purdy, Rob Roy, ed. *The Fugitives' Reunion: Conversations at Vanderbilt*. Nashville: Vanderbilt University Press, 1959.

Robertson, James I., Jr. Review of *The Civil War: A Narrative*. *Civil War History* 21 (June 1975): 172–75.

———. Review of *The Civil War: A Narrative*, vol. 2. *American Historical Review* 69 (April 1964): 790–91.

Rubin, Louis D., Jr. *The Edge of the Swamp: A Study in the Literature and Society of the Old South*. Baton Rouge: Louisiana State University Press, 1989.

———. "*I'll Take My Stand*: The Literary Tradition." In *A Band of Prophets: The Vanderbilt*

Agrarians after Fifty Years, edited by William C. Havard and Walter Sullivan. Baton Rouge: Louisiana State University Press, 1982.

———. "Shelby Foote's Civil War." In *A Gallery of Southerners*. Baton Rouge: Louisiana State University Press, 1982.

———. "Simms, Charleston, and the Profession of Letters." In *"Long Years of Neglect": The Work and Reputation of William Gilmore Simms*, edited by John Caldwell Guilds. Fayetteville: University of Arkansas Press, 1988.

———. *The Wary Fugitives: Four Poets and the South*. Baton Rouge: Louisiana State University Press, 1978.

Simms, William Gilmore. "*Domestic Manners of the Americans*, by Mrs. Trollope." *American Quarterly Review* 12 (September 1832): 110.

———. *The History of South Carolina*. Rev. ed. Charleston: Russell and Jones, 1860.

———. *The Letters of William Gilmore Simms*. 6 vols. Edited by Mary C. Simms Oliphant, Alfred Taylor Odell, and T. C. Duncan Eaves. Columbia: University of South Carolina Press, 1952–82.

———. *The Life of Captain John Smith*. New York: Geo. F. Cooledge, 1846.

———. *The Life of Chevalier Bayard*. New York: Harper, 1847.

———. *The Life of Francis Marion*. New York: Langley, 1844.

———. "Miss Martineau on Slavery." *Southern Literary Messenger* 3 (1837): 641–57.

———. *The Partisan: A Romance of the Revolution*. 1835. New York: Redfield, 1856.

———. *Sack and Destruction of the City of Columbia, S.C.* Columbia, SC: Daily Phoenix, 1865.

———. *The Social Principle: The True Source of National Permanence*. Tuscaloosa: Erosophic Society of the University of Alabama, 1843.

———. *The Sources of American Independence. An Oration*. Aiken, SC: Aiken Town Council, 1844.

———. *South Carolina in the Revolutionary War: Being a Reply to Certain Misrepresentations and Mistakes of Recent Writers, in Relation to the Course and Conduct of this State*. Charleston, SC: Walker and James, 1853.

———. *Views and Reviews in American Literature, History and Fiction: First Series*. Edited by C. Hugh Holman. Cambridge, MA: Belknap Press, 1962.

Simpson, Lewis P. *The Brazen Face of History: Studies in the Literary Consciousness of America*. Baton Rouge: Louisiana State University Press, 1980.

———. *The Dispossessed Garden: Pastoral and History in Southern Literature*. Athens: University of Georgia Press, 1975.

———. *The Fable of the Southern Writer*. Baton Rouge: Louisiana State University Press, 1994.

———. *The Man of Letters in New England and the South: Essays on the History of the Literary Vocation in America*. Baton Rouge: Louisiana State University Press, 1973.

———. *Mind and the American Civil War: A Meditation on Lost Causes*. Baton Rouge: Louisiana State University Press, 1989.

Singal, Daniel. *The War Within: From Victorian to Modernist Thought in the South, 1919–1945.* Chapel Hill: University of North Carolina Press, 1982.

Skei, Hans. "History as Novel: Shelby Foote's *The Civil War: A Narrative.*" *Notes on Mississippi Writers* 13 (1981): 45–63.

Smith, Lillian. *Killers of the Dream.* New York: Norton, 1949.

Squires, Radcliffe. *Allen Tate: A Literary Biography.* New York: Pegasus, 1971.

Strandberg, Victor. *The Poetic Vision of Robert Penn Warren.* Lexington: University Press of Kentucky, 1977.

Sundquist, Eric. "The Literature of Slavery and African American Culture." In *The Cambridge History of American Literature*, vol. 2, *American Prose Writing, 1820–1862.* Cambridge: Cambridge University Press, 1995.

Tate, Allen. *Essays of Four Decades.* New York: William Morrow, 1968.

———. *Jefferson Davis: His Rise and Fall.* New York: Minton, Balch, 1929.

———. *Poems.* New York: Charles Scribner's Sons, 1960.

———. *Stonewall Jackson: The Good Soldier.* New York: Minton, Balch, 1928. Nashville: J. S. Sanders, 1991.

Taylor, William R. *Cavalier and Yankee: The Old South and the American National Character.* New York: George Braziller, 1961.

Tolson, Jay, ed. *The Correspondence of Shelby Foote and Walker Percy.* Durham, NC: DoubleTake, 1997.

[Tucker, Nathaniel Beverly]. "Literary Notices." *Southern Literary Messenger* 1 (June 1835): 591.

Turner, Arlin, ed. *The Negro Question: A Selection of Writings on Civil Rights in the South by George W. Cable.* New York: Norton, 1958.

Twelve Southerners. *I'll Take My Stand: The South and the Agrarian Tradition.* New York: Harper, 1930.

Underwood, Thomas A. *Allen Tate: Orphan of the South.* Princeton, NJ: Princeton University Press, 2000.

Van Tassel, David D. *Recording America's Past: An Interpretation of the Development of Historical Studies in America, 1607–1884.* Chicago: University of Chicago Press, 1960.

Voegelin, Eric. *The New Science of Politics: An Introduction.* Chicago: University of Chicago Press, 1952.

Wagner, Frederick. "Simms's Editing of *The Life of Nathanael Greene.*" *Southern Literary Journal* 11 (Fall 1978): 40–43.

Wakelyn, Jon L. *The Politics of a Literary Man: William Gilmore Simms.* Westport, CT: Greenwood Press, 1973.

Warren, Robert Penn. *All the King's Men.* HBJ Modern Classics ed. New York: Harcourt Brace Jovanovich, 1974.

———. *Brother to Dragons: A Tale in Verse and Voices.* New York: Random House, 1953.

———. *Collected Poems of Robert Penn Warren*. Edited by John Burt. Louisiana State University Press, 1998.

———. *Democracy and Poetry*. Cambridge, MA: Harvard University Press, 1975.

———. Introduction to *Selected Poems of Herman Melville: A Reader's Edition*. New York: Random House, 1970.

———. *John Brown: The Making of a Martyr*. New York: Payson and Clark, 1929.

———. *The Legacy of the Civil War: Meditations on the Centennial*. New York: Random House, 1961.

———. *Portrait of a Father*. Lexington: University Press of Kentucky, 1988.

———. "The Use of the Past." In *New and Selected Essays*. New York: Random House, 1989.

———. *Who Speaks for the Negro?* New York: Random House, 1965.

Watson, Charles S. *From Nationalism to Secessionism: The Changing Fiction of William Gilmore Simms*. Westport, CT: Greenwood Press, 1993.

Weaver, Richard. *The Southern Essays of Richard M. Weaver*. Edited by George M. Curtis III and James J. Thompson Jr. Indianapolis: Liberty Fund, 1987.

White, Hayden. *Metahistory: The Historical Imagination in Nineteenth-Century Europe*. Baltimore: Johns Hopkins University Press, 1973.

———. *Tropics of Discourse: Essays in Cultural Criticism*. Baltimore: Johns Hopkins University Press, 1978.

White, Helen, and Redding Sugg. *Shelby Foote*. Boston: Twayne, 1982.

Williams, T. Harry. *Lincoln and the Radicals*. Madison: University of Wisconsin Press, 1941.

Williams, Wirt. "Shelby Foote's *Civil War*: The Novelist as Humanistic Historian." *Mississippi Quarterly* 24 (Fall 1971): 429–36.

Wimsatt, Mary Ann. *The Major Fiction of William Gilmore Simms: Cultural Traditions and Literary Form*. Baton Rouge: Louisiana State University Press, 1989.

Woodward, C. Vann, *The Burden of Southern History*. Rev. ed. Baton Rouge: Louisiana State University Press, 1968.

———. "The Great American Butchery." Review of *The Civil War: A Narrative*, vol. 3. *New York Review of Books*, March 6, 1975, 12.

———. *Origins of the New South, 1877–1913*. Vol. 9, *The History of the South*. Edited by Wendell Holmes Stephenson and E. Merton Coulter. Baton Rouge: Louisiana State University Press, 1951.

———. Preface to *John Brown: The Making of a Martyr*, by Robert Penn Warren. 1929. Nashville: J. S. Sanders, 1993.

Young, Thomas Daniel, and John J. Hindle, eds. *The Republic of Letters in America: The Correspondence of John Peale Bishop and Allen Tate*. Lexington: University Press of Kentucky, 1981.

INDEX